Cross Country and Road Running

Cross Country
and Road Running

Cliff Temple

Stanley Paul
London Melbourne Sydney Auckland Johannesburg

Stanley Paul & Co. Ltd

An imprint of the Hutchinson Publishing Group

17–21 Conway Street, London W1P 6JD

Hutchinson Group (Australia) Pty Ltd
30–32 Cremorne Street, Richmond South, Victoria 3121
PO Box 151, Broadway, New South Wales 2007

Hutchinson Group (NZ) Ltd
32–34 View Road, PO Box 40–086, Glenfield, Auckland 10

Hutchinson Group (SA) (Pty) Ltd
PO Box 337, Bergvlei 2012, South Africa

First published 1980. Reprinted 1982

Set in Monotype Baskerville

Printed in Great Britain by
The Anchor Press Ltd and bound by
Wm Brendon & Son Ltd, both of Tiptree, Essex

British Library Cataloguing in Publication Data
Temple, Cliff
    Cross country and road running.
    1. Running
    I. Title
    796.4'26   GV1063
        ISBN 0 09 141521 7

Contents

Preface

Most of this book is based upon what I, as one individual, have seen, heard, read, discussed, learnt, experienced, abandoned and retained during my twenty years in athletics as a competitor and coach.

There is an old saying that 'Those who can, do. Those who cannot, coach'! A few coaches might even take offence at that suggestion, but personally I feel it succinctly sums up why some of us feel at least as much fulfilment in coaching as we ever did as competitive athletes.

I do not believe that one necessarily needs to have been a much decorated competitor in order to be able to coach, any more than a doctor needs actually to have suffered every illness he cures. I like to think that such a coach is sometimes even more sensitive to need, and more sympathetic towards those who would like to run faster, regardless of standard.

However, this book would not be complete without also reflecting the views and experiences of some dedicated and talented athletes who have reached the heights and, to the following, who were among those who kindly took the time and trouble to discuss their own training and race preparation with me during the writing of this book, I am especially grateful:

Gillian Adams, Christine Benning, David Black, Christina Boxer, Dave Chettle (Australia), Sebastian Coe, Bernie Ford, Brendan Foster, Hilary Hollick, Mike McLeod, David Moorcroft, Nat Muir, Keith Penny, Bill Rodgers (USA), Tony Simmons, Joyce Smith, Ian Thompson, John Treacy (Eire), Grete Waitz (Norway), Barry Watson.

Cliff Temple
Hythe, Kent
February 1980

Acknowledgements

The author would like to thank the following for their help during the preparation of this book:

Ron Holman (BAAB National Event Coach, Long Distance), Harold Lee, F.R.C.S. (Chairman and Past President, Road Runners Club), and Bryan Smith (BAAB Senior Coach), for reading sections of the manuscript.

John Jewell (Past President, Road Runners Club).

And, for their assistance, particularly in the compilation of Chapter 10: Barry Wallman (Hon. Secretary, English Cross Country Union), Mrs Vera Duerdin (Hon. Secretary, Women's Cross Country Association), Robert Dalgleish (General Secretary, Scottish Cross Country Union), Mrs June Ward (Hon. Secretary, Scottish Women's Cross Country Union), Leslie Jones (Hon. Secretary, Northern Ireland AAA), Mrs Maeve Kyle (Hon. Secretary, Northern Ireland Women's AAA), John Collins (Hon. Secretary, Welsh Cross Country Association).

John Holt (General Secretary, International Amateur Athletic Federation), Miss Marea Hartman M.B.E. (Chairman, Women's Commission, IAAF), Jon Wigley (Information Officer, IAAF).

Neal Dickinson (Hon. Secretary, English Schools Athletic Association), John McGhie (Hon. Secretary, Scottish Schools Athletic Association), James Shaw (Hon. Secretary, Ulster Secondary Schools Athletic Association), Norman George (Hon. Secretary, Welsh Schools Athletic Association), Peter Luke (Hon. Secretary, British Schools International Athletic Board).

Les Edwards (Hon. Secretary, Counties Athletic Union), Les Golding (Chairman, General Committee, Amateur Athletic Association), Mrs Dorette Nelson Neal (Hon. Secretary, Midland Counties Women's AAA), Ray Scruton (Hon. Secretary, Southern Counties Women's CC and RWA), Don Shelley (Hon. Secretary,

British Marathon Runners Club), Clive Williams (Editor, *Welsh Athletics*), Mrs Jessie Jones, London Olympiades AC, and Ron and Madge Merrie, Bournemouth AC.

All-Sport, Tim Pike, Don Rose, Mark Shearman and Mike Street for permission to use copyright photographs.

Note: As will be seen from the above list, a great number of different associations control various areas of cross country and road running in the UK. Each has its own set of rules, which are being reviewed from time to time, and consequently no responsibility can be accepted by the author or publisher for references to rules which may change during the lifetime of this book. However, every effort has been made to ensure their accuracy at time of going to press.

Prologue

The first smell is usually liniment, wafting through the corridor of the changing rooms as you try to find a spare peg or a corner in one of the crowded dressing rooms to put down your bag. You hear snatches of conversation above the chatter of preparing athletes. . . .

'Only managed 72 miles last week. . . .'

'Had this twinge in my knee after 17 miles of the Poly Marathon. . . .'

'Building up for the Hog's Back race . . . doing a flat-out 15 miler on Sunday morning with Bernie. . . .'

At that moment you feel you are the least trained, most ill-prepared entrant in today's race. Visions of darkness falling and of officials out with torches looking for you flash across your mind. The hour or so before a race is usually your least confident. You'd pull out now, but you've come all this way. . . .

You collect your number. 'There's a map of the course over there,' says the official at the numbers table. You drift over to look at the map, a photocopied Ordnance Survey with coloured arrows added in felt-tipped pen. If you are going to be in the lead, you'll need to know the way. But you aren't. On the other hand, when darkness is falling. . . .

You don't need a map to find the toilets. Then, outside, time for a glance at the multi-coloured running shoes being sold from the back of someone's car. 'Haven't got your size with me, but if I take your name and address. . . .'

A jog. Have you eaten too late? Too early? Are you tired? Have you trained too much this week? Too little? Funny how negative things keep floating to the surface of your mind when you've been through this dozens of times before. It's only a road race, isn't it?

Two laps, 5 miles each. If it gets too hard, you can always drop

out after one lap and get out of the changing rooms before the
rest come back and ask how you got on. But you've come all this
way. . . .

A shaky line forms for the start. Must be 200 here. Serious faces
at the front: lean, tight-skinned, hungry-looking runners. Never
seen *that* sort of shoes before. At the back of the assembly, the
banter. Talking, laughing – probably all be facing the wrong way
when the gun goes.

'Hold it, lads . . . just one picture for the local paper. Now here's
the mayor to start you off.'

At the third attempt the gun fires. Doesn't seem too bad. A
mile gone, lots of runners in front of you, but lots behind you too.
3 miles: overtaking a few, being overtaken by a few. The figures
you pass are the young, inexperienced runners who started too
fast. The ones coming past are the older runners, slower to start,
but whose pace probably won't fluctuate by more than a few
seconds a mile all the way, and who will keep overtaking relent-
lessly until the finish.

Halfway. Inside the half-hour anyway, feeling okay. The
possibility of dropping out seems ludicrous now. You instinctively
speed up slightly as you pass the knot of spectators, then tell
yourself to ease back into what was a comfortable pace.

7, 8, 9 miles. You're going to finish. You try to pick it up a little
on the final mile, and as you cross the line you feel a weight being
lifted from your chest and a momentary urge to be sick over the
timekeeper's clipboard. Swallow hard.

Your legs feel suddenly numb and sweat trickles into your eyes,
as you try to find your tracksuit among the abandoned garments
by the side of the road. Wonder who won?

Tracksuit on. You jog another half-mile back down the course.
Just coming in is the voice who 'only managed 72 miles last week'.
Behind him comes the '17 mile knee twinge in the Poly,' just
getting the better of 'flat-out 15 miler with Bernie on Sunday.'

You're glad you came all this way.

A clearing in the wood. Leaves scrunch underfoot but there is a
stillness in the air. In the distance voices can be heard. 'Come on,
get up with them!'

Footsteps, laboured breathing, then suddenly a lanky boy in a red vest and blue shorts runs across the clearing and disappears down the path opposite. For a few seconds silence descends again. Then another boy, stockier, in a yellow and green vest, follows the first across the clearing and down the path.

Two more, together, both in blue, appear; then suddenly the whole pack. There must be well over 150, running two and three abreast, winding through the wood like a multi-coloured streamer, and not one of them older than fifteen.

Coaches in tracksuits and mothers in headscarves pop out from behind trees, yelling at the puffing youngsters, and then disappear again in search of the shortest cut back to the finish.

The streamer slowly fades into one or two stragglers. Then a tiny lad in a vest three sizes too big for him appears, walking and holding his side. He sees you, and starts running again. 'Stitch,' he gasps, half defensively, half apologetically.

'Never mind,' you say. 'Keep at it.'

Going up the second hill, all she can see is a winding file of muddy legs in front of her and then, as she comes over the top of the climb, she can spot the leader in the distance, already 200 perhaps 300 yards ahead. It's probably that Jane whatsername who won the Southern title, she thinks; that girl with the loud mother. Like to see her lose for once but she seems to win everything.

Half a mile further on, and some of the girls around her are almost walking. Not her, though. She'll keep running until the end, despite the mud and the hills. Last year she was 264th in this race, and she wants to do better this time. That's what she's been training for, isn't it? Her Dad said she could have a new tracksuit if she got into the first 200. She thinks her Dad will probably get her the new tracksuit anyway if she really wants it, but she'd like to earn it properly.

Good old Dad. He drives her all over the country to different races, and he's never seen her win anything. Yet. But he'll be there at the finish, like he always is, holding her tracksuit and training shoes, and he'll say what he always says: 'All right, dear? Never mind, you'll beat them all next time.'

Coming up to the finish now . . . she can see the crowds, and she is aware that the runners around her are trying to sprint, which is almost impossible on this mud. Several go past her, but then wilt again and one girl actually stops and walks within sight of the finish. Voices are screaming encouragement from both sides. It's all right for *them* to say, 'Sprint now!' *They* haven't got to run.

Across the line, she takes a metal disc. An official shouts at her to keep moving and she follows the file of gasping athletes down the roped-off funnel, her hands on the shoulders of the girl in front for support. She feels the hands of the girl behind on her shoulders, but she is too tired to turn and look. Hope no one falls over, or we'll all go down, she thinks.

At the other end of the funnel she sees Jane whatsername posing for a photographer, already back in her tracksuit and looking as though she's been out for an afternoon stroll. Jane's mother is talking in a loud voice to no one in particular about there being 'no opposition'.

She glances down at her own muddy legs, then remembers to look at the disc she is still clutching in her right hand. It is stamped 176.

Then, alongside her, a voice. 'All right, dear? Never mind, you'll beat them all next time.'

The flags aren't really needed, because the crowd, three or four deep in places, lines the course, straining for the first view of the runners. They started 12 minutes ago to the muffled explosion of that maroon, which sent over 1600 runners sprinting into their 9 mile journey. They'll be slowing by now, but the English National Cross Country Championship always has a spectacular, colourful and fast start.

There is a buzz among those spectators who can actually look round the clump of bushes not 60 yards away, and some shouts, getting nearer. Then this huge mass of humanity, squeezing into every available inch, comes pouring round the corner, filling the gap between the rows of spectators with a sea of colour punctuated by the fleshy streaks of arms and legs, all pumping furiously.

In the lead, it's . . . no, it's . . . well, at least twenty of them. Familiar faces, most of them winners in their own patch with giant local reputations but fighting today for a place in the first ten, or even hundred. They came in cars and coaches and special trains with their wives and girlfriends, parents and club officials, who know only too well that Saturdays in winter are spent waiting for muddy runners to appear around clumps of bushes.

How many thousands and thousands and thousands of training miles have gone into the preparation for this frenzied 9? In Bury and Exeter, Hastings and Tamworth, Sunderland and Shanklin, the training has been faithfully logged. On sunny Sunday mornings and bleak Monday nights, along slippery footpaths or partially lit back streets, these men have woven their own route to this moment, when all of them would come together on common ground and brush elbows in getting round three long laps.

A mass of runners, still passing. Surely the leaders will be round again in a minute, and yet we haven't seen the last man through. The faces tell you little of the real story. How many of these runners are having the race of their lives, far in excess of anything they could have hoped, and are at this moment living an experience which they will be recounting to their clubmates on the long Sunday morning runs for years to come? How many are enduring a private hell, wondering why, today of all days, their legs will not respond, leaving them so frustratingly far down on their norm?

How many of these runners will be having their final race today, retiring tonight in disgust, and perhaps making a comeback next week? How many will be so encouraged by the little figure stamped on the cold metal disc they will take as they cross the finishing line that their running careers will henceforth be given greater momentum, as they decide to devote even more of their life to pursuing a gold medal, or something less definable?

So this was the English National Cross Country Championship. It started at three o'clock and it will be over for many of them by four. They ran thousands of miles individually before today, yet more than one life will have been altered by the 9 miles they have just run together.

The Olympic Stadium. Every seat filled. The runners have been gone over 2 hours now. There were sixty-five starters, but we hear they're down to forty-nine now. No progress reports for 25 minutes, though. We've seen the relays, seen the 1500 metres and the 5000 metres finals in the stadium while they have been out there on the road.

The announcer says the leader is within a kilometre of the stadium now. We can hear the cheering outside, as the thousands of people who could not get tickets at least see part of one of the classic Olympic events. The accompanying motorcyclists will leave him when they get up to the stadium gates and he will be alone for 50 metres through the tunnel, 50 metres in which he will hear only his own echoing footsteps. He will be momentarily isolated from a world in which 80,000 pairs of eyes in the stadium and 200 million viewers watching television are staring at the other end of the tunnel, waiting and wondering.

The noise as he emerges from that tunnel envelopes him like a blanket. Some know instantly who he is; others will have to search for his number in their programmes. But his plan to break from the field when he did has worked. He was near exhaustion until his entrance to the world's greatest sporting arena gave him a new lease of life, a massive burst of adrenalin which will see him safely around the final lap of the track he had left just over 2 hours earlier at the start of his 26 mile journey.

His sweat-soaked vest is stuck to his skinny body, his hair plastered to his head, but the thousands of miles he has run since he was that scraggy boy, trailing in the cross country race in a vest three sizes too big for him, have paid off in the best possible way. He crosses the line and he is among the immortals: the Olympic marathon champion.

1

The Boom in Running

To run, says *The Concise Oxford Dictionary*, is to 'progress by advancing each foot alternately, never having both feet on the ground at once'. Even the dryness of the definition cannot fully submerge the exhilaration of the activity. Never having both feet on the ground at once. Just reading the words stimulates your legs into imaginary action – the echo of runs remembered and anticipation of runs to come.

For running is as old as man himself. And while it was certainly an effective means of getting away from anything hostile, or simply for getting from A to B, opportunities it provides for sporting competition were appreciated by the Ancient Greeks. There have always been challenges and races and, while modern competitive athletics may have its roots only as far back as the nineteenth century, the interest in finding out who was the fastest runner in the town or the country goes much further back than that. Now we can discover the fastest runners in the world too.

Since the inaugural modern Olympic Games, held at Athens in 1896, the swiftest runner has become a universal hero. A Greek shepherd named Spiridon Louis was greeted with almost hysterical acclaim in Athens when he won that first marathon race and with it Greece's first Olympic title.

In the years that followed names like Paavo Nurmi, Emil Zatopek, Vladimir Kuts and Lasse Viren have transcended the political and language barriers and become famous worldwide for an ability to run just that little bit faster than their contemporaries. And as time passes other names will become similarly well known simply because of the speed with which they can 'progress by advancing each foot alternately, never having both feet on the ground at once'.

But, while the keenest students of the sport engage in endless hours of inconclusive argument about the stars of past and present, and whether the 1952 triple Olympic champion Emil Zatopek would have beaten the 1972–76 double Olympic champion Lasse Viren, a whole basic attitude has altered, grown and developed during the 1970s.

The signs are all around us. That man in the tracksuit puffing down the road last night. Not exactly flying, was he? But he'll be there again tonight. That group of girls jogging in the local park: laughing, giggling, but jogging and enjoying it. All those boys you saw competing in a cross country race on the common last Saturday afternoon. There were hundreds of all shapes and sizes, and some of them obviously finding it harder work than others. But did it really matter that some took 15 minutes to run the course, and others took 25 minutes? Not at all.

For now at last there is a new realization among the many thousands of runners the world over who are not destined to win an Olympic gold medal or to break a world record. Their role in running need not be confined merely to sitting in open-mouthed amazement at the exploits of that fraction of 1 per cent who are simply more gifted or more dedicated to the pursuit of excellence. To reach the heights is an admirable achievement certainly, but it is not the *only* achievement available to those who run.

In the past decade, a definite and glorious backlash has been growing against that often expressed view that 'winning is everything, second place is nothing, silver medals are for losers, and who cares who was runner-up anyway'.

As a dogma for those whose livelihoods depended upon success, like the highly pressurized US college coaches, who may not have invented it but certainly help to preserve it, the win-at-all-costs attitude may even have worked to a certain degree. Or, if the results did not come, then the attitude could at least serve as a sign to their employers that the failure was not for want of motivation.

But for the rest of us whose limited running ability meant that no one was scrambling to sign us up for their athletics club or track scholarship, to hear this view persistently repeated during the 1960s by the coaches, the spectators and the stars themselves, seemed like being constantly hit on the head with a hammer. You reached the stage where you almost felt a fraud just pulling on a pair of running shoes if you could not break 4 minutes for the mile, and you tended to go out training late at night, after dark, in case someone saw you and word got round that you were getting ideas above your station.

It was not just an athletics inferiority complex, self-generated by those of us who had difficulty breaking 5 minutes for the mile, let alone 4. It was simply that we *were* athletically inferior, and we knew it. Or if we did not, there was generally someone around with a lot of badges on their tracksuit and a loud voice to make sure that we soon did. (I wonder what happened to them all? I suppose they just became so wonderful that one day they floated away on a cloud.)

But during the seventies an almost revolutionary idea that success in competition was not really vital as long as you took part and enjoyed it gained popularity. And although it did not emanate entirely from the USA – the land of win, win, win – it gathered a lot of its momentum there.

The growing concern about the spiralling heart-attack fatalities of the 1960s certainly contributed to this popularity, particularly as the medical authorities were blaming obesity, lack of exercise and too much soft living as some of the prime causes. Jogging and running became new discoveries in a nation which was used to driving everywhere. A boom started.

At first everyone was jogging, because it was a simple, cheap and effective way of retaining (or regaining) health, losing weight and physically stretching yourself. Before that, stretching was something a lot of Americans did mainly in bed.

Then the victory of Frank Shorter in the 1972 Olympic marathon at Munich, and the success of a book entitled *Aerobics* by Dr Kenneth Cooper, which gave measurable values to different levels of gentle exercise, became two big boosting influences. Shorter's win, unexpected as it was, earned a lot of coast-to-coast television time, and suddenly all the joggers following the advice in Cooper's best-selling book became Frank Shorter striding to victory.

An over-simplification, perhaps, but road race fields began to increase, providing as they did an incentive beyond jogging, a thermometer for those who needed a target at which to aim. Marathons became particularly popular, however long they took to complete. Finishing was the goal, never mind the time.

The benefits of exercise were enough to sell running. The word of mouth praise it was suddenly receiving for the consequent weight loss, the regained vitality, the new awareness, the lowered pulse and blood pressure, and 'getting a fresh start in life' sold it more effectively than any Madison Avenue campaign could have done. The same people who had cried win, win, win, were now muffled by the commotion over a re-discovered exercise, and instead they looked down at their own paunches, felt their own galloping pulses, and started jogging themselves.

No longer did it matter about winning. As long as you were running you were doing something positive to aid your health, and increasing your chances of living longer. The day that running took off was the day that losing became respectable.

Hundreds of new road races sprang up throughout the USA. The New York City Marathon was first held in 1970 with 126 competitors; by 1979 it had 14,153. The Mayor Daley Marathon in Chicago doubled its entry in one year with 10,000 runners in 1978. Major commercial companies realized that sponsorship of road races was a good way to reach thousands of people, and began pouring money into staging their own road races in conjunction with local athletics clubs and groups, who were in turn almost overwhelmed by the attention suddenly shown to, and the funds available for, an activity which they had been carrying on for years on a shoestring.

Runner's World, the US magazine which both recorded and helped to promote the boom, noted that:

During 1977 there was a tendency to look at the astonishing numbers involved in running marathons and to assume that the marathon boom had peaked and that it couldn't possibly go any higher. However, in America when a trend begins it often takes a great deal of time to slow down. So it was with marathoning. Especially in the marathons that, through major sponsorship, could garner media attention and could manage to modify themselves to handle larger fields, there was a continuation of the tendency to double in size.

And in numbers. In 1978 the same magazine listed 171 marathons scheduled to be held in the USA that year. In 1979 the total had risen to 270.

Even the long-established races, like the Boston Marathon, which was first held in 1897, were bursting at the seams, despite strict time standards introduced from 1970 in an effort to curtail the unmanageable numbers. In 1968, with no standards in force, 1103 runners took part. In the 1979 race, with a qualifying standard of 3 hours for men and $3\frac{1}{4}$ hours for women and men over forty, there were 8000 official competitors taking part, plus an estimated 3000 unqualified gatecrashers, who just joined in.

Runner's World itself reflected the changing decade. In 1970 it was a bi-monthly black and white photo-litho magazine with forty-eight pages. By 1979 it had become a glossy, full-colour monthly magazine with up to 194 pages.

The running boom was at its most marked in the USA, but elsewhere similar, if less dramatic, growth was taking place. 'Fun runs' were becoming popular the world over. The fun run is a kind of halfway house for the jogger who wants to try something with a little more of a challenge, but does not yet feel ready to tackle organized athletics events. People of all ages and abilities run a relatively short course (perhaps 1¼ miles) in what is strictly speaking a run and not a race. Certificates are awarded for finishing, not for winning, which reinforces the concept of taking part regardless of ability.

Such events are often organized by sports councils or similar bodies, and attract hundreds of participants. At a major centre of running, like Gateshead, the total can be in four figures, while the *Sunday Times* stages a National Fun Run in Hyde Park, London, in which 15,000 people took part in 1979, running round a 4 kilometre grassland course. In Auckland, New Zealand, 32,000 people have taken part in a single 6½ mile run, while in Milan a half-marathon attracted no less than 55,000!

In Britain more and more athletics clubs are opening up jogging sections. A National Jogging Association has been formed, and many cross-country and road-race meetings now include a 'family fun run' in the programme for parents, friends, coaches and officials to take part in before the serious racing begins.

The effect of this upsurge of interest in jogging and fun runs has shown itself in the mushrooming numbers of competitors taking part in hundreds of inter-club and open-road and cross-country events staged every weekend throughout Britain. And if there is one main competitive celebration of cross-country running which has in itself reflected the growth of the sport, it must be the English National Men's Championships, staged each March.

In the main event, the Senior 9 mile race, the most humble club runner can find himself lining up and jostling elbows with the top internationals in the country over the first mile in what is always a colourful and spectacular start. You can even feel the ground tremble beneath your feet as the swarm of runners passes by.

To appreciate the growth of cross country, consider these figures.

In 1974 there were 968 finishers in the race, a splendid total in itself. Just five years later, in 1979, there were 1555 finishers (and 1672 starters) – a 50 per cent increase. Yet, potentially, it could be many times larger because each club can field only nine runners at the most, and some clubs have literally hundreds of runners from which to choose their nine-man team. So, whichever way you look at it, the sport is enormous. And growing.

Why? Partly because of the increasing understanding of the need for exercise in some form or other simply to maintain health. Partly because there will always be a percentage of achievers anyway – runners who do want to be winners, who find that running is something at which they excel or want to excel, and who find through the sport a means of self-expression. But particularly, I believe, because of the emphatic, and still growing, rejection of the win-at-all-costs idea, and the acceptance that just to take part at your own level is more important than having a grandstand seat to watch someone else.

This changing attitude has encouraged more runners who have only limited time or ambition to take part, knowing that for them success and improvement are totally individual targets and that there is now a much greater, and healthier, respect for that. More runners are encouraged to continue in the sport, too, whereas before they might have felt obliged to stop altogether when business or family commitments forced them to reduce their training. One experienced club runner recalls:

Some years ago there was an attitude that if you couldn't give running your full commitment, then it wasn't worth doing. Now most people realize that any running is better than no running, and that it really is possible to want to run for your health and not simply because you want to win a gold medal at the next Olympics.

The days when there was a tacit understanding that unless you were as good as the best you might as well stick to dominoes are over, and that feeling is reflected both at club level and among the champion runners of today.

Brendan Foster, who has experienced the whole running spectrum from the level of the sixties 'scrubber' who was afraid to race because he was running so badly in training, up to becoming an Olympic medallist and record breaker in 1976, summed up the changing attitude after winning the English National Cross Country title in 1977:

If winning is everything, then I will be the only bloke here today who is pleased, and the 1500 runners I beat will all have to go home miserable. But I bet there are some runners today who may have improved from 1300th last year to 1250th this year, and they are probably even more delighted than I am. It's wrong to think that every race has only one winner. Running is about improving yourself, and if you ran faster or finished higher than last time, then you're a winner, no matter how many others finished in front of you.

If changing attitudes are partly responsible for the increase in popularity, what, apart from the health aspect, are the particular attractions of road running and cross country themselves? Both after all are strenuous physical activities and, although they also include team scoring events, unlike soccer and rugby you cannot pass the blame for your own poor performance on to your team-mates. The individual stands alone.

The first attraction must be its simplicity. You do not have to book a court, or find an opponent or a team-mate before you can practice. You just run. And the longer and more often you run, the stronger you become and more likely to do well in a branch of athletics which, after all, tests simply your strength and ability to run a long way, and not your technical skill or your capability at using specialist equipment.

Improvement is directly related to the amount of time and effort you put into training, and if you have not trained you will have no one but yourself to blame. This aspect was the one which always appealed to me most when I was at school, where the main sports we played were rugby, cricket and athletics. I was hopeless at rugby because without my glasses I found it difficult to differentiate between my team-mates and opponents, and from time to time made some splendid runs in the wrong direction!

Cricket was too slow and too much of a team game inasmuch as I never felt there was enough I could do on my own to influence the result.

Running was quite different, however, and with a pair of spiked shoes on my feet I was a total disaster! In my first ever cross country race, as a thirteen-year-old, I ran in a 2 mile event for my school against Shaftesbury Harriers at a horribly muddy place called Brook Farm at Totteridge in North London, and was left so far behind that I got lost because the officials did not believe there could be anyone else still out on the course, and so collected in all the marker flags.

Yet even then the attraction of a sport for which you could train, alone, any time, anywhere, and in which the results depended upon your perseverance, was as strong then as it remains now, twenty years later. Unlike gymnastics or ice skating, you do not have to rely on someone else's opinion of your ability. Unlike soccer or rugby you do not have to rely on your team-mates. Unlike boxing you do not have to rely on meeting the right opponent at the right time, and being seen by the right person. Instead, I found that by reading a couple of books from the library at Wembley, where I then lived, and undertaking a few training sessions on my own around the local King Edward's Park I could actually become a better runner.

Not a world beater, not a record breaker, but a better runner. At school the boys who used to romp away with every race still did so, unchallenged by me and probably totally unaware that I was making even a tiny dent in their vast lead every week. (I once worked out that if I continued to improve at the same rate as I did in the first week of my training, then we would all be forty-eight years old before I caught them!) But if I did not appear to be troubling the outstanding runners, I did seem to be making progress over those unfortunates who were about my own natural athletic standard – and most of whom were recognizable by only having one leg or weighing 18 stones.

There was an inner pleasure in lining up for each successive race knowing that I was slightly fitter than last week and perhaps ready to beat someone else whom I had never beaten before. The fact that they were not spending their evenings training, while I was, seemed irrelevant; they had the same chance to do so. And later, as the opposition began to include a higher percentage of those runners who did train instead of relying on their natural ability, so the aim was to do more training more often than they did, and so close the gap that way.

It had such a satisfying simplicity about it, and such an open-ended future. In running everything depends on the individual, and looking back now I can honestly say that the only reason I did not break the world 10,000 metres record was not because I did not have contacts in the right places, or that a particular official did not like me; it was just that I wasn't good enough. And that really is the best, most satisfying reason.

In running, everyone can reach their own natural peak. It does not matter whether you live in Penzance or the Outer Hebrides,

Birmingham or London. The only criterion as to whether you can break the world record or win a gold medal is whether you can run fast enough. Running is a great leveller. Social background, income, political beliefs and rank are all forgotten when you line up for a race. Instead, training and determination take over, and in the Army Championships a private can outrun a field marshal.

Even the actual process of training for distance running can be reduced to very basic practical terms. You can change into your running kit, go out of your front door, run for as long as you want to, and end up at your front door again. A 20-minute run can take 20 minutes, an hour's run can take an hour. That may not be ideal, because many doctors feel you should spend some time on mobility exercises before you run to try to avoid possible injury. In fact, I wonder how many runners actually do, because the feeling of many is that they would rather use the time for an extra 2 or 3 miles' running, and take the risk of injury.

Not the ideal attitude, perhaps, but it does highlight why road running is such a popular participant sport and method of training. Although, like all amateur sports, the demand on one's limited spare time is regular, in running it can be reduced to the bare minimum. Home by six o'clock, out running by 6.15 p.m., back by 7.15 p.m., showered and dressed not long after 7.30 p.m., with another 8 miles or so to put in the diary. Those who participate in other sports, or even some other branches of athletics, may have to travel to a ground or stadium, then wait for others to arrive, and travel home afterwards, often tripling the total time that they actually spend on training.

To go out and run at a steady pace is not merely a preparation for races. In itself it can be relaxing and therapeutic, easing away the stresses and tensions of the day, with its benefits for racing being only by-products for some people. But in sufficient quantity, and with reasonable regularity, it will enable the average healthy man or woman to get comfortably through a road or cross country race, as it does for thousands of runners throughout Britain every week.

And it is these athletes, who are content to run at a comfortable pace over a range of distances from 2 to 20 miles or more at a time, who form the vast majority of the road and cross country running population of Britain. They train and race at a constant level in clubs, and are perfectly happy to do so with no dreams of Olympic glory.

Many of them seldom race on the track, for two main reasons. Firstly, there are adequate open road races available in most parts of the country all year round, as well as cross country races throughout the winter, and these cater for all standards of runner. Being longer and slower in overall pace than track races, they are more attractive to the steady speed athlete, who would rather run in the middle of a 10 mile road race field at a top speed of six or seven minutes a mile, than to run very little faster in a 5000 metre track race, and probably be lapped by the winner two or three times.

Secondly, to do well in track races normally involves the inclusion of speed work as an extra or alternative training session – a type of running which is often unacceptably uncomfortable to some recreational club runners. They prefer to stick with their programme of enjoyable steady running in which they get pleasantly tired without pushing themselves up against any limits.

The world of cross country and road running can count the vast majority of active athletes in this country among its participants. The rewards of racing can be an all-expenses-paid trip to the other side of the world to race internationally, or just a shared mug of tea and a piece of home-made cake after an inter-club race. But, whatever your motivation and your ambition, the joy of running is that the choice, the target, and the means, are always yours and yours alone.

2
The World of Cross Country

Of all forms of running, cross country is the most basic, back-to-nature exercise. The track and road are, after all, simply artificial surfaces developed by man, but the grass and mud of cross country really provides the athlete with a tough, challenging and absolutely natural carpet on which to run.

The elements may make the mud heavier, cover the course in deep snow, or leave it bone hard. The hills provide their own specific challenge. But they will still be there when today's runners have gone; the very grass itself, perhaps churned into mud by hundreds of pairs of feet on the Saturday afternoon, will grow green again when the athletes have packed their kit and left.

While some runners use cross country running and racing merely as a stamina builder for the summer track season, others treat it as a serious form of racing (indeed, often *the* serious form of racing). But, for all of them, the soft surfaces build up leg strength and endurance and help reduce the possibility of injury during a time of year which is usually spent putting in a large amount of background mileage, much of its necessarily on the road after dark.

In the British winter, Saturday and Sunday offer the only chance for many runners to train in the daylight and, if Sunday is traditionally kept for the long, steady road run, then what better mental and physical contrast than to spend Saturday afternoon running cross country and to feel the ground for once yielding beneath your feet?

Organized cross country running has its roots in the mid-nineteenth century when it began as a winter pursuit for members of the Thames Rowing Club which met at Roehampton in Surrey. They decided to take runs on the nearby Wimbledon Common to keep fit, and in 1868 began to organize paperchases. These events involved several runners setting off as 'hares' and laying trails of pieces of paper cut like confetti, while the other runners had to

follow as 'hounds' and there was a prize for the first hound to
reach each hare.

From this the club's running section became known, as it still
is today, as the Thames Hare and Hounds. The club founder,
Walter Rye, was the first president of the English Cross Country
Union when it was established in 1883, and he described the club's
activities in the 1880s:

The distance run varies much, and usually consists of a ring of 8–10
miles from the clubhouse, which is generally an old-fashioned suburban
inn. The longest run we remember was about 24 miles in a little over
3 hours.

Hares and hounds alike should run in the colours of their club.
Canvas shoes with india-rubber soles, worsted socks, flannel knicker-
bockers, and white or dark blue waterman's sweaters are the best thing
to wear for winter, for if a brook has to be forded, or a river swum, the
warm wet wool prevents any chill being taken in the coldest weather.
And those who have tried it are aware that it *is* cold after sunset,
running over 2 miles of heath, fagged out, in wet things.

When the run is over, the tub – lukewarm if it can be had – is in
universal request, followed, if possible, by a cold douche by means of a
bucketful of water from the hands of a stable helper.

If the run has been extra wet or cold, a steaming glass of port negus
may be wisely taken as a precaution. But it is a singular thing that both
before and after the meal that terminates the evening, ginger beer and
gin is the favourite drink, having probably been found by long experience to best carry off the extra heat of the body caused by a long run.
. . . Tea and a sing-song used to close the evening very pleasantly.

Even earlier, in 1837, a tough cross country race known as The
Crick Run had been originated at Rugby School. It was a cross
country event too which led to the modern 3000 metre steeplechase.
The story is that in 1850 an undergraduate of Exeter College,
Oxford, named Halifax Wyatt, was discussing with some colleagues
a horse-racing steeplechase in which his own mount had fallen.

'I'd rather go round the course on foot than ride that animal
again,' said Wyatt. This casual remark was taken up by his friends,
and later that year a 2 mile foot steeplechase was held on marshy
farmland at Binsey, near Oxford. There were twenty-four fences
to be jumped and the winner, appropriately, was Wyatt himself.
By 1879, a track steeplechase had been established, and that particular type of event was destined to become part of the summer
athletics programme. Until recent years the hurdle on the take-off

side of the steeplechase water jump even used to incorporate a permanent hedge but now at the majority of tracks it has been replaced by canvas, boards, or just thin air, and so the steeplechase has consequently lost some of its original spirit.

The first English Cross Country Championships as such were staged in Epping Forest in 1876, with all thirty-two competitors going off course and the race being declared void. (Over a century later, the same thing occasionally happens in club races!) The inaugural National Championship is therefore considered to have been the 1877 race, held over 11¼ miles at Roehampton, and won by Percy Stenning from thirty-two other starters on 24 February 1877.

The sport grew, and there were more than 100 starters in the 1881 Championship, 252 in 1908, 544 in 1955, 1046 in 1969, and ten years later, in 1979, no less than 1672 runners took part in the Senior Championship event and a total of nearly 6000 athletes entered three different age group races.

For a short time cross country was included in the Olympic Games programme, but the occurrences at the 1924 Games in Paris led to its removal. The Olympic race, over a 10,000 metre course which followed the banks of the River Seine for some considerable distance (and was described by one English competitor as 'like a disused brickyard'), was held on a scorching hot July day when the temperature was breaking records itself at 45 degrees centigrade (113 degrees fahrenheit). Many of the competitors suffered heat stroke, dehydration, and several were rumoured to have died, though fortunately these stories proved untrue. But many ran themselves into an advanced and dangerous state of exhaustion in the highly unsuitable conditions, and only fifteen of the original thirty-nine starters finished. Of these, a number were in a very poor state, reeling insensibly around the track at Colombes Stadium, where the race finished, and one competitor actually slumped to the track just 50 yards from the line.

Only the legendary Finn Paavo Nurmi, who won the race by nearly 1¼ minutes and took a total of four gold medals in those Games, appeared unaffected by the weather. Late into the evening officials were searching the course for runners who were still missing, and the scenes at Colombes had so shocked Olympic officials that cross country running was dropped from future Games.

There are now moves afoot, nearly sixty years later, to have it re-admitted to the Olympics and with the considerably greater

knowledge of both officials and athletes regarding extremes of
temperature it is unlikely that there could ever be a repeat of the
Paris race. Cross country running, although essentially a winter
sport, is already in the Games in one respect, of course, as part of
the modern pentathlon programme.

But exactly what constitutes 'cross country' has been open to
many different interpretations over the years. Even the current
International Amateur Athletic Federation (IAAF) rules for cross
country events are prefaced by the following statement:

Owing to the extremely varying circumstances in which cross country
running is practised throughout the world, especially in regard to
different seasons, climatic conditions and distances, it is impossible to
lay down any rigid legislation for international standardisation of this
sport.

Its own definition of a cross country course for championship
and international events states:

The race shall be run over a course confined, as far as possible, to
open country, fields, heathland, commons and grassland. A limited
amount of ploughed land may be included. If the course passes
through woodland without any clearly defined path or track, it must
be clearly marked for the runners. The traversing of road of any description should be limited to the minimum.

The World Cross Country Championships, which were started
in modest form in 1903 but only came under the IAAF wing in
1973, have been staged on both soft sandy courses with artificial
mounds, like Rabat, Morocco, in 1975, and the glutinous mud and
steep climbs and descents of a Glasgow park in 1978.

Often, though, they have been held on horse-racing courses,
resulting in a long, twisting, mainly flat, event, which is fine for the
spectators and television cameras, but perhaps less interesting for
the runners themselves, and more like a long grass-track race.

And this is the dilemma. The more important the race, the
greater the number of people who want to see it, either in person
or on television, which means that the course has to be reasonably
open and accessible. Yet some of the best cross country courses in
England from a runner's point of view are those provided at
smaller inter-club meetings involving perhaps 100 or fewer
runners. Then narrow paths, stiles, woodland and fences can be
included, and one of the best cross country courses on which I
have ever competed is that used for the Orion Harriers 15 mile

invitation race in Epping Forest. It involves just one big lap, but it is not a good course for spectators, whose best method of following the race would probably be to run alongside the leaders!

Some sort of compromise between variety and the necessity of the shop-window effect has been reached in recent years with the televising by the BBC of invitation cross country events at Gateshead and Crystal Palace, using a number of circuits on a course of around ¾ mile to 1 mile.

But, as John Shrewsbury, the senior BBC producer responsible for athletics and cross country, says:

Even with the shorter circuits, the terrain can still be a problem You must be able to see the runners at all times. The commentator can't say, 'Oh dear, they've gone out of sight now'. The viewers expect to see the whole race, so in preparing to televise any cross country event I walk the course well in advance to decide how best to cover it. If a section of it is fairly open, it may need only two cameras to follow the runners for ¼ mile. But in a wooded section, it may need three cameras to cover even a 100 yard stretch.

Usually I use nine cameras to cover the Crystal Palace cross country course, and five at Gateshead, which is a more open circuit.

But, in 1983, if the World Championships are held at Gateshead, a bigger course would be in operation and then we'd need nine. You've also got to plan for the ultimate emergency, such as losing a camera at the finishing line through a technical fault, so you have to have another standing by, because twenty or twenty-five other countries may be taking pictures from us.

Shrewsbury directed live coverage of the World Championships at Chepstow in 1976 and Glasgow in 1978 ('when the weather was so bad, the cameramen could hardly hold their cameras still'), and expects that in 1983 a crew of around ninety to 100 on site alone would be needed to get the pictures back to the viewer at home, compared to the forty or fifty necessary in providing coverage of even an invitation event shown in *Grandstand*.

The biggest problem in any televised cross country race is identification of the runners, especially on a very muddy day, with a large field and some teams wearing the same colours. The commentators have to rely on their monitor sets for most of the race, and they are seeing exactly the same picture as the viewer at home. So if they miss something, don't throw the cat at your TV set.

Although its history is shorter than for men, cross country running for women in Britain goes back further than many people

think. It is more than half a century since the first Women's AAA
National Cross Country Championship was held, in terrible
weather, at Luton in 1927, when A. Williams of Littlehampton
beat no less than 107 rivals. Even five years before that the ladies
of Birchfield Harriers and London Olympiades AC were including
cross country as part of their winter training, while in France a
women's national championship had been held since at least
1923. In 1931 an international three-sided match between England,
France and Belgium at Douai, France, was staged with Gladys
Lunn of Birchfield Harriers leading England to team victory.

Although cross country came under the umbrella of the Women's
AAA, a number of enthusiasts felt that it should have its own
association and a meeting in Birmingham on 16 September1950
brought about the formation of the Women's Cross Country and
Race Walking Association, with Mrs Dorette Nelson Neal as
chairman. The Women's AAA subsequently delegated to the
WCC & RWA responsibility for cross country and race walking,
and road running, and it has remained there ever since as the
winter activity increased dramatically. In 1979 there was a record
total entry in four age groups of over 2000 for the WCC and RWA
National Cross Country Championships. The following year the
Association became known simply as the Women's Cross
Country Association.

As with many amateur sports, a confusingly large number of
associations exists in athletics generally, but the main organizing
bodies for cross country in the UK are:

Men	Women
English Cross Country Union	Women's Cross Country Association
Scottish Cross Country Union	Scottish Women's Cross Country Union
Welsh Cross Country Association	Welsh Cross Country Association
Northern Ireland AAA	Northern Ireland Women's AAA

These in turn comprise smaller bodies. The English CCU, for
example, includes the Eastern Counties CCA, Midland Counties
Amateur CCA, Northern Counties CCA and Southern CCA,
while the Women's Cross Country Association comprises three
districts: the Southern Women's CC & RWA, the Midlands
Women's AAA, and the Northern Women's CC & RWA.

The various associations have their own regulations regarding minimum and/or maximum distances and ages for competition. The following tables summarize these as they apply in the UK.

Men's Cross Country – Age Groups in the UK
England and Wales

Group	Definition	Maximum distance
Colts	Confined to competitors who are eleven or twelve years of age on 1 September immediately prior to competition.	2½ miles
Boys	Confined to competitors who are thirteen or fourteen years of age on 1 September immediately prior to competition.	3 miles
Youths	Confined to competitors who are fifteen or sixteen years of age on 1 September immediately prior to competition.	4 miles
Juniors	Confined to competitors who are seventeen, eighteen or nineteen years of age on 1 September immediately prior to competition.	6 miles
Seniors	A competitor in a Senior cross country race must be twenty years of age or over on 1 September immediately prior to the event. A competitor in an Open cross country race, or a cross country relay race where the race or section does not exceed 9½ miles (15 kilometres), must be at least seventeen years of age on the day of the competition. For a race or section exceeding 9½ miles, but not exceeding 15½ miles (25 kilometres) eighteen years of age; for a race or section exceeding 15½ miles but not exceeding 21¾ miles (35 kilometres) nineteen years of age; for a race or section exceeding 21¾ miles twenty years of age (all on day of competition).	
Veterans	Confined to competitors who are at least forty years of age on the day of the competition: Class 1 – forty to forty-nine Class 2 – fifty to fifty-nine Class 3 – sixty to sixty-nine Class 4 – over seventy	

Scotland

Group	Definition	Maximum distance
Junior Boys	Eleven years of age or over, but under thirteen as at the preceding 1 April.	2 miles
Senior Boys	Thirteen years of age or over, but under fifteen as at the preceding 1 April.	3 miles
Youths	Fifteen years of age or over, but under seventeen as at the preceding 1 April.	4 miles
Juniors	Seventeen years of age or over, but under twenty as at the preceding 1 April.	6 miles
Seniors	Twenty years of age or over, as at the preceding 1 April.	
Veterans	Forty years of age or over.	

Northern Ireland

N.B. There are no set age groups in Northern Ireland, and a promoting club is able to set its own definitions, but the following age groupings are enforced for the annual Northern Ireland National Cross Country Championships, all of which are held after 1 January.

Group	Definition	Maximum distance
Colts	Under fourteen at midnight on 31 August/1 September in year of competition	There is a maximum distance of 10 miles for athletes under sixteen, although usually events for young athletes rarely exceed 3 miles. An athlete must be eighteen to compete as a Senior.
Boys	Under sixteen at midnight on 31 August/1 September in year of competition	
Youths	Under eighteen at midnight on 31 August/1 September in year of competition	
Juniors	Under twenty at midnight on 31 August/1 September in year of competition	
Seniors	Over eighteen at midnight on 31 August/1 September in year of competition	
Veterans	Over forty on day of competition	

Women's Cross-Country – Age Groups in the UK

England and Wales

Group	Definition	Maximum distance
Girls	Eleven years and under thirteen years at midnight on 31 August/1 September preceding the competition. (Younger girls will be permitted to compete during the season provided they are eleven years of age on the day of competition.)	2500 metres
Juniors	Thirteen years and under fifteen years at midnight on 31 August/1 September preceding the competition.	3000 metres
Intermediates	Fifteen years and under seventeen years at midnight on 31 August/1 September preceding the competition.	4000 metres
Seniors	Seventeen years and over at midnight on 31 August/1 September preceding the competition. Long distance road running – confined to Seniors only. Under eighteen years – not to exceed 5 miles. Under nineteen years – not to exceed 7 miles. Under twenty years – not to exceed 10 miles.	
Veterans	Over thirty-five years on day of competition.	

NB: Juniors and Girls may not compete in other than their own age group. In National and Area championships, Intermediates may compete only in Intermediate events. In other competitions, where permitted by promoting or organizing bodies, Intermediates may compete in Senior events, providing that the distance of the race, or the stage of the race, does not exceed 4000 metres ($2\frac{1}{2}$ miles). Competitors may not compete in Intermediate and Senior events on the same day.

Scotland

Group	Definition	Distance
Minor Girls	Nine years and under eleven at midnight on 31 August/1 September preceding the competition.	Minimum and Maximum: ¾ mile
Girls	Eleven years and under thirteen at midnight on 31 August/1 September preceding the competition.	Minimum: 1 mile Maximum: 1¾ miles
Juniors	Thirteen years and under fifteen at midnight on 31 August/1 September preceding the competition.	Minimum: 1 mile Maximum: 2 miles
Intermediates	Fifteen years and under seventeen at midnight on 31 August/1 September preceding the competition.	Minimum: 2 miles Maximum: 3 miles
Seniors	Over seventeen years at midnight on 31 August/1 September preceding the competition.	Minimum: 3 miles Maximum: 4 miles for cross-country only
Veterans	Thirty-five years on day of competition.	

Northern Ireland

Group	Definition	Maximum distance
Minor Girls	Eleven, but under thirteen as at 1 January in winter of competition.	2000 metres
Juniors	Under fifteen as at 1 January in winter of competition.	3000 metres
Intermediates	Under seventeen as at 1 January in winter of competition.	3500 metres
Seniors	Over seventeen as at 1 January in winter of competition.	–

So both men's and women's sides of the sport have a strong tradition and substantial organizational network, and over the years the sport has catered for younger and younger athletes. In England, for example, it is theoretically possible for a girl to win a national Junior Cross Country title on her eleventh birthday; in Scotland there is a National Championship for nine- and ten-year-old girls.

But whatever the age, sex, standard or ambition of the runner, and however important or insignificant an event may seem, certain basic approaches to any cross country event apply equally if runners want to get the best out of themselves on the day of a race.

Before the race

Knowledge of the course, its climbs and its descents, surface condition and so forth is of immense value to the cross country runner, and a jog round it can be used as at least part of your warm-up before the race. There is usually a map on display at the changing rooms or near the start (and at larger events, in the programme) setting out the route and distance. Examine this carefully, because sometimes when more than one age group is involved at the same meeting, each age group has its own combination of laps.

There might be a 'small' lap, which leaves out part of the complete circuit, itself known as the 'large' lap. Because different maximum distances are laid out in the rules for each age group, varying lengths of course are needed. For instance, at a women's cross country meeting, the Minors and Juniors might run two 'small' laps, the Intermediates might run one 'small' and one 'large' lap, and the Seniors two 'large' laps. At a men's meeting similarly the Colts, Boys, Youths, Juniors and Seniors might all have different combinations of laps for their respective races.

Consequently, each athlete has to study the map and relate the information given to their own age group. Usually the course is explained before the start of the race by an official anyway, but it only needs a barking dog or an untimely bout of coughing for you to miss every word of his graphic description. But if you have any doubts just before the start, this is the moment to express them, not halfway round the course, if at all avoidable.

Usually the course is marked by flags of a vivid colour, such as orange or red, strung out in such a way that as the runner reaches each one, the next should be visible. Arrows are sometimes employed too, and it is essential to ensure you know beforehand just what type and colour of markers are being used for your event. Otherwise you might inadvertently start following the signs for a sponsored walk or a guided tour of the New Forest. If the course is indicated along a natural and well-defined path, then you can usually assume that you simply follow the natural line of path until another marker appears. The Scottish CCU has a specific rule which states that competitors have to keep within 10 yards of the markers or risk disqualification, and all over Britain corner-cutting occurs far too often in cross country races. Athletes can be, and sometimes are, disqualified for such an offence if it is deliberate.

Human markers are often posted at strategic or potentially confusing points on a course to ensure that everyone goes the right way, and the best organized races have a profusion of human and static markers around the course. In the unfortunate circumstance that you do go astray, however, it is always better to re-trace your steps once you are sure you are off course, rather than to go on, hoping that you will stumble across the path again. This is partly to minimize the extra distance you will have to run, and partly to avoid leading others off course.

Some events employ the use of one or more runners to act as 'hares', not taking part in the race itself but instead running ahead of the field and leading them round. It is a useful additional method of indicating the route but, if the hare is to be relied upon entirely, there can be hazards. The possibility of the hare losing his way is slight but not unknown, and of course he has to be a reasonable runner himself, especially if senior athletes are involved. It is no good them overtaking him after $\frac{1}{2}$ mile and then having to wait for him to come puffing up at every junction before they are able to continue. I remember one race where the hare injured his leg after 1 mile and the entire race had to come to a halt while he was helped back to the start, and a new hare was hastily re-cruited from the refreshment room.

Far better, then, to study the map, to jog round the course and be absolutely clear in your own mind where you are going. For it is not only the leader who can use the information. Even if you know you are going to be well back in the pack, it is preferable to know exactly how far you have left to run, what hazards if any still remain (are there any more steep hills? any ploughed fields?) rather than come across them as a nasty surprise when you had just imagined that you ought to be finishing. By knowing the course you can spread your effort as efficiently as possible, just as you would in a track race. In that way you can achieve your own best result, which after all is the main aim, whether you are ninth or ninety-ninth.

Bernie Ford, one of Britain's most successful and consistent cross country runners, says:

I always inspect the course beforehand, looking for possible bottlenecks and places where I could make a break. Or I try to guess where someone else might make a break so that I can ensure I'm in a good position to go with them if they do.

Former International cross country champion Joyce Smith tries to arrive at a race venue in plenty of time to walk the course before she starts warming up, for the same reason:

If there is a very narrow section and you're badly positioned, runners in front of you could hold you up while the leaders get away. I also look at the muddy parts to see if there is a choice of paths, and if so which has the firmer footing.

Track world record breaker Sebastian Coe says he is not a great cross country enthusiast because he feels the mud hinders his light style, but he recognizes its value for the summer and takes part in winter races for strength training:

If you are checking your shoes on a muddy path and your own race is going to be the third or fourth of the day, you have to remember that it could be ten or twelve times worse when you come to race on it, because 2000 runners may have gone over it.

Tony Simmons, another very experienced and successful international cross country runner, says:

It may sound funny, but the first thing I look for when I arrive at a course is the toilet. I get very nervous before a race, and I may need to go four or five times in an hour prior to the event. It's actually a serious problem for some people, and the facilities are often inadequately marked, which is why you see so many runners disappearing behind the bushes.

Brendan Foster recalls the time when a close inspection of the course even helped him win the National Cross Country title.

When I came down for the Championships in London in 1977, I wasn't very confident because it had been raining all week at home in Gateshead. I expected it to be very muddy at Parliament Hill, and I never run well on mud. But when I arrived early at the course, I found that it was surprisingly firm, which suited me. I went all round it, and when I started the race I was in a much more confident mood than I might otherwise have been. Just taking the trouble to look at the course surface that day played a positive part in my victory.

Because cross country is a winter sport, the pre-race warm-up ought to be slightly longer than before summer races. The colder weather means muscles take longer to loosen up, and with any sort of race it is essential to be warm and ready at the start, however bitter the day. If it is very cold, additional tracksuits, sweaters and other clothing should be used to keep warm; it is no use standing around shivering and saying 'isn't it cold?' to anyone who will listen. You have to overcome the problem, not discuss it.

There is no limit to how much extra clothing a runner can wear, and some feel the cold more than others. Both Sebastian Coe and Joyce Smith sometimes put olive oil on their legs to try to maintain some warmth on a bitter day, while Joyce adds that she cannot recall ever *not* running a cross country race in long sleeves. She feels the cold so much that she often wears gloves too. 'I always feel that with a long sleeve vest you can push the sleeves up if you're too hot, and throw the gloves off. You can still run if you're hot, but not if you're cold.' Bernie Ford, on the other hand (or on both hands, come to that), cannot stand wearing gloves for more than a mile at the most.

It is very much a matter of personal taste, and there is no need to feel that others will think you 'soft' if you wear long-sleeved jumpers, extra tee-shirts, mittens, a woollen hat, even tights, if they keep you warm. The body performs much more efficiently when warm, and there is little value in shivering on an icy day in a thin vest and shorts which, in a low temperature, will prevent you from running well. Through experience you will get to know just how much to wear in the different weather extremes so that you will be neither uncomfortably hot nor depressingly cold during the race.

Extremes of temperature and choice of kit are discussed more fully in Chapter 6, but one thing to remember is that, in most club events, and certainly championship races, you have to wear your club colours when competing, and athletes have been disqualified from important races for not doing so. This means that you must decide how many layers of clothing you want to wear in the race, and then put your club vest on top of them, with your number pinned on to it.

Don't worry that you have got a long-sleeved sweater underneath and that the arms of it show! As long as your club colours are on top, with your number clearly visible, you are not breaking any rules.

Put your warm-up gear (i.e. the outer tracksuit in which you will warm up beforehand and discard before the race starts) over the top, and do not take it off until the race is due to start. When you do, try to remove it as calmly as possible! You may be in a highly nervous state, particularly if it is an important race, or you are a relative newcomer to the sport, but there is nothing worse than trying to rush and getting in a panic when a zip sticks as you are trying to get your tracksuit trousers off over spiked shoes. You may end up hopping around on one foot, falling in the mud and rolling around like a demented chicken, while 200 other runners shiver on the starting line waiting for the impromptu cabaret to end.

The warm-up itself varies from athlete to athlete. The intention is to reach a state where you can immediately start racing confidently and efficiently, and this state arrives more quickly for some than others.

Grete Waitz of Norway, the World Women's Cross Country Champion in 1978 and 1979, uses the same warm-up for cross country as for the track:

I start jogging about 45 minutes before the start and continue for 15–20 minutes. Then I do 10 minutes of faster strides and exercises, before putting on my racing shoes and doing a few more fast strides.

David Black, the English National Champion in 1975 and another of our most experienced internationals, finds a total of half an hour, including jogging for 20 minutes, a few faster strides and exercises sufficient for him, while Joyce Smith allows twice as long for her warm up:

By the time you have jogged a couple of miles easily, visited the toilets, put your spikes on and done a few strides, it takes nearly that long.

Sebastian Coe starts his winter warm-up about fifty minutes before the race:

I start moving very easily, walking, bending, stretching, and then jogging. On very cold days if you can do any of your warm-up anywhere indoors, it can save so much time and wasted effort. Warming up outside in the freezing cold is a matter of continually trying to keep warm, and the second you stop, you're often back to where you started. At least indoors you don't feel you have to continually keep moving.

Time must be allowed during the warm-up to stop and change from your warm-up shoes, which will probably be training flats, to your racing shoes. During the warm-up you can assess whether the course surface calls for short or long spikes, or even no spikes at all.

Most modern racing shoes have screw-in spikes, sets of which can be bought in packets in different lengths and are fitted into the sole with a special spanner. It is a relatively easy job to change spikes, but you have to ensure that they are screwed quite tightly in and will not work loose during the race. Conversely, you must be prepared, if trying to unscrew spikes, that one or more may appear to be stuck fast. A pair of pliers can help to shift stubborn spikes, and should become another part of the competitive athlete's permanent kit.

If the course is very wet and muddy, long spikes – say 12 millimetres ($\frac{1}{2}$ inch), or even 15 millimetres ($\frac{5}{8}$ inch) – should ensure a better grip. But if it is dry or frozen then obviously such long spikes may not go very far into the ground and you would feel instead that you were running around on stilts. In that case, shorter spikes (perhaps 9.5 millimetres/$\frac{3}{8}$ inch) will be more suitable. Or even waffles.

In the running shoe sense, waffles are not something that you eat, but rather a special type of shoe sole originally developed in the USA by the famous Oregon coach, Bill Bowerman. It is covered with dozens of small rubber studs which give good traction on most surfaces, and cushioning on hard surfaces by expanding into the space around them. They also have the advantage of providing a uniform grip over the whole of the sole, unlike spikes where the main traction is concentrated to the front of the sole. As distance runners tend to land on their heels first, the advantages of a waffle sole on courses where there are short sections of gravel path or road are clear. Such surfaces are usually discouraged in cross country races, but sometimes inevitable. The latest development is a special cross country shoe which combines the best of both worlds – a waffle sole with spikes. Bernie Ford says:

I have run continental cross country races in needle spikes, or even flat shoes because their courses are so fast, but usually in Britain spikes are needed, although in the autumn I have worn waffles on dry cross country courses. If it is very muddy, it doesn't really matter what length you wear because you may not get a great deal of grip anyway. But I avoid wearing long spikes on courses with long grass, because when you're getting tired you're not lifting your feet up so high, and you could easily trip.

David Black takes two or three different pairs of shoes to races and waits to see the course condition:

Sometimes I wear 12 millimetre spikes, on less mud 9 millimetre. If there are sections of road included, I run in spikes and just hope the road is not too long!

Grete Waitz normally runs in 12 millimetre spikes for cross country:

If you use any longer spikes, you may pick up all sorts of mud and grass. But if it is very dry, or there are sections of road in the course, I may wear 9 millimetre.

Sebastian Coe uses 6 or 8 millimetre spikes on a crisp, dry surface, or 12 millimetre 'if it's soft and gooey'.

Joyce Smith, with a history of tendon trouble, always wears spikes with a built-up wedge heel, and so does Dave Moorcroft, the 1978 Commonwealth Games 1500 metre champion who has also excelled on the country at distances from $1\frac{1}{4}$ to 9 miles. He says:

I always wear a wedge heel because once I ran the National Championship without a heel and was in agony for ages afterwards with strained tendons.

Inter-changeable spikes, and a big bag of alternatives, are essential. But I think the less time you spend in your racing shoes the better, because mentally when you put on a pair of lightweight racing shoes after warming up in heavy ones, you feel great.

So, when you have made yourself familiar with the course, warmed up thoroughly, and decided what you will wear in the race on your body and your feet, only one other thing remains. The race.

Most cross country races usually begin too fast for the simple reason that the widest part of the course is often the starting area itself. Thus if you are ambitious to do well in a race, it is of little value to get left behind early on, as you will then have to spend the next couple of miles overtaking slower runners. And, if the course gets very narrow in parts, as some do, the overtaking opportunities will be limited, leaving you with frustrations similar to those of a sports car driver who finds himself following a slow-moving load of hay down a country lane. And all the time the leaders are getting further ahead.

In a small inter-club race it may be less of a problem than at the start of the English National Senior Championship where the starting line may be nearly 200 yards long and accommodating 1700 athletes. And in that race when the starting maroon explodes (no point in using a pistol) the men who want to get up to the sharp end of the race quickly set off to cover the opening mile in close to 4 minutes 20 seconds, even though there are still 8 more miles to cover afterwards. Thus, although even-paced running is physiologically the most economical method of running any distance race, in practical terms the bigger the race the faster you have to start, even if it means getting into oxygen debt for a while. Brendan Foster says:

The start of the National is always a bit crazy. Everyone runs much too fast for the first mile, but if you're not going to get left back in 500th place, you've just got to go with them.

Bernie Ford, the most consistent runner in the National in recent years, with two victories and four second places between 1974 and 1979, admits:

The start is the only problem with the National. If I can get up there and the first mile is over, then I know I'm all right. But that race is a great leveller. It doesn't matter who you are, anything can happen to you in that initial dash. I'm really scared before it starts, because I'd hate to fall over in front of that lot.

I'm sure I must run close to my best for 800 metres, or even 400 metres, in that first flat-out dash. You *can* come through the field steadily, but you're not going to be involved in the winning of it if you are not up there after a mile.

Dave Moorcroft comments:

If you are 4 or 5 seconds down after 1 minute, which is not much really, you are probably 200 or 300 positions down on the leaders. So for those extra few seconds you have to go hard to get up there. It's a case of what level you think you're at. If you really think you're going to be in there with a shout, then you've got to be up there all the way. But if you are aware that 9 miles is a very long way, and have no pretensions to being in the first fifty, you've got to run it very sensibly. It would be ideal if everyone agreed to start off at the pace they were eventually going to settle down to, but although one or two might agree, the other 1699 wouldn't!

The National poses its unique problem just once a year, but there are athletes, like Grete Waitz, who prefer to run fast from the start regardless of the size of the race:

I always start quickly because I don't have much speed at the finish.

If you are fit, you can start fast and hold on, but if you are not in such good condition then it is much wiser to start more cautiously.

Scoring

The team scoring system in cross country is very simple. If the rules state that, say, three athletes per club will score in the overall result then the judges add together the positions of the first three finishers from each team, and the club with the *lowest* total is the winning side. This result, from a 1979 Kent League race, illustrates the three-to-score system:

Seniors

Place		Time
1	D. Goble (*Dartford*)	10.14
2	L. Hall (*Ashford*)	10.20
3	J. Boorman (*Medway*)	10.58
4	K. Hughes (*Medway*)	11.33
5	J. Brown (*Ashford*)	11.44
6	D. Lowings (*East Kent*)	11.59
7	S. Reed (*Wigmore*)	12.13
8	R. Moies (*Wigmore*)	12.35
9	J. Mawgan (*Ashford*)	12.39
10	M. Dye (*Medway*)	13.05
11	J. Ralph (*East Kent*)	13.11
12	L. Dray (*Dartford*)	13.39
13	J. Godden (*Dartford*)	14.05
14	P. Horner (*Wigmore*)	14.27
15	J. Banks (*East Kent*)	15.55

Teams

Place		Score
1	Ashford (2, 5, 9)	16
2	Medway (3, 4, 10)	17
3	Dartford (1, 12, 13)	26
4	Wigmore (7, 8, 14)	29
5	East Kent (6, 11, 15)	32

With relatively small fields, officials can note the finishing position and number of each athlete and work out the team scores afterwards quite quickly. In much larger fields, however, the disc system of scoring is more practical, although it does rely on the co-operation and understanding of every team manager and athlete for it to work efficiently at an event like the English National Championships, where it was first introduced in 1929.

Here, in the Senior 9 mile race, for example, with a six-to-score system, each club is allowed to enter up to fifteen athletes, who will all appear on the programme (Figure X). On the day, however, a maximum of only nine from that fifteen are actually permitted to compete and the club's team manager has to state on a declaration card (Figure Y) handed in to officials before the race starts which nine runners will be taking part for his club. And of those nine, only the first six to finish from each club will be included in the scoring.

As each runner crosses the finishing line he is given a metal disc, about the size of a ten pence piece, on which is stamped his overall position. He hands this to his team manager, who puts all of the discs received by his club's scoring runners into an official envelope (Figure Z), on the outside of which is printed a special form where he must list the competitors' numbers and their finishing position.

On a separate envelope (Figure Z) he writes down the positions of his 'non-scoring' runners, and when all of the envelopes have been collected in and checked, race officials can sometimes announce the provisional team result before the last runner has even finished the race.

FOLKESTONE AC., Light Blue/Black Lettering   118

922 Allsworth B.	926 French A. K.	929 Temple C. G.
923 Callwell M.	927 Rumsey D.	930 Thompson D. J.
924 Dyer M.	928 Shaxted S.	931 Walsh I.
925 Figgins W. A.		

FRODSHAM H., Black/Orange Badge   68

932 Jones G. C. H.	937 Wood R.	942 Rowland P.
933 Rose J.	938 Gaynor J.	943 Mather K.
934 Nichelson D.	939 Ratcliffe W.	944 Hayes K.
935 Lloyd P.	940 Butterworth J.	945 Cottrell L.
936 Webster R.	941 Proudfoot C.	946 Stott P.

GATESHEAD H. AC., White Vest, 4" Red Band   59

947 Foster B.	952 Irvine S.	957 Trainor J.
948 Smith B.	953 Mills J.	958 Coleby M.
949 Coates D.	954 Myatt J.	959 Amos A.
950 Spedding C.	955 Baggaley B.	960 Winter S.
951 Cannon D.	956 Leddicote B.	961 Ainslie H.

Figure X: An excerpt from the English National Cross Country programme 1979. In clubs like Gateshead Harriers there is great competition to make even the 'National' team; clubs like Folkestone AC have to be a little less selective. But both have their place in the race. (The numbers on the right-hand side are those of the starting pens.)

ENGLISH CROSS-COUNTRY SENIOR CHAMPIONSHIP, 197

TEAM CARD

Club .....GATESHEAD HARRIERS.....

The Competitors running in this team are numbered as under:

947   948   950   952   954

955   956   958   961

Signed..

This card must be properly filled in and handed to the Competitor's Steward

Numbers must be given — not names

Figure Y: Before the race the team manager has to hand in this card declaring which runners from those entered will actually be competing.

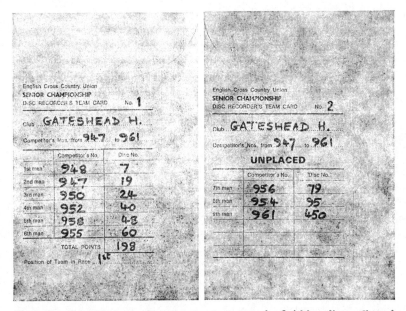

Figure Z: After the race, the team manager puts the finishing discs collected by his athletes into these envelopes, and returns them to the race recorders.

In the event of a tie, with two clubs having the same total points score, the last scoring man home decides which club is placed higher. If, for example, Gateshead Harriers and Folkestone AC both totalled 198 points, but Gateshead's sixth scorer finished sixtieth and Folkestone's sixty-first, then Gateshead would be placed higher.

Knowing that every single place counts gives an added incentive to the later finishing competitors, and even those who know they are not actually in their team's scoring six can assist their club-mates by getting ahead of another club's runners who may be in *their* scoring six and thus push up the total score of their rivals.

A club does not have to field nine runners to score in the team race: six is the minimum in the English Senior Championships. If, through injury, illness or other circumstances, they cannot even manage six, the surviving athletes can still compete and will receive their discs, but the club will not count in the overall scoring. Likewise, if a club does not have enough runners even to enter a team, it may enter anything from one to five individuals, who will all run and receive discs, which they will hand in to a special steward responsible for collecting the discs of all the individual entries after the race.

Because individual positions play such an important part in cross country scoring, and as in a big race large groups of runners may be finishing very fast and close together, a special system of ensuring their positions are accurately recorded is used. It is the funnel system, and involves the use of roped-off corridors down which the runners are directed as they cross the finishing line.

The narrow part of the funnel is only about 2 feet across, which means it is just wide enough for one athlete at a time, and judges try to ensure that the runners go down the funnel in single file in the same order in which they crossed the finishing line. At the far end of the funnel, which is normally about 30 yards long, officials note down the finishing order of the competitors.

The advantage of the funnel system is that it avoids a bottleneck at the finishing line itself, where it would be impossible to control hundreds of fast-finishing and exhausted runners and still judge them accurately. Indeed as some of them would not quite reach the finishing line before having to come to a halt, they would not receive an accurate official time. This can still happen if the process is delayed.

As the funnel or chute fills up with runners, so a second parallel

funnel can be brought into operation, and then a third and a
fourth, with as many as eight funnels or more in operation for the
biggest events. By the time the last funnel is filled, the first one
should be empty again as the runners have filed through and had
their finishing order recorded.

The only disadvantage of the system is that in some international
events an unscrupulous runner occasionally tries to move up a
couple of places in the funnel itself, which is blatant cheating because the race officially finishes before the funnel entrance is
reached. That is where the times are recorded to be matched up
later to the finishing order.

But on the short journey to the other end of the funnel, despite
its narrowness, an unfair improvement has occasionally been made,
with weary runners, many foreign tongues, the general confusion
and an unending stream of finishing runners often enabling the
action to go unnoticed, or at any rate unpunished.

The IAAF has been investigating ways of tightening up the race
finish procedure to eliminate this happening, and fortunately it is
a rare occurrence in Britain. But, if you are competing abroad,
keep your wits about you in the funnel, because the race might
not quite be over!

Bernie Ford, a regular competitor in races all over Europe as
well as Britain during the winter months, sums up some of the
other differences:

You have to remember that the continental version of cross country
means anything that is not on a track – from a road race, to climbing
up the side of a mountain, or running round a rubbish tip.

The first thing I learnt when I started running cross country races
abroad was never to take any notice of the blurb they send you about
the course being 'suitable for short spikes', or whatever. You just have
to take a good selection of spikes with you, then look round the course
and make up your own mind. At one race in France, where the course
was mainly cinder and gravel paths, there was a section of road, but
they covered it with strips of Tartan track!

They also tend to use lots of short laps, and even after going round
five times you're in danger of being confused and disorientated, so it is
vitally important to find a point at which you know just how far there
is to run before the finish.

You've got to be very careful about the start too, because they're not
as controlled as in Britain. You've really got to be warmed up, stripped
off, in the front rank and facing the right way 5 minutes before the gun
is scheduled to fire, and ready to run at any moment. Then, when the

others go, you have to go with them, even if the gun hasn't fired, because they won't be called back.

Tony Simmons, a similarly experienced competitor in European cross country events, agrees:

It's no good waiting for the gun to go because you'll be left 30 seconds behind in some races. On one of my first ever trips abroad, to a race in Marseilles, I was still lacing up my shoes when the race started. Ever since then I've never believed a continental starter when he says he won't let the race go until everyone is behind the starting line.

Brendan Foster has also suffered from unpredictable starts:

To be realistic, the starting in many cross country races abroad is disgraceful, but it's better to be at the front of a group of disgraceful runners than at the back saying 'how disgraceful!'

In some countries they just don't believe in having fair starts, so you have to watch the earlier races to see how they get off, and what warning they get.

But, as Tony Simmons points out:

One of the big advantages of racing abroad regularly is that you get to know your opposition. You get to know what training they're doing, what stage of preparation they're at, and what their views are. Above all, you get to see them as human beings, who eat and sleep the same as everyone else.

When I first ran internationally I used to think 'Oh my God, there's so-and-so. I shouldn't even be in the same race as him.' But you learn that everyone has their ups and downs too, and when you come to a major championship race they don't seem quite so superhuman.

People often get overawed by past records or reputations. I remember an inter-club race at home once where I hadn't been training very much beforehand and some athletes who should have beaten me that time let me win simply because they seemed to think that there was no point in trying to beat me. I should have lost, but it was nothing I did which won me that race. They did it all to themselves!

3

The World of Road Running

Q. Why did the chicken cross the road?
A. To get the bend in its favour.

'Mummy!' cried the little girl, rushing indoors from the front garden. 'There are a lot of men outside taking their trousers off in the middle of the road!'

'It's all right, dear,' reassured her mother, as she surveyed the scene from the front door. 'They're not men. They're runners.'

Road running takes sport to the most unlikely arena: your own doorstep. Any quiet suburban road is liable to become part of a racecourse, as 200 or 300 runners line up across Lobelia Avenue at three o'clock on a Saturday afternoon for the start of a road race (only to have to part again like the Red Sea a few seconds later to let Mrs Dingleby from number 38 chug through in her Morris Minor, blissfully unaware that she has only just missed crushing one or two well known feet).

Fortunately, few residents seem to object – vocally, anyway – to the use of their road as a race track. Many come out to watch, a few are oblivious to any sporting event which is not being shown on their TV screens, and just one or two may complain, quite understandably, if they find athletes sitting on their front walls, using their tree branches as coat hooks, or even watering their flowers.

Sadly, some athletes do forget that they are within inches of other people's homes, and treat the surrounding area like a changing room. Tracksuits left on walls or fences without prior permission can be particularly annoying to the residents.

One runner finished a road race to find that his tracksuit trousers had been blown by the wind from a low wall over which he had draped them on to a front lawn, where the owner was mowing the grass. As they were green, explained the gardener to the runner afterwards, only half convincingly, he hadn't seen them and . . .

Then there was the tale of a group of runners who left their tracksuits uninvited on a garden fence during a 10 mile road race and returned to find that the house owner had collected them up and given them to the vicar for his jumble sale. One of the runners had to queue up outside the church hall the following Sunday and buy them all back for five pence each.

But road running, both training and racing, is the most basic and simple activity within the sport of athletics, and perhaps within any sport. And while you can understand pole vaulters and hammer throwers complaining about the lack of facilities in Britain, a road runner would get little sympathy for complaining that 'those East Germans have got more roads than we have'.

Its sheer simplicity makes it an attraction for a great many club level athletes who seldom if ever set foot on a conventional running track either for training or racing. It is also a particularly satisfying area for those of us with little or no basic speed, for stamina accumulated through regular training can compensate for the inherent lack of swiftness. Most senior club runners can break 6 minutes for the mile, but far fewer can crack the hour for 10 miles. The difference is not speed, but having or gaining the stamina to sustain that limited speed.

The accumulation of stamina results not from any great skill, but simply from regular runs of graduating length and intensity until the body is sufficiently well-trained to achieve the target set for it. After running 10 miles in 1 hour, running 20 miles in $2\frac{1}{4}$ hours or a marathon in $3\frac{1}{4}$ hours could be targets at which to aim, or your target could simply be to run those 10 miles faster.

Whatever the goal, achieving it is down to the simplest and fairest give-and-take deal in sport. If you run often, you run faster. All the money in the world, all the friends in high places, all the fast talking and wheeling and dealing that you could imagine, cannot substitute for the only way to prepare to run a long way. Only going out and actually running can do that.

There are, of course, many races shorter than the marathon, and it is in the 5 and 10 mile events that adult beginners are best advised to obtain their early road running experience before even contemplating a marathon. Details of most of the open road races in the UK (with 'open' meaning open to entry by any amateur runner in the relevant age groups, not a description of the surroundings) are advertised in specialist magazines like *Athletics Weekly*, from which the runner can obtain a great deal of advance information about both road and cross country events, and indeed any athletics events.

The Road Runners Club (RRC), which is a national organization of runners from clubs in different locations but with a common interest in road events, publishes for its members an annual fixture list with details of over 100 races of 10 miles and more, with their closing date for entries, entry fee, starting time, and the address of the race secretary.

The RRC itself, with a UK membership of around 2500, has really played a significant part in the development of this area of the sport, particularly in the long distance events, since its foundation in 1952. For, although road running had taken place in England since at least 1907, and there were many well-established races long before the early 1950s, interest had not extended very much beyond the classic marathon distance of 26 miles 385 yards.

The father of long distance road running in Britain is acknowledged to have been Arthur Newton, whose exploits in South Africa thirty years earlier were eventually to lead to the foundation of the RRC. Newton, the son of a Norfolk clergyman, was born in 1883 and settled in South Africa in 1901, later buying a farm which produced first-grade cotton and tobacco. He had no background in athletics, and seemed set for a prosperous life as a farmer until a change in government in South Africa put the land he owned and had developed into a 'native territory' belt in 1922, which ended his farming endeavours without compensation.

Searching for a method of getting into the public eye, in an effort to bring attention to his plight, and realizing that successful sportsmen were well-known figures, he decided to enter the Comrades Marathon, a 54 mile event run on rough roads between Durban and Pietermaritzburg. He was thirty-nine and a complete novice at running but, with five months of carefully thought out, graduated, daily training, he managed to win the race and went on to retain the title for the next three years.

Sadly, his success did nothing to help his farming situation, but it did set him off as a prodigious record breaker at long distances, both in South Africa and on return trips to England. He set a world 50 miles best of 5 hours 38 minutes 42 seconds on the London to Brighton road in 1924, and 100 miles best of 14 hours 6 minutes in 1934.

Newton's ideas, developed through practical experience and his particularly sharp, reasoning mind, led to the publication of four books and innumerable magazine articles on all aspects of long distance running, although he was not without his critics. Yet even when well into his sixties he would get up at 5.00 a.m. for, 12 mile runs, and at his home in north-west London on Sunday afternoons he would hold gatherings of long distance enthusiasts, his disciples.

It was through such meetings that some of his followers had the idea of trying to emulate his feats on the London to Brighton road, which winds for over 50 miles through Croydon, Redhill, Horley, Crawley, Bolney and Pyecombe, taking in three waves of hills.

Ernest Neville, an athletics official with a lifetime of association with that particular road through many walking events held along the route, became involved in organizing a running race from London to Brighton and, with sponsorship from the now defunct *News Chronicle* newspaper, the race was held as part of the Festival of Britain celebrations on 11 August 1951. There were fifty-six entrants, forty-seven starters and thirty-two finishers, with Lew Piper of Blackheath Harriers, a forty-year-old insurance clerk, winning in 6 hours 18 minutes 40 seconds after running the $51\frac{3}{4}$ miles from Westminster Bridge through wind and rain.

The race was a success, and the only residual problem was to find the means to make it an annual event. Consequently, Neville decided to found a new body, the Road Runners Club, to undertake this task, with the immediate object being to promote the 1952 race. The inaugural meeting of the RRC was held at the Regent Street Polytechnic in London on 30 June 1952, and was addressed by Arthur Newton, who lived to see the race grow from strength to strength before his death at the age of seventy-six in 1959.

Such a long race as the London to Brighton appealed, however, to only a small proportion of those athletes who ran on the road, and so the scope of the newly-formed body was subsequently enlarged to cover the whole range of distance events from 10 miles upwards. The aim of the RRC was, and still is, 'To bring together all those interested in long distance running, to serve their interests, and to act as a forum for all enthusiasts.'

To this end, the RRC has been a watchdog on such aspects of the sport as course measurement, and has developed a standards scheme; it also publishes a high standard triennial newsletter,

operates an insurance scheme, and organizes film shows as well
as a select number of long distance races, including the annual
London to Brighton race each September, which was, after all, the
raison d'etre of the club.

As with cross country, the actual jurisdiction of road running
comes under various regional and national bodies throughout the
UK. In England and Wales it comes under the control of the
Amateur Athletic Association for men, and in England under the
Women's Cross Country Association for the ladies. The AAA rules
for competition concerning road running begin as follows, with
the corresponding WCCA Rules being virtually the same:

Road races, including Marathon Races, shall be run on roads, and
permission of the local Police Authority must be obtained when public
highways are used. Runners must follow the traffic rules of the road as
laid down by the local Police Authority, especially at roundabouts;
when traffic or similar circumstances make it unsuitable, the course,
duly marked, may be on a bicycle path or on a footpath alongside the
road, but should not be on soft ground such as verges or the like. The
start and finish may be in an enclosed ground or athletic arena.

Note: The course shall be measured one metre from the left-hand verge
of the road in the running direction.

Men's Road Running – Age Groups in the UK

England and Wales

Group	Definition	Maximum distance
Colts	Confined to competitors who are twelve and thirteen years of age on 1 April for competitions held between 1 April and 31 August, or on 31 August for competitions held between 1 September and 31 March.	2½ miles
Boys	Confined to competitors who are fourteen and fifteen years of age on 1 April for competitions held between 1 April and 31 August, or on 31 August for competitions held between 1 September and 31 March.	3 miles
Youths	Confined to competitors who are sixteen and seventeen years of age on 1 April for competitions held between 1 April and 31 August, or 31 August for competitions held between 1 September and 31 March.	4 miles

Group	Definition	Maximum distance
Juniors	Confined to competitors who are eighteen or nineteen years of age on 1 April for competitions held between 1 April or 31 August, or 31 August for competitions held between 1 September and 31 March.	6 miles
Seniors	A competitor in a Senior road race or road relay where the race or section does not exceed 15 kilometres (9½ miles) must be at least seventeen years of age on the day of competition. For a race or section exceeding 15 kilometres, but not exceeding 25 kilometres (15½ miles) eighteen years of age. For a race or section exceeding 25 kilometres but not exceeding 35 kilometres (21¾ miles) nineteen years of age. For a race or section exceeding 35 kilometres twenty years of age (all on day of competition).	
Veterans	Confined to competitors who are at least forty years of age on the day of competition: Class 1 – forty to forty-nine Class 2 – fifty to fifty-nine Class 3 – sixty to sixty-nine Class 4 – over seventy	

Scotland

Group	Definition	Maximum distance
Junior Boys	Eleven years or over, but under thirteen years on 1 April preceding competition	3000 metres/ 2 miles
Senior Boys	Thirteen years or over, but under fifteen years on 1 April preceding competition	5000 metres/ 3 miles
Youths	Fifteen years or over, but under seventeen years on 1 April preceding competition	6500 metres/ 4 miles
Junior Men	Seventeen years or over, but under nineteen years on 1 April preceding competition	10,000 metres/ 6 miles
Senior Men	Under Scottish AAA rules, a competitor taking part in an Open race must have reached the age of nineteen if the event is beyond 10,000 metres, and must have reached the age of twenty-one if the event is beyond 10 miles	
Veterans	Over forty on the day of competition	

Northern Ireland

As with cross country, there are no hard and fast rules concerning age groupings in Northern Ireland, with the clubs being able to decide their own limits. However, there is a maximum distance of 10 miles for an athlete under sixteen (although there are few races beyond 3 miles for the younger runners), and an athlete has to be eighteen years of age to run as a Senior.

Women's Road Running – Age Groups in the UK

The age groups in respect of women's road running in the UK are the same as the cross country age groups, and these can be found on page 35.

The responsibility for choosing, measuring and marking the route of a road race rests with the race organizers, and the chief concern of the competitor is simply to run as well as possible. But advance knowledge of the route and the terrain to be covered are, at the least, helpful to any competitor, and positively essential to the ambitious runner. Quite apart from the possible pitfall of leading 200 other runners into a cul-de-sac, it would be quite conceivable on an unfamiliar course for a runner to make a hard effort to get away from the field and then, just as he was intending to ease off slightly to recover, be suddenly faced with an unexpected hill with no apparent top.

So get to know the course. Most races display some form of course map at the changing rooms to show competitors the direction and shape of the route. But such diagrams do not always indicate the uphill and downhill sections, and a quick trip round the course by car can be illuminating if it can be arranged. Make mental notes of where the inclines begin and end, where you can get some form of respite on a down slope, and what to look for towards the end of the race (or lap, if several laps are used). There is nothing worse than gathering yourself up for a final effort towards what you imagine is the finish and then, as your eyes search in vain for the timekeepers, to be told, 'Only 2 miles to go!'

It is always possible to jog some of the course as your warm up, and in any case the route will be marked in one or more ways. For instance, a pilot car may drive ahead of the field, and as long as the driver keeps clear enough of the front runners, so that they do not spend the entire race breathing in exhaust fumes, this is a good method, as it also warns oncoming traffic of the approach of a race.

It is not always ideal, however, if the race has to pass through narrow lanes. I once agreed to pilot a race through a country area and, while leading the runners down a single track road, met a car coming the other way. Its driver refused to budge, and I had no alternative but to reverse up to a passing place some 40 yards back and, while the offending car went past in the opposite direction, the entire race overtook me, leaving me at the wrong end of a road race field which would be steaming merrily through 20 or 30 miles of little-used Kent countryside if it was not turned left at the next junction. Fortunately, judicious use of another lane just about saved the day.

Police patrol cars and motorcyclists, if the local force can spare the manpower and are asked in plenty of time, are sometimes willing to act as race pilots, while another alternative is the pedal cyclist, as long as there are not too many hills. At a Northern marathon several years back the leading runner was surprised to see the pilot cyclist he had been following for a long way suddenly get off his bike and go into a house. It turned out one of the tyres had punctured and he had gone home to mend it, little realizing that the runners were still following him!

As in cross country, static markers, human or otherwise, are usually positioned at each important junction in a race, and the general rule should be to keep straight on the road you are following until you are directed off. The directions may come from an official, or from arrows, posters or even chalk marks on the road, and again it is essential to familiarize yourself early on with the specific type of markers to be used in that race.

In most events up to 10 miles or so, for the majority of runners it is usually a case of follow-the-leader anyway, but in longer events it is often possible even for big fields to become well stretched out, and then you have to depend solely on how the course is marked. Which brings me back to the original point: knowledge of the course you are about to run can be a great asset in helping to spread your effort most economically over the route and thus improve your time and placing.

So when you are at a race you have never run before, and you hear a lot of changing room talk and nervous jokes about 'Deadman's Hill', or whatever, find out from other runners what they mean. At the Rochester 5 mile road race, for instance, which is one of the country's oldest events, the course starts with a mile long steady climb and then, just when you think you have reached the top, you are suddenly directed up an even steeper slope called Cookham Hill. It can be a nasty shock if you are not expecting it!

Joyce Smith usually goes round a road race course by car beforehand to familiarize herself with the terrain. 'If it is just one big lap, then sometimes I may take it as it comes, but I always make sure I see a map of the course and ask where the hills are.'

David Black takes special note of the finishing area, 'especially if the race ends on a track, as some road races do. I like to ensure that I know exactly where the entrance is, and which way round we go.'

In races over 10 miles, refreshment stations may be provided (and in marathons *have* to be provided), together with the provision of water and sponges. A refreshment station in this instance does not mean somewhere you can buy a cup of tea and piece of cake. That comes after the race. During the event it consists instead of a roadside table on which plastic cups of water, orange squash, lemon squash, cold sweet tea and even de-fizzed Coke may be provided for the runners.

Apart from the obvious revitalizing value, they are there for the more serious reason that on a hot day dehydration could occur in a long race as the body squeezes out its fluid through sweating in an effort to cool the skin surface. Taking drinks during the race helps to replace the liquid lost, and the hotter the day the earlier drinks should be taken – even before you feel the need, and this is discussed in more detail in Chapter 6.

In marathons the first refreshment station comes at around 3 miles (5 kilometres) and at approximately similar intervals thereafter, with sponging stations interspersed between them. In races longer than 10 miles, but not a full marathon, refreshments are provided at the 10 mile point and at 5-mile intervals afterwards, with water and sponging points in between.

Anyone who saw the classic marathon scenes in Kon Ichikawa's documentary film of the 1964 Olympic Games, *Tokyo Olympiad*, will remember how easy the great Ethiopian runner, the late Abebe Bikila, made taking a drink during a marathon seem.

The vivid scenes showed Bikila heading down a long, straight motorway-like road with the Olympic flame at the stadium in the distance as his goal. He came to a refreshment station, grabbed a cup of water, drank the contents and threw it down without disturbing the pattern of his effortless running. I always used to think it was as easy as that until I first tried it! Instead of the Bikila smoothness, I found orange squash sloshing from side to side in the cup as I ran, spilling over the sides and sticking my fingers together for the rest of the race. And, when I went to try to drink it, it was swirling about so much that most of it went either up my nose or down my chin, with just a few drops going in my mouth, as I desperately tried to keep running.

It is reassuring to find that it even happens to the stars too. When Bill Rodgers, the American marathon runner, first won the Boston Marathon in 1975, he stopped – completely – several times in the closing stages of the race to take drinks, even though he was running just inside the course record for this classic event.

'I know everyone thinks I'm crazy to stop, but I think it helps me,' he says. 'If I don't stop, I can't drink – it just splashes.' His point was that it was more important to ensure that he took in some of the liquid rather than just a few drops and then risk dehydrating in the final miles.

Ian Thompson, the 1974 Commonwealth and European Marathon Champion tries to stem the waste by putting his hand over the top of the cup and letting the liquid slosh against it. 'That way you can control to some degree how much comes out.'

Actually taking the drink sometimes poses a problem too, as Thompson says:

> If there is a group of runners together, you often have to make a grab and the chances are that most of the liquid is going to go all over the floor, which is rather frustrating. The best thing is to try to arrange for someone to be at the refreshment station to hand it to you, even if they have to run alongside for a short way.

One method of overcoming the spillage problems in marathons, where competitors can hand in their own drinks beforehand to be put out at specific refreshment stations around the course, is the use of small plastic bottles with a squirting top. With these it is possible to squeeze the liquid in a jet into your mouth and thus remove the need to suck in a drink while trying to maintain your breathing rhythm.

Special bottles for this purpose are now sold in some sports shops, although a number of runners have successfully used the type of hair spray bottles which can be bought (empty!) at many chemists, enlarging the hole through which the jet comes if necessary.

The pre-filled bottles have to be marked with your race number so that officials at the various refreshment stations can identify them and hand them to you, or at least put them in a prominent position on the table as you approach; trying to find your own drink among dozens of different bottles in the closing stages of a long race on a hot day can be a challenge in itself.

At the 1979 Sandbach Marathon a complex system was in operation whereby every runner who had handed in personal drinks beforehand had a yellow circle on their race number. Officials with walkie-talkie radios were positioned 100 yards down the road from the refreshment table, and as the runners passed them they relayed the numbers of all approaching competitors with yellow circles ahead to the table officials who then put the corresponding drinks to the front.

After you have finished with the plastic bottles or cups, you simply drop them on the pavement or in the gutter, from where they will be collected up. The bottles are usually returned to the finish, although you can expect to lose one or two of these relatively inexpensive items per race.

Sponging points, situated between the refreshment stations, are where officials establish a line of buckets of water into which they dip a host of sponges and hold them out to competitors as they pass (the sponges, not the buckets). If you take one (a sponge, not a bucket) it can be quite refreshing to wipe your face, neck and shoulders with it, but in general it is not too good an idea to try to drink water from such a sponge unless you are in great need of the liquid. The sponges, like the cups, are often dropped in the gutter when they have served their purpose, and usually they are collected up by hordes of enthusiastic youngsters who rush them back to the buckets. By the time a few dozen dropped sponges have been dipped into the water, it begins to get some-what gritty and dirty, and there is not always time or opportunity for the officials to change it. A cold sponge can be reviving, but the water it contains is often less than palatable, and if there is a lot of grit around it can be like wiping your face with a Brillo pad.

Safety

If we accept that every time we set foot on the road we are entering an arena in which thousands of motorists and pedestrians are killed and injured every year in this country alone, then it is obvious that the appearance of several hundred runners on the scene, if not directly posing danger, is not exactly making the roads safer either.

Road running started before the First World War, when there were few motorized vehicles about, and if the sport has grown considerably since then it is a small expansion compared to the increase in traffic over the same period. Some traditional road races, including the London to Brighton clubs relay, have been discontinued partly because of the traffic problems they created. Others, like the Finchley 20 mile road race, have had to restrict their entry and to switch from a Saturday to Sunday to conform with local police requirements.

Many other races continue on public roads, usually without incident, but sometimes a few near misses. And occasionally a runner is injured. At the 1979 Cambridge Harriers road relay in Bexley, one of our leading veteran runners, Ken Harland, was hit by a passing car and suffered a compound fracture of the leg.

Only a month or two earlier, international Keith Penny fell trying to avoid a van while leading the Mitcham 25 kilometre road race, and had to drop out. Both are experienced road runners, and yet even they could not avoid the traffic hazard.

Occasionally the problem arises even more unexpectedly. Bolton international Steve Kenyon was leading the Eastham Burco 7 mile road race at Fleetwood in 1978 when a well-built spectator inadvertently crossed the road in his path, collided with the slight Kenyon, and sent him somersaulting to land on his head in the road, opening a gash which needed five stitches.

They are the sort of incidents which can never be totally eliminated from the sport, any more than one could have predicted that a rhinoceros would chase Bournemouth's Chris Stewart after 2 miles of a 15 mile road race in Kenya. But there are some common sense rules which can at least help to keep traffic incidents to an absolute minimum.

The most obvious of these is to keep left during races. Yet at many events you can see runners drifting from side to side on the road, often without looking round, to try to take advantage of the bend all the time. Quite apart from the traffic danger this poses, it actually contravenes the rules, because the course is measured 1 metre from the left-hand verge of the road, and to go to the other side is equivalent to cutting the course.

When training for road running, use the pavement as much as possible and, if you have to run on the road where there is no pavement, at least try to face the traffic whenever you can so that you can assess oncoming vehicles. A single runner on a narrow country lane is far more vulnerable to a fast car rounding a bend than when he is running alongside a main road.

At night, wearing a light-coloured (preferably white) tracksuit top or jumper will help motorists to see you, while an alternative is to use fluorescent patches on your tracksuit, or diagonal belts of the type worn by motorcyclists and cyclists.

There are moves afoot to try to transfer, in the interests of safety, as many road races as possible to enclosed circuits in parks or private grounds, and the old motor racing circuit at Crystal Palace National Sports Centre has been successfully used for road races and relays.

But even if it were possible to transfer every road race to traffic-free courses, thousands of runners would still have to train during the week on public roads. As a driver, I have cursed the foolishness of fellow-runners out training when they have suddenly darted across the road, or when I have narrowly missed hitting them because they were running down the middle of the road at night wearing a navy blue tracksuit.

Conversely, as a runner, I have cursed those car drivers whose main ambition in life seems to be to drive as close and as a fast as possible to me when out training. In fact, there is probably a proportion of blame on both sides. But the unprotected human body is likely to fare far worse than a mass of fast-moving metal in the event of any collision, and the safest course is for the runner to treat every car driver as a lunatic and to choose the training routes carefully.

Likewise, although training in a group or pack can be particularly enjoyable, you must take care that amid all the backchat and banter which usually accompanies such runs you are not posing a traffic hazard by taking up too much room, straying wide into the road around blind bends, or simply paying insufficient attention to prevailing traffic conditions.

Above all, the runner about to set out on a training run around the local roads can always expect to meet traffic. A driver, on the other hand, will scarcely be setting out on his journey expecting to meet a runner.

4
Types of Training

Like a building, any training programme needs good, solid foundations. It is no use trying to run substantial distances fast until you can run the same distances slowly first, and even the most ambitious international starts a year's training cycle with a large amount of steady paced running. This method of training has been popularized by the New Zealand coach Arthur Lydiard, a former marathon runner who coached Peter Snell and Murray Halberg to Olympic track gold medals in the early 1960s, and whose views on the importance of 'conditioning' for all middle- and long-distance runners are now subscribed to, either directly or indirectly, by the majority of the world's leading runners.

Lydiard by no means invented the system, but refined it and held that the key to success was a basic conditioning programme of 100 miles a week of steady running through the winter, followed by a transitional period which brought in hill training, and then moved on to track work. Even for 800 metres runners like Snell, Lydiard prescribed this programme on the basis that speed was inborn but that additional strength obtained through conditioning gave athletes the ability to sustain their top speed for longer, and with less effort.

But the eventual success of any training programme depends on striking the right balance with perhaps a dozen or more variables, including stamina running, speed running, the correct racing programme, diet, and sufficient rest. Every single athlete is a special case, and no two are ever exactly alike in their background, ability and mental approach. If two athletes undertake identical training, they may still both improve, but the chances are that at least one of them will not be training to optimum effect.

This never-ending search to find the training programme which is exactly suited to the athlete and his current condition is one which involves the coach and athlete in a lot of thought, study and, it must be admitted, occasional guesswork. But the aim is to cut the guesswork to the absolute minimum.

For the serious athlete, it can sometimes be like playing a fruit machine – trying to get three oranges in a line. You may get the first and third, but miss the second; you may have stamina and be free of injury, but be short on speed. You may have the second and third, but lose the first; your speed is good, you are injury free, but you lack stamina. And so on, until finally the day comes when you do manage to get all the oranges in a line and hit the jackpot. Except, of course, that there are probably nearer to twelve oranges than three, and that makes it even more difficult. The Olympic champion is the athlete who, on the day, has more oranges in line than anyone else: his speed, stamina and confidence are all good, his racing programme has been right, he is rested, injury-free and has no dietary problems or illness. And the final most elusive orange of all is a little thing called luck, which even the best prepared athletes need on the big day, whether it is in an Olympic stadium or at the local cross country championships.

You cannot legislate for luck, nor is it possible to state conclusively in a book that 'this is the exact training programme that *you* need'. No one will ever be able to write a book like that, containing the ultimate answer for every athlete, which in itself points to the very fascination of running: 'Have I got the formula exactly right this time?' or 'How many oranges will I get in a line this Saturday?'.

For, even if two runners have the same personal best time for 10 miles on the road, they could need completely different training programmes to improve their performance in the most efficient and effective way. If, for example, you have run 10 miles in 60 minutes on regular weekly training of around 40 miles a week, and you step your mileage up to 60, then the chances are quite good that you will eventually improve your time for 10 miles. But a closer examination of your training might reveal that you would also benefit from some speedwork once a week, to compete in some shorter races occasionally, or to undertake some hill running. You might have an uneconomical style for road running, and you might be over-striding or under-striding. It might turn out that instead of easing down, you are running a flat-out 10 miles time trial the night before a race (as I heard of one runner doing) to make sure you can get the distance!

Any of these aspects, and more, could be adjusted to improve your 10 miles time while still retaining your 40 miles a week. And if you made the adjustments, and also picked up your training level to 60 miles a week, then the improvement should be considerable. The most successful runners do not just go out and run haphazardly. They evolve, through thought, study and self-criticism, the best possible training programme to suit them.

This chapter examines in general some of the types of training in common use by distance runners the world over, while the next chapter considers how athletes of different ages and backgrounds could build up their own training programme.

But I stress now that these chapters are not, and could never be, because of the complex nature of preparing for competition, designed to be more than the basic materials and examples with which you can build, the planks of wood from which *you* must finally make the table which either stands up or collapses.

The other point to make here is that the spectrum of running is enormous, and to generalize too much can be dangerous and misleading. Thus I trust that coaches and parents of the youngest runners will appreciate that in this chapter I am concerning myself specifically with the more senior and experienced runners and, while the broad policies and types of training apply similarly across the board, the details of mileages and times are not designed for younger athletes. Instead, a separate section aimed specifically for younger athletes is included in the next chapter.

Running is a simple process. Oxygen is breathed in from the air, absorbed into the blood through the lungs, and taken by the blood to the muscles to assist them perform the activity required of them, which in this case is to run. That is a greatly simplified version of what actually happens, but the limitations on running are very much governed by the ability of the body to carry out the oxygen transportation process efficiently and continuously.

Through regular training, though, it is possible to increase that ability considerably and thus raise the level of athletic performance. For example, nearly 6 litres of air can be processed in a single breath by even an averagely trained distance runner, while an untrained person would probably manage less than 5 litres. A trained runner also has more red blood cells and in each cell more haemoglobin (an iron-containing protein which provides the colour and the bulk of the contents of the cells, and is responsible for the transport of oxygen) than an untrained person, and can thus absorb and move more oxygen from the lungs to the muscle tissues.

As a result of training, the heart, which is itself a muscle, enlarges and strengthens to the point where it can pump a much greater volume of blood with more efficiency. The runner's resting pulse rate becomes correspondingly slower the fitter he gets, as the heart needs to beat less often to move the same amount of blood at rest. An average healthy non-runner might have a resting pulse rate of 72–74 beats per minute, whereas a well-trained runner may have a resting pulse of only 40, or even lower. Some people are born with a relatively low pulse rate, and these are often the lucky individuals who have a 'natural' talent for winning races at school.

But, unless they undertake some form of training themselves, the day will come when the regularly training runner will surpass their natural ability. It may take years, but the runner with only modest talent can continually improve his condition and his ability to shift oxygen around the body while a rival with natural ability but a reluctance to train will remain at a constant level.

The training effect, achieved through regular running, is simply a form of adaptation made by the body to be able to cope with the work asked of it. The adaptation is a response to the stress imposed by running, and once a certain level of fitness is achieved, the 'stress' has to be increased by graduating the amount of intensity of training, to keep the body constantly adapting to a higher degree of fitness.

All the time, the volume of air that can be taken in and processed through the lungs, and the rate at which it happens, the oxygen-carrying capacity of the blood, and the ability of the circulatory system to transport oxygenated blood to the muscle tissues are being greatly increased. Muscles become stronger and more efficient. Stamina increases. Body fat, which hinders the processes, is being burned up and reduced to a minimum. On every training run you are becoming a fitter, stronger, better-prepared athlete

During a 20 mile run, for example, massive amounts of blood are moved around the body, the pulse is kept at a reasonably high and steady level (thus providing the type of 'stress' to which the cardiovascular system will adapt and strengthen for the future)

and greater capillarization occurs, allowing the blood more routes to get oxygen to the muscles.

Sometimes in short, fast training runs, or in certain sections of a relatively short road or cross-country race, particularly going uphill, you will be in a situation where the blood just cannot get enough oxygen to the muscles because the demands being made are too high. In that situation, a state of 'oxygen debt' is said to exist, and the muscles begin to accumulate lactic acid, the waste product of the exercise and which can only be tolerated without loss of pace for a short while. As the lactic acid level increases, so the muscles become hindered in their movement until an easing off is essential to allow the oxygen supply to catch up with the demand and repay the debt. Track races up to 800 metres are run at top level almost entirely in this anaerobic (without oxygen) state, and the ambitious 800 metres runner has no choice but to adapt to running anaerobically and tolerating enormous oxygen debts in the closing stages of the race without losing too much speed.

As the distance of an event increases, the balance between anaerobic and aerobic (with oxygen) running tips more and more towards the type of running in which the supply of oxygen is equal to the demand, until one reaches the marathon, which is considered to be a 99 per cent aerobic event. In other words, unlike the 800 metres it is not a lack of oxygen in the muscles which slows the runner in the closing stages of a marathon but rather the sheer fatigue of running continuously for several hours.

Obviously, the more the runner has to run anaerobically in his or her chosen event, then the greater proportion of their time will be spent in training anaerobically. In other words, they will deliberately put themselves into oxygen debt a number of times in training sessions, and by doing so their body will adapt to the situation and allow them a greater tolerance of such discomfort in the future. On a session of hard 10×400 metres runs on the track, for example, the athlete has the chance to experience severe oxygen debt ten times, with suitable recovery (and repayment of the debt) in between.

Mentally, as well as physically, it is nevertheless a very hard form of training, and one not to be repeated too often. But then training is very much a rehearsal of the race. It would be of little value, for instance, to run a great distance at a very slow speed and then expect that on the race day you will subsequently be able to run 800 metres very fast. By the same token, a marathon runner who did little but endless repetition sprints of 200 metres would not be improving their preparation for an event which is over 200 times longer.

The human body is deaf, dumb and blind. You can talk to it, write letters to it, or even draw it diagrams, but the only way it can really understand what you want it to do in races is if you take it carefully, patiently and regularly through the motions in training.

LSD

The form of training which has become known as LSD has nothing to do with pre-decimal money, nor drugs. Instead, LSD stands for Long Slow Distance, and became known as such after the publication of a successful book in 1969 written by the American author Joe Henderson. A prolific writer on the subject of running, and a long time competitor of self-admitted modest ability, Henderson entitled his work *Long Slow Distance – The Humane Way to Train.*

He did not claim to have invented LSD, which involves running steadily for long periods at a pace of 7–8 minutes a mile or slower in order to gain strength and endurance. But some might say he re-invented it at a time when there had been an over-emphasis on speed. At least he gave reassurance to those who had discovered by themselves, as Henderson did, that they seemed to gain far more, both mentally and physically, from relaxed aerobic running than from constant sessions of speedwork.

Now, more than a decade later, Henderson says he wishes he had left the word 'train' out of the original title, because some people have misconstrued his aim as trying to promote LSD as the best method of training for *racing*. He readily admits that in itself it is not, and that instead the right proportion of distance running as a base, and speedwork as a tune-up, is more effective for racing.

What he *was* promoting was simply an enjoyable way of running, and he now says:

When I wrote in 1969 about casual, gentle, light-hearted running, it wasn't intended for people who view their running the opposite way. I never said everyone would like it. I never meant to imply that it was *the* method, only *a* method – an alternative for those who were sick of the idea that running had to hurt all the time. It was a fairly common attitude ten years ago.

Henderson explains that his own interest in switching to LSD was:

... finding an immediate way to make training a little less painful. My racing times had sunk to terrible levels, and my lower legs ached continuously. With the Boston Marathon as a convenient goal eight months away, I decided to make training comfortable enough to enjoy and run races long enough to yield satisfaction – no matter how long they took. I had neither enjoyment nor satisfaction just then, and LSD looked like a handy route for achieving both.

Undiluted LSD has worked in sometimes strange ways, but it hasn't produced a bad trip at all. Anything that gives a 4 minutes 27 seconds mile (compared to a 4 minute 44 seconds in my last race before the change), and a 2 hour 49 minutes marathon (I couldn't have run one before the change), and is fun too, can't be bad. I'm anxious to get out and run, which is saying a lot at 6.15 in the morning. What a nice change it is padding softly and slowly along the side roads, either involved in conversation or in solitary thoughts unconnected with how, and why, I'll take another step. Racing, in these circumstances, is threatening to become an unnecessary incidental – except as a social event.

It is important to understand the background and value of LSD running because it has been misrepresented in the past, and whether distance runners agree with Henderson's views or not, it forms a substantial part of nearly all their training programmes. You might be a twelve-year-old running 3 miles on a Sunday morning, or a senior international marathoner covering 28 or 30 miles at a time, but you cannot be a distance runner without running distance.

The choice which faces the uncommitted runner, though, is whether to settle for a training programme made up exclusively of LSD, which can be less painful and more relaxing than any other type of running, or whether to include alternative elements of faster work. LSD builds an excellent stamina base, strengthens the cardiovascular system, lowers the resting pulse rate, develops muscular endurance, keeps down weight and can even help ward off possible heart disease in the older runner. It also enables the runner to get comfortably, and often very successfully, through distance races, although obviously the longer the race the more running will be needed in preparation.

But on its own it is never likely to allow the runner to reach his or her fullest potential at distances below, or perhaps even including, the marathon. I won't say that it will prevent the gaining of success, because success is relative, and I am sure that it would be possible for runners of a certain standard even to win races of reasonable magnitude on the basis of just LSD running. But winning a race does not necessarily equate to reaching full potential.

Serious athletes really need to include some other, faster types of running in their training, to place the kind of stress on their system which will allow the body to adapt to the feel of a fast race. This applied stress is absent from a programme that is totally orientated to LSD – a fact which the ambitious runner would regard as a drawback and which many others would say was a positive recommendation.

Fartlek

One method of providing the change of pace missing from LSD without undertaking too great a commitment to formal speed training is to introduce what is known as *fartlek* into the pro-gramme. This is a form of running which can be relaxing and enjoyable, but also as physically taxing and beneficial as you wish to make it, according to how the mood takes you.

The word is Swedish, and means 'speedplay'. The concept was developed over thirty years ago by the Swedish Olympic coach Gosta Holmer at a time when Swedish runners like Gunder Haegg and Arne Andersson were dominating world middle-distance running. There was naturally a lot of interest in their training methods, which had originally been evolved to beat the Swedes' great rivals, the Finns, and Holmer's original fartlek routine went like this:

1 Easy running for 5 to 10 minutes (as a warm-up).
2 Steady, hard speed for ¾ mile to 1¼ miles.
3 Rapid walking for about 5 minutes.
4 Easy running, interspersed with wind sprints of 50–60 yards, and repeated until a little tired.
5 Easy running with three or four 'swift steps' now and then (trying to simulate the sudden speeding up to avoid being overtaken by another runner!).
6 Full speed uphill for 175–200 yards.
7 Immediately, fast pace for 1 minute.

8 The whole routine was then repeated until the total time prescribed had elapsed. 'But every athlete must remember that he
must not feel tired, but rather stimulated by the training,'
Holmer wrote.

'Always finish by running on the track from one to five laps,
depending upon what distance you run in competition.'

Holmer submitted that the benefits of this type of training were
as follows:

Fartlek brings us back to the games of our childhood where nature
decided that we should expose our inner organs to much effort, so that
our bodies will develop. A child plays while sitting, walks some steps,
runs to its mother, walks or runs back to the playground, makes a
longer excursion to get a toy etc. To keep its balance, a child prefers
running to walking. The swift, but short, runs dominate, and develop
the inner organs.

The runner gets to learn his ability. He doesn't tie himself up on a
certain task (such as a run of two English miles on the track, or three
separate 220 yards sprints at a certain pace) but he is forced to explore.
It is not the fixed courses that make a Professor out of a student, but the
student's spirit of exploration, his studies of other explorers and his
friends with them. It is the same thing with an athlete. Fartlek is such
a field of investigation. Fartlek is rich in contests. Richer for the athlete
with a creative power and the ability of deciding where there is a limit
for his strength. That is to say, the ability to decide for himself when the
training is no longer improving him, but destroying him instead.

If Holmer's exact schedule for fartlek running and his parallels
with childhood behaviour have been rather clouded by the mists
of time, the spirit of it remains. Because its very nature allows such
a range of components, it is impossible to say emphatically that
it now consists of *this*. But generally speaking it involves alternate
fast and slow running of any distances over a course that has not
been specifically predetermined.

Natural markers, like trees or pillar boxes, can act as starting
and finishing lines for hard efforts. The session is usually for a
duration of time such as 20 minutes or 45 minutes, rather than a
particular distance, and the runner alternately sprints, jogs and
sustains racing or steady speed for as long as he wishes. Obviously
the beneficial effects depend very much on the mental attitude of
the individual, and it would be easy to jog for an hour, sprinting
just 50 metres in the middle, and then writing down '60 minutes'
fartlek' in your training diary. Its value would be rather limited.

But in the same time it might be possible to insert any number of hard bursts of 200, 300, 600, 800 metres or more, with recovery jogs as long or as short as you felt you needed in between.

For instance, you might run through a park and decide to run hard from 'the main gate as far as that little old lady sitting on the bench over there'. As long as the little old lady doesn't think you are about to mug her and start jogging off rapidly in the opposite direction, such natural markers are ideal.

The basis of fartlek is to alleviate some of the physical hardship by introducing an air of mental relaxation into your training; to make it more interesting, you could possibly decide to increase your pace considerably from the time you first met a man with a dog until such time as you met another man with another dog! As long as you don't cheat and start the session outside Cruft's, it can be a valuable exercise, especially if the first dog is an Alsatian which looks ready to bite you.

This might seem a flippant example, and in some respects it is, but you can translate it into serious racing terms: a rival suddenly decides to put in a hard burst, and you have to go with him. You don't know how long he will sustain that burst, but you have to be ready for it to last a long while. In the same way, you don't know whether the next man-and-dog duo are just around the next corner or still at home debating whether or not to go out for a walk.

These faster sections of running raise the pulse in the same way as a racing effort, they lengthen the stride, and help to break up the monotony of the week's training. Twice a week is probably the maximum that it should be used in preference to more formal sessions unless you have an iron will in forcing yourself to the limit, but it is a refreshing alternative when you are feeling jaded or stale.

Interval training

Another classic method of race preparation is interval training and, although to some runners this instantly conjures up a picture of toiling round a track, that is certainly not the only place it can be done. But it is a more rigidly controlled form of training than fartlek running, and calls on the athlete to run a predetermined number of times over a given distance, with a specific recovery, or 'interval', between each run.

It was this type of training which was favoured by Roger

Bannister in his preparations to become the first 4 minute miler in 1954, although it should be added that a scarcity of time from his medical studies precluded him from adopting anything more time consuming than a diet of specifically high quality track work.

Its value is in pushing the pulse rate up to around 180–200 beats a minute, near the maximum, during the run itself, and allowing it to drop down to nearer 120 during the recovery period, before pushing it up again with the next hard run. Obviously it is primarily a form of training for the runner who is basically fit to begin with rather than for someone who is trying to get fit.

The variations possible are enormous. How many runs altogether? Over what distance? At what speed? With what recovery?

For instance, a runner might start off the season by running 12 × 400 metres in 75 seconds, with a 2 minute walk recovery. If he can handle that comfortably, he might increase the volume in later sessions to 15, and then 20, runs of 400 metres in 75 seconds. Or he might stick with the total of 12 and then try to run each one faster than 75 seconds. Or he might just cut the recovery time down to 1½ minutes walk. Or change the recovery from a walk to a jog. The combinations are endless.

Another variation is the 'up the clock' or 'pyramid' session, in which the individual runs become longer each time. The athlete runs 100 metres hard, followed by a 100 metres jog, then 200 metres hard and 200 metres jog, followed by 300 metres hard, and so on. He increases the distance up to a given limit – say 600 metres – and then starts reducing them, with 500 metres, 400 metres, down to 100 metres again. The possible combinations in interval running are endless, and although the up the clock session may seem complicated, it keeps the athlete's mind constantly occupied in working out where each successive run and recovery will start and finish on the track. It also gives a wide variation of pace in one session.

'Interval' distances can be anything from as short as 50 metres to 1200 metres, a mile, or even more. Lasse Viren, the Finnish Olympic 5000 and 10,000 metres winner, has done a 5000 metres track training session in which he alternately sprinted and eased for 50 metres sections, which, particularly on the later laps, is a very hard exercise. It contained more violent pace changes than he would ever be likely to meet in any race, and the total time it took, 13 minutes 32 seconds, was not a great deal slower than he would run with more even pacing in a top class race.

Interval training on the track also helps to develop pace judgement, both for those runners who include some track races as part of their training for road and cross country races, and for those who simply like to have a clear idea of the pace they are running when there is no other way of accurately assessing distance.

If a regular interval session on the track is being used as an integral part of a long-term build-up for a particular race, then it is a good idea to have at least one specific session which, carried out every two or three weeks, can give you a guide to your progress. You might, for instance, choose a session of 15×400 metres with a 2 minutes' walking recovery. Then, if you have no coach to assist you, you should try to find someone to time each run, note it down for you and time the recovery.

It is possible to do it all yourself, but running with a stopwatch in your hand can be slightly distracting and does not always give you the most accurate record of your run. You may anticipate the start, or the finish, of the run and whether that would give you a faster or slower time is irrelevant; the point is that it is inaccurate. Also you may find that, as occasionally happens, you have inadvertently stopped the watch during the hard effort and run yourself flat out only to discover that you apparently took just 8.6 seconds for that 400 metres!

Accuracy is of paramount importance in what could be your only timed runs of the week. And, if you accidentally slice off an odd $\frac{1}{10}$ of a second here and there, it will only make it more difficult to improve next week, while the value of the timed session as a progress pointer will have been negated.

The same misleading effect occurs if you allow yourself to stray away from your pre-set recovery time. 2 minutes may actually seem a long time after the first couple of runs, and you may be tempted to cut 10 or 15 seconds off the recovery. But by the sixth or seventh run you will be glad of every second, and by the eleventh or twelfth you may even be tempted to re-tie your shoes just as the recovery time is up, to delay the next hard effort. But it really is in your own interest to stick rigidly to your pattern, even if you wonder 'What difference will another 15 seconds' rest make?' quite apart from strengthening your self-discipline, which is a vital part of any successful runner's make-up, to shorten or extend the recovery period means that you cannot make an accurate comparison next time you do the same session.

We are talking about the use of interval running in that sense not only as a training method, but also as a kind of thermometer to check progress. But, of course, not every type of interval training needs to be timed at all. While some runners prefer the rigid framework of a track session, others are happier using paths, stretches of parkland, or any other suitable area. If the actual running is carried out with the same intensity, then it doesn't matter whether the distance actually covered is a nice round figure, like 400 metres, or something obscure like 369⅞ metres. The object remains the same: to raise the pulse as high as possible let it drop in recovery, then repeat the exercise to bring about the adaptations of training the body to cope with physical stress.

During the winter even those fortunate enough to live near a track may find it impossible to use because of lack of floodlighting or, if it is a cinder track, because of the condition of the surface. For them, and for anyone who prefers not to use the track anyway, it is important to discover local facilities and areas which, with a little imagination, lend themselves to interval running.

For instance, I have solved the problem of winter interval work with my own group of athletes in Folkestone by taking them on to the Leas, which for more than 100 years has been a popular cliff-top promenade overlooking the English Channel. In the summer it is usually crowded with holidaymakers and visitors, but on winter Thursday nights we have it to ourselves, and it forms an ideal training site. It is wide, traffic-free, and slopes gently for about ¾ mile.

At somewhat irregular distances all along the Leas, ranging from around 50 metres to 100 metres, there are lamp-posts which not only provide our 'floodlighting', but are also the markers for the interval session we do there. The athletes start at one end of the Leas, sprint past the first two lamp-posts, turn and jog back past just one lamp-post, then turn again and sprint another two lamp-posts, and so on. That way, they gradually make their way along the Leas, always sprinting up the slight slope and jogging back down it, until they reach the end of the path. Then they turn and stride back down to the starting point and repeat the whole session two or three times.

Eventually the athletes have, in effect, run hard efforts on anything up to thirty-six repetitions at distances varying each time between 100 and 200 metres, with an average recovery jog of around 80–100 metres. Performed on a track, even with the flat ground, it would be a hard session both mentally and physically but, because we are using a natural setting, with the distances varying slightly on every run, the runners say that it never seems as hard as track training.

Not everyone, of course, has such an ideal facility on their doorsteps, though I hasten to add that it also has its drawbacks. The wind blowing off the Channel in winter can sometimes be bitter, and one night the temperature dropped well below freezing point during an interval session, turning the path into a skating rink. But, wherever you choose to run, remember that while *all* training is preparation for racing, some types are, in themselves, more like a dress rehearsal for the real thing than others.

Interval running, and to a lesser extent fartlek, gives you the chance to run to the limit, and experience the fatigue and the oxygen debt you will meet in races. Not just once, but ten or twelve or twenty times in a session. And, each time you force yourself to experience that limit, the more your body will be adapting to the stresses of needing more oxygen urgently in the muscles and coping with the other demands being made of it. For that reason, the ambitious cross country and road racer should include such a session at least once a week in his or her training programme.

Mentally, it is sometimes a hard task to keep putting your body on the rack in this way. But, if you understand the value, and indeed the need and the place in the training plan for such a session, then you will be less likely to drop it from your schedule each week and substitute instead a few more miles of steady running. Some aspects of training cannot be replaced.

Resistance training

Those who think that this section is about blowing up bridges will be disappointed, because the resistance in this case is that felt by your own body as it tries to run up, over or through some form of difficult terrain or substance which has been chosen to force it to work that much harder.

The most obvious form is hill running, in which the athlete has to increase his work rate considerably to maintain even a steady pace, and some specific alterations to the running action have to be made to assist with the added work load. The athlete runs more on the toes and leans slightly into the hill; the knees have to come up higher and the arms have to drive harder. What is virtually a sprinter's action has to be adopted and, if the hill is long enough, some form of oxygen debt will be incurred; certainly the pulse will be raised considerably.

But strength and power will be gained from the exercise and, although a cross country or road runner may rarely be called upon in a race to run *flat out* up a hill, he or she will nevertheless have to race up hills at some stage, and this form of training can develop good technique and economy in doing so. In training the aim should be to reach the top of the hill as tired as possible; in racing it is to reach the top of the hill as fresh as possible. The first, repeated often enough, can lead to the second.

Unless it is unavoidable, a session in which the athlete charges up a hill with all guns blazing, stops on reaching the top and then turns to jog meekly back down again, is not the most beneficial. Physiologically, of course, it will have a solid training effect, raising and lowering the pulse as it does, and developing muscular power. But it also builds in an unhelpful mental reflex if repeated time after time, week after week, that 'when I reach the top of this hill I can stop or ease off'.

Unfortunately, in races there is no such respite. You reach the top and have to carry on running. Thus, a hill 'circuit' in which the athlete runs over the top and then continues the pace for another 50–100 metres, perhaps turning left or right, before jogging back down on a separate route, is ideal. Certainly it is essential if a group of athletes are training together, because inevitably they will become strung out and would probably end up with the descending and ascending athletes running into each other, unless the hill is wide.

In this respect, natural 'bowls' and paths in woods or parkland can be used to work out a challenging, yet mentally stimulating, circuit. Although the total distance may only be estimated, the runner can occasionally try to cover as many circuits as possible within a given time limit, although he should resist the temptation to turn every hill session into such a time trial.

Even if the use of a circuit is impractical, as it may well be on a midwinter evening, and the athlete has to resort to running up and down the same hill, at least every possible session should incorporate running on beyond the top of the hill.

One precaution with hill work, particularly if it is being used as a transitional stage from a period of long, steady running, is to include only a modest amount of uphill running at first and gradually build it up on each session. To rush into a great volume of hill work all at once is to invite shin soreness and strained Achilles tendons, which need time to adapt to being fully stretched again. The mobility exercises outlined later in the chapter are of particular value before hill training.

Incidentally, although running uphill produces undoubted benefits, I have also found some value in an occasional session of 10×150–200 metres down a gentle slope on grass. This session, which can be performed in bare feet if the surface is suitable, flatters the speed but it increases the cadence of the stride and can be quite exhilarating and mentally refreshing at a time of year when so much of the training can seem like pure slog. But it must be down a slope, not a hill, and on grass rather than road, which causes too much jarring in the ankles, knees and lower back.

Most runners have hills near them, although several of the athletes in my own group live on the pancake-flat Romney Marsh and often train in sweat-shirts emblazoned 'Romney Marsh Mountain Rescue Team' as an ironic reminder that they do not. What they do have in their vicinity, though, is the sea and the sand of the south coast, and both can be used effectively for resistance work.

On beaches which do not drop away too sharply it is possible to run hard through waves at ankle to knee height for stretches of 100–200 metres, which is far more tiring than on dry land, especially when repeated a considerable number of times in a session. On every single stride the knees have to come up high, and there is a drag resistance on the feet as they go in and out of the water. The arms have to pump extra hard to help the leg drive, and the abdominal muscles particularly benefit. Take any lazy strides and you are likely to fall flat on your face in the sea!

A drier form of resistance training is sandhill running, which gained particular popularity when the 1960 Olympic 1500 metres champion Herb Elliott of Australia attributed a great deal of his success to running in sand dunes. The principle is the same: instead of reaching the required level of stress by running fast or long, the athlete quickly reaches a fatigued state sufficient for the training effect to occur by the resistance of running in loose sand, particularly up hills. A popular training camp for athletes at Merthyr Mawr, in South Wales, has access to particularly challenging sand dunes which were blown in from the sea 300 years ago. One is known as the Big Dipper which, with its 1 in 3 gradient, is thought to be the highest in Europe.

Again the effort needed to run up such dunes involves exaggerated knee lift and aggressive arm drive if you are to make any progress in the shifting sand. But sand can be effective, and the young Cornish runner Jeremy Lothian reached Junior International Cross Country level on a background of training on the Gwithian Towans, a long stretch of dunes on the south-west coast of Cornwall. Lothian, from the village of Ludgvan, near Penzance, was a good example of the point that where you live matters far less than how fast you can run and how hard you are prepared to train.

He did, however, have the dunes within reasonable reach and became used to running on them regularly over a long period. But an athlete with little or no sand experience must be careful not to overdo dune running at the first opportunity he gets to run on sandhills. The heels sink much deeper into the loose surface than he will be used to, and like any form of uphill running there is a danger that the Achilles tendons will become over-stretched unless they can adapt gradually to the extra range of movement.

Weight training is another form of resistance training popular in athletics generally. But, while it has its place for sprinters and at the shorter end of the middle-distance scale, my own opinion is that cross country and road runners will gain more specific benefits from actually running than from lifting weights. Few leading distance runners use weights, preferring to use the time instead to increase their training mileage, and this is a valid point. If runners wish to include weight training in their programme (and there are a number of good publications on the subject) then it should only be as an addition to their running programme, and not as a substitute for part of it.

Altitude

For those athletes bordering on international level, altitude training is another aspect of preparation for competition which they may wish to consider. Its particular problems and benefits came into focus during the mid-sixties as the world prepared for the 1968 Olympic Games, which had been controversially awarded to 7200 feet high Mexico City.

At such heights the natural air pressure is reduced, which allows improvement in performance at the short, explosive events like the sprints and jumps. But the lower concentration of oxygen in the air makes things very difficult for the endurance event competitors who normally live at sea level and who, without sufficient acclimatization, cannot get enough oxygen circulating to the muscles, causing an inevitable drop-off in performance. Such runners might be able to perform a series of repetition runs at a relatively short distance, say 200 metres, and apparently be running really well, although an abnormally long recovery between efforts might be needed. But, when the same athletes came to run a distance which involved a more sustained effort, they would find it much more difficult than usual, until acclimatization had taken place. Normally this may take up to a fortnight even to begin to occur noticeably, and so not surprisingly athletes who were born or had lived for most of their lives at altitudes of 5000 feet and above did particularly well at the 1968 Olympics, being able to cope with the difficulties much better than even acclimatized lowlanders.

But what has carried over from the research done at the time is the realization that a sea-level competitor who returns from a prolonged period spent at altitude has a supercharge of red blood cells produced naturally by the body as a means of dealing with the inadequate oxygen supply. Having these extra blood cells at sea level means that more oxygen than normal can be transported to the muscles, and a temporary improvement in performance may follow. Consequently, some leading athletes now spend considerable periods of time training at altitude in preparation for a major event, deliberately to increase their oxygen carrying capacity, even though the event itself is being held at sea level.

As this seems such a good way of using nature to improve performance, why does not every top runner subscribe to altitude training?

The answer is that it does not suit everyone. Some athletes find that even at a relatively modest altitude of 5000 feet they suffer headaches, nose bleeding and nausea. Others find that it just does not seem to benefit them sufficiently to justify the expense and disruption of living at altitude in Switzerland, Kenya, the USA or wherever. Also, there is still a lot of research to be done, particularly concerning the ideal length of time to come down from altitude before competition.

A short period of re-adjustment at sea level is needed, but after two or three weeks the benefits begin to diminish, so good timing is critical, as some members of the 1972 British Olympic team which trained at altitude in St Moritz before those Games discovered. A number of athletes who stayed at altitude for what was thought to be the correct amount of time before their events went down to Munich and performed rather disappointingly. But in meetings held in the immediate post-Games period the same athletes set lifetime bests, indicating that they had undergone insufficient re-adjustment before the Games.

But one girl athlete, who had become bored with staying at altitude and left St Moritz for Munich before the recommended time, ran well in excess of all reasonable expectations at the Games and set a UK 1500 metres record which stood for seven years.

Thus, as each athlete may take a different shoe size, so each one may need a different period of adjustment at sea level before achieving their optimum performance, which could be seven to fourteen days or even longer after 'coming down'. Consequently, in considering whether altitude training can help you in a certain race, you have to be fairly sure of your own particular requirements before committing yourself. Instead of helping your performance, it could actually hinder it, so some form of experimentation, using a minor event, is preferable to taking the risk of ending up, as one of those 1972 Olympians remarked, 'throwing away four years of hard work'.

It is also thought that for athletes who do respond to altitude training well, the more frequently time can be spent there, the more benefit will accrue. However, as most runners have jobs, families and other considerations, it takes a particularly ambitious and single-minded athlete to live for regular extended periods away from home, often in a foreign country and with an unfamiliar diet, simply trying to boost their total number of red blood cells.

For what has to be set against the physical benefits are what can be the inestimable negative effects of boredom and change of routine. Sitting around waiting for your next training session for weeks on end, while hoping that your blood cells are duly multiplying, is scarcely the most fascinating of pastimes. The ability to cope mentally plays a big part in the success of altitude training.

Of course, circumstances can be favourably adjusted. Members of the athlete's family or close friends could possible go to altitude too, employment could be found locally, and so on. But it all involves a major upheaval, not to mention an expensive one, because British athletes would inevitably have to go abroad.

Altitudes of at least 5000, and up to 8000, feet are generally considered to be the most beneficial for distance running purposes, so even jogging on the spot at the top of Ben Nevis (4406 feet) while taking deep breaths, won't help a great deal.

In the USA the 1972 Olympic marathon champion Frank Shorter is in the ideal situation, having moved with his wife to Boulder, Colorado (5350 feet) in 1975, first as a lawyer and then operating his own business, selling running gear. He says:

I've lived at altitude since 1967, and it's worked for me. It's simply harder to run up here – there's more of a training effect, or return for a given effort. Besides, you tend to train best where you're happiest, and if you like the mountains, you'll probably do well there.

The place is almost perfect. Apart from the altitude of Boulder itself, nearby Flagstaff Mountain rises to 7200 feet, the weather is generally good and, even if it is not, then Boulder's University of Colorado offers indoor training facilities. More and more of the top US runners have moved to Boulder, and some of them have found local employment working in Shorter's shop.

But, while there is no doubt that altitude training can, and has, produced excellent results for some runners, the difference between training at altitude away from your home environment and creating your own home environment at altitude, as Shorter did, are among the many aspects of this type of training which the athlete must consider thoroughly before it is judged as being the universal answer it may at first appear.

And one very important point must never be overlooked: training, even at altitude, still has to be hard, correctly planned, regularly executed, and allied to the right racing programme as effectively as at sea level to produce the results on the day that matters.

'Blood packing'

One related grey area which has inevitably crept into discussions about preparation for international races during the past decade has been the subject of 'blood packing' or, as it is sometimes misleadingly called, 'blood doping'. Most information on this process is based only on rumour and speculation, and little hard evidence is available, and I mention it here by no means as a recommendation but merely to complete the picture.

In blood packing, an amount of blood is withdrawn from the athlete and the cells are packed and stored. Within a few weeks, and assisted by a high-protein diet, the body will have made up the deficiency, and the stored cells are then returned to the body a day or so before the competition, theoretically producing in a few minutes the 'supercharge' effect created naturally by having lived for long periods at altitude.

Tests on blood packing have been carried out in Sweden, apparently with successful results, and rumours have been flying around for years pointing at specific athletes who are allegedly supposed to have used the method to obtain their success. Every accusation has been denied, and no one has admitted achieving good results after having used blood packing techniques, even though in theory the use of one's own natural blood would not contravene any of the international rules about doping substances. Ethically, of course, it could be construed as cheating but proof would be virtually impossible to obtain as there is nothing to 'detect'.

Fortunately for the sake of the sport, there is increasing evidence to suggest that the process can be dangerous and will not work. One physiological view, put forward by the UK National Event Coach for Long Distance Running, Ron Holman, who has carried out research in this field, is that because a red blood cell substrate known as 2-3-diphosphoglycerate rapidly diminishes within hours of being withdrawn in a quantity of blood from a fit person, the replaced cells are not fully effective.

A leading Canadian sports doctor has also put forward a theory that to replace haemoglobin could possibly introduce infection and cause severe illness or even death.

A further view comes from a Finn, Dr Pekka Peltokallio, who is the personal doctor of Lasse Viren, at whom the suspicious finger has been pointed more than most because of his ability to peak so successfully at the Olympic Games. Peltokallio says that Viren, like many athletes, takes a gram of Vitamin E every day, a gram of Vitamin C three times a day, a multivitamin pill with trace minerals, and bee pollen. Viren has an abnormally large heart, capable of pumping huge amounts of blood on every stroke. But he does not blood pack, because his haemoglobin content is already at a maximum level.

The haemoglobin level in the blood is usually expressed in grams per 100 millilitres, with 14·8 grams per 100 millilitres being a normal healthy level in men, and 14·0 for women. Peltokallio says:

There can be no use in adding red blood cells if one's haemoglobin count is above 15.0, and Viren's is normally 14.4 to 15.6. That is close to optimum level. Any less and you carry less oxygen. But any *more*, and the blood becomes too thick. It can't work as well. There is a disease where the blood becomes too thick and people who have it can get congestive heart failure. They can't pump it. So it is crazy for most runners to try blood exchanges. It is sad that these suspicions take away from Lasse's greatness. He needs no trick. Why do they single him out?

It is reported that the experiments which have been carried out have proved relatively successful, but only on people who were anaemic or unfit. As far as the benefits of blood packing for a fit athlete are concerned, the evidence seems to point to a considerable number of risks and no demonstrable advantages.

Exercises

Distance runners tend to be greatly lacking in mobility, which can cause an unnecessarily restricted running action and sometimes even lead to injury. A few extra minutes before each training session spent on some simple exercises, such as those outlined below and illustrated later on, can improve running style by 'unlocking' the muscles, and help to prevent injury by ensuring that the body really is ready to run. Trying to run hard with insufficient preparation is to ask the muscles to perform without giving them a chance to warm up, and that is when the muscle fibres rebel and tear. It is like asking someone to be at their brightest, most cheerful and creative just moments after being rudely awakened.

But if the muscles are gently stretched by exercises to at least the maximum level to which they will work in running, and slightly beyond, then there is little chance of running causing the over-stretching of cold, contracted, reluctant muscles.

Astride stretch

Stand with left leg forward, the knee bent, and the right leg back with the right knee just resting on the ground. With the hands on the left knee, keeping the right knee on the ground, lean right forward and hold for 15 seconds. Repeat with the opposite leg and then do the whole exercise again. Particular benefit to hip, hamstring and groin.

Quarter-squat

Bend the knees slightly and hold quarter-squat position for 20 seconds. Repeat three times. This stretches the quadriceps (front of the upper leg) and relaxes the hamstrings (rear of the upper leg).

Wall push-up

Stand facing a wall, about 3 feet away from it. Lean on it with straight arms, and then bend the arms to lean as far into the wall as you can, while keeping the feet flat on the ground. Hold for 20 seconds and then push away from wall. Repeat six times. Particular benefit to calves and Achilles tendons.

Kerb stretch

Stand on the edge of a kerb or step, facing inwards, with the heels 2–3 inches over the edge. Gently lower the heels about $\frac{1}{2}$ inch at first, and then raise again. Repeat ten times each day, gradually increasing the amount of stretch. Particular benefit to Achilles tendons.

Bent leg sit-up

Lie on your back on the ground, with the knees well bent and the hands behind your head. Perform ten sit-ups, while trying to keep the feet on the ground. Particular benefit to abdomen and back.

Rest

What, you may wonder, is a section on rest doing in a chapter specifically dealing with different types of training methods? It is here because I believe that rest plays just as important and constructive a part in the preparation of a runner as any of the other aspects discussed earlier. Yet it is something to which few pay much attention, other than just to accept that to rest the day before a race will probably result in a better performance than carrying out another hard training session.

Others actually resent resting, feeling that to do so is to throw away valuable time which could otherwise be used to put in yet more miles. But, if that was the case, the best runner would be the one who trained non-stop for 24 hours a day . . . obviously impossible, so once again it is a question of striking the right balance.

In the short term, hard training, either in quantity or quality, is destructive. It tears down muscle tissues, accumulates waste products in the blood, can cause dehydration which in turn can upset the balance of electrolytes required for functioning of nerves and muscles, and reduces both the amount of energy-giving glycogen in the muscles and the level of blood sugar.

Nature repairs the damage, but it takes time. On each occasion that the body is subjected to hard training, it is eventually set back up again a little stronger than before. But if it is constantly being hammered by hard training without the process of repair ever being completed, it may eventually break down altogether. It is like a house being damaged by a storm. If the builders get to work they can make the house better prepared to face another storm. But if the next storm arrives before they have finished the job, and then another and another, the original damage may be made much worse.

For the runner, sleeping and eating regularly and well helps promote the recuperation, or repair. Alternating 'hard' and 'easy' training sessions also assists, for the demands of modern distance running tend to crowd out the possibility of complete recovery after every session. What has to be avoided is reaching the extreme level of fatigue in which susceptibility to injury or illness is greatly increased.

As Gosta Holmer said of fartlek training, 'the athlete has to decide for himself when the training is no longer improving him, but destroying him instead'.

But relaxing activities, like taking a sauna, a massage, yoga or easy swimming can help the regeneration process by stimulating the circulation without aggravating the temporary damage caused by the running training.

Time and again there have been examples of athletes who have been almost fanatical in their training and whose careers were interrupted by the inevitable breakdown injury brought on by overloading their systems. After an enforced rest, which they usually hated and resented, they often came back to competition on the minimum of training and produced superb performances. Not all of them realized that the performance probably resulted from their original training plus the rest working together. Instead they spent a very long time anguishing over what they could actually have achieved 'if the injury hadn't halted my training'.

The American writer and medical researcher Ned Frederick feels that too many runners treat their bodies as just another obstacle to overcome in their quest for success, and he tells a particularly significant story in explaining the theory that hard work plus rest equals success.

Two climbers reached the peak of a famous mountain together, but when they came down they had different tales about their exploit. One spoke of 'conquering the mountain'. The other put it more humbly: 'The mountain and I together attained the heights.' In the same way, it is not the athlete *against* his body. It is the athlete *and* his body against his rivals.

5

Preparing for Competition

There is a saying, which should not be taken too seriously, that a sprinter is an athlete who has speed but no strength, a marathon runner is an athlete who has strength but no speed, and a middle-distance runner is an athlete who has neither strength nor speed. It does, though, highlight the problem facing most athletes training for cross country and road running. Both forms of competition require stamina, but the shorter distances especially require some element of speed too.

Stamina can be accumulated by regular long runs at a steady pace, and the more frequently you run, the stronger you become. But, if you want to include some speed work too, then a place has to be found during the week for that. And what about hills? Inevitably you will face hills of varying gradients during the competitive season, and training on hills at least once a week will help you to cope with them. Then of course there is the need for rest, and easing down before competition. . . .

How on earth do you fit it all in? If you are keen to build up your mileage to gain stamina, then you will not be too anxious to spend a great deal of time on speed work which does not add up to many miles. But if the race is short, what point is there in being strong and slow? So the dilemma continues, with the athlete or coach facing a constant struggle to fit a quart's worth of training into a pint's worth of time, and still come up fresh and smiling on Saturday for a race.

In this section, we examine some of the possibilities facing the athlete, and for convenience it is separated into three broad sections: the senior male athlete, the senior female athlete, and the young athlete.

Men

The first important decision to be made is the level at which you hope to be competing in the forthcoming season. If your ambition is to challenge for a place in the national team for the World Cross Country Championships in March, then your approach will be quite different from the club runner who is quite happy maintaining a reasonable level of fitness which will help him get through a weekly succession of low-key road and cross country races without too much discomfort.

But let's start with the ambitious runner, whose planning will have begun before the previous track season had ended. Through his club officials, he will know the dates of all the major cross country championships of the winter, most of which come after Christmas, with the English National Championships normally held on the first Saturday in March.

From that, he can work backwards and decide how many weeks he is going to allow himself to build up for such races. For the National, for example, the period from the middle of September to the end of February would give him twenty-four weeks, with another week of easing down before the race itself. In the initial period he will want to gradually build up his training mileage towards, and perhaps above, its previous highest ceiling, and then once he has put a lot of miles 'in the bank', he will introduce more sessions involving faster running and his overall mileage total may fall slightly.

That twenty-four-week period could be subdivided, perhaps just into two periods of twelve weeks each, with speed work being introduced in the second period. Or it could be further divided into four periods of six weeks each, with one week's training repeated six times and then amended. Or, to get a wider variety of training, a fourteen-day cycle could be repeated three times over a six-week period, and then amended. The latter could look something like the table on pages 92-3.

The schedule is only a guide, of course, and some runners have achieved a great deal on less; others have had to do a lot more. Adjustments also have to be made for mid-season races in which the athlete wants to do well, and will therefore have to ease down, for you cannot train at your greatest volume and compete at your highest level simultaneously. When you are building up your training mileage, you will be tired for most of the time. You will be tired before you train, you will be tired afterwards and, if you line up for a race on Saturday afternoon, you will probably still be tired.

Thus the races which are included in the training programme shown are not those of great importance, but rather the low-key inter-club events which will provide a mental break from training. If the athlete feels particularly strongly about going into a race in which he knows he will probably not do particularly well because of residual fatigue, then he can easily substitute a training run for the race.

In fact, it is now a frequent and rather ironic sight to see the number of athletes busy training round a cross country course on a Saturday afternoon, cheering on their clubmates, but not joining in the race themselves because they are 'too busy training'! As long as the athlete is honest with himself, and the reason genuinely is one of fatigue, then it can be justifiable for him to become a mobile spectator in this way. Pushing your body to the limit in training two or three times a day, particularly in winter, can be a very trying exercise, guaranteed to test the resolution and fortitude of any athlete, regardless of the eventual results it produces. But perspective must always be maintained.

It can be harder still for the summer-minded athlete, of course, as he tries to improve his track ability by increasing his winter training volume. But take heart from the fact that even Brendan Foster admits he had his blackest moments during his winter preparation for the 10,000 metres at the 1976 Montreal Olympic Games, where he eventually was Britain's only athletics medallist, and also broke the Olympic record in the 5000 metres.

'Very tired tonight' and 'very fatigued over last few miles' were the sort of comments he was putting in his training diary as he logged over 130 miles week after week. But when he eased down again, it all paid off, as he knew it would from his years of experience as a club runner and an international.

Foster had built up over fourteen years to reach that level of 130 miles a week, and the worst thing the club runner could do would be to faithfully copy that amount simply 'because Brendan Foster does it'. A gradual increase in your average mileage over the winter is always the safest and most sensible way of improving and trying to stay clear of the injury you will almost certainly sustain by suddenly jumping from, say, 50 miles to 100 miles a week.

Day	Period One Mid-Sept. to Oct.	Period Two Nov. to mid-Dec.	Period Three Mid-Dec. to Jan.	Period Four Feb. to mid-March
1 Sunday	Long run: 15 miles	Long run: 16 miles	Long run: 18 miles	Long run: 20 miles
2 Monday	(a.m.) 5 miles (p.m.) 8 miles	(a.m.) 5 miles (p.m.) 10 miles	(a.m.) 8 miles (p.m.) 10 miles	(a.m.) 5 miles (p.m.) 8 miles, including hills
3 Tuesday	(a.m.) 5 miles (p.m.) 12 miles	(a.m.) 5 miles (p.m.) 12 miles	(a.m.) 5 miles (p.m.) 12 miles	(a.m.) 5 miles (p.m.) 12 miles
4 Wednesday	2 × 5 miles	3 × 5 miles	(a.m.) 8 miles (p.m.) 10 miles	(a.m.) 5 miles (p.m.) 5 miles, including 3 × 1200 metres fast
5 Thursday	(a.m.) 5 miles (p.m.) 10 miles	(a.m.) 5 miles (p.m.) 10 miles	2 × 5 miles, including 4 × 600 metres strides	(a.m.) 5 miles (p.m.) 10 miles
6 Friday	7 miles	(a.m.) 5 miles (p.m.) 7 miles	1 hour fartlek	(a.m.) 5 miles
7 Saturday	Race, or 10–12 miles cross-country	Race, or 12 miles cross-country	Race, or 12 miles cross-country	(a.m.) 5 miles (p.m.) Race or 10 miles (or 12 × 400 metres) on country
8 Sunday	Long run: 17 miles	Long run: 18–20 miles	Long run: 20 miles, hilly course	Long run: 15 miles hilly course

Day				
9 Monday	(a.m.) 5 miles (p.m.) 8–10 miles	(a.m.) 5 miles (p.m.) 10 miles	(a.m.) 5 miles (p.m.) 10 miles	(a.m.) 5 miles (p.m.) 1 hour fartlek
10 Tuesday	(a.m.) 5 miles (p.m.) 1 hour fartlek	(a.m.) 5 miles (p.m.) 90 mins. fartlek	(a.m.) 6 miles (p.m.) 12 miles	(a.m.) 5 miles (p.m.) 12 miles steady
11 Wednesday	(a.m.) 5 miles (p.m.) 12 miles	(a.m.) 5 miles (p.m.) 10 miles	(a.m.) 5 miles (p.m.) 8 miles	(a.m.) 5 miles (p.m.) 8 miles fast
12 Thursday	2 × 5 miles	3 × 5 miles	(a.m.) 5 miles (p.m.) 10 miles	(a.m.) 5 miles, including hills (p.m.) 10 miles
13 Friday	Rest	Rest	Rest	Rest
14 Saturday	Race	Race	(a.m.) 5 miles low-key (p.m.) Race	(a.m.) 5 miles (p.m.) Race or 10 miles cross-country
	Average: 85 miles a week	Average: 96 miles a week	Average: 97 miles a week	Average: 91½ miles a week
	Repeat cycle three times	Repeat cycle three times	Repeat cycle three times	Repeat cycle three times

A sample twenty-four week winter training plan for an athlete aiming to race well in the National Cross Country Championships (see page 90).

Just consider: if you increased your average winter mileage from
50 to 70, a reasonably large jump in one season, then over a six
months period you would still have run well over 500 miles more
than the last winter. But the chances are that if you tried to go
from 50 to 100 miles a week you might manage it for three weeks,
get injured, and end up with an actual average nearer 25! Gradual
improvement over a long period has been the story of anyone who
has made a lasting impression in distance running at any level.
And remember, the world is not generally expected to end tomorrow.

Obviously, though, the higher the total mileage you undertake,
the more your life has to revolve around running instead of the
other way round. Each athlete develops a training pattern which
suits him individually, even if it may not suit anybody else. Many
of our leading runners adopt programmes which are similar in
volume but different in detailed breakdown.

Some manage to involve the journey to work and back as part
of their daily training, like Dave Black:

During the week I run about 6 miles to work at eight o'clock in the
morning, then do a longer run home in the evening – about 10 miles
fartlek. On Saturdays, if I haven't got a race, I'll do 10 miles in the
morning and 5 in the afternoon, while on Sundays, like most other
people, I do a long run. In the past it's been about 15 miles, but I'm
gradually lengthening it to 22 miles with thoughts of the marathon.

In all, my weekly winter mileage totals about 90 or 100, which very
rarely includes any hill work. I do interval work, on grass in spikes,
about three times a week in summer, when my mileage drops to about
80 but, although I feel I ought to do some in winter too, when I run
home in the dark I tend to just stick to fartlek for my speed work.

I don't take any rest days if I can help it, though I may train only
once the day before a big race. In winter, I often run 16 miles the day
before a race, and train on the morning of the race too, if it isn't that
important.

Mike McLeod has been successful as both a track runner (winner
of the 1979 IAAF Golden 10,000 metres) and a cross country
runner (1979 English National Champion), but his coach Alan
Storey feels he will eventually specialize in road running, where
he has already made a considerable mark. His training for all
three branches of competition is based on a twice-a-day winter
regime which totals 80–100 miles a week on average, but occasionally reaches 120.

In the morning I run between 4 and 8 miles at 8.00 a.m., and again in the late afternoon, around 3.30 p.m., anything from 7 to 15 miles. Sometimes it's fartlek, and sometimes just steady running, according to how I feel. Most of it is done on dirt tracks or around the hilly cross country circuit in Gateshead, where I live.

On Sunday mornings I do a long run, which could be from 10 to 20 miles, depending on how much beer I drank the previous night! And twice a year, when there are no important races coming up, I run a 24 miler when I visit my coach in Durham.

I like to get out for my Sunday morning run about 8.30, so I'm back by 10.30 and have the rest of the day to enjoy myself. I've got a lot of other hobbies, like photography, skin-diving and water ski-ing, and I prefer not to spend all my time talking about running, like some people do.

Athletes like McLeod, and in recent years Dave Bedford and Ian Stewart, have shown that it is possible to race effectively at different times of the year, although normally easing down their high-volume work when they wished to peak for an important event.

Bedford reached new levels in terms of bulk, approaching weekly mileages of 180–200 (around 28 miles a day), but his outstanding performances on road, track and country persuaded many other runners to try to build up to similar levels, often with overuse injuries as a result.

A previously published extract from Bedford's 1971 training diary indicates the work he was undertaking:

Monday: 10 miles in morning; 6 miles at 12.30 p.m.; 12 miles fartlek in evening.

Tuesday: 10 miles in morning; 6 miles at 12.30 p.m.; 5 miles in evening; 8 × 800 metres in 2 minutes 12 seconds.

Wednesday: 10 miles in morning; 6 miles at 12.30 p.m.; 10 miles in evening.

Thursday: 10 miles in morning; 6 miles at 12.30 p.m.; 9 miles in evening with 30 × 200 metres.

Friday: 5 miles in morning; 6 miles at 12.30 p.m.; 15 miles in evening.

Saturday: 5 miles in morning; 15 miles at 11.00 a.m.; 10 miles fartlek (p.m.).

Sunday: 5 miles in morning; 20 miles at 10.30 a.m.; 5 miles evening.

Did Bedford go over the top in terms of volume, or was he simply ahead of his time? It may take another ten or twenty years before anyone can answer that accurately.

Bernie Ford is less concerned than some runners about using his winter training to prepare for the track. He says:

I'm not someone who says in September or October, 'Right, I'm going to start planning next track season now'. I like cross-country and road racing as much, if not more, than the track, and maybe that is why I don't do so well in the summer.

I can probably train for six weeks for a specific race, two months at the most, without a race, but usually I need competition regularly. If you race nearly every week in the winter, it helps it go so much quicker!

I never specifically start training for the big cross-country races like the National until after Christmas. I race most weeks, or every other week at least, until Christmas, and use the races as my speedwork, with just 85–100 miles a week of steady running.

Then around January I start building up for the National and the other major events. Before what I consider my best ever cross country race in England, winning the 1978 National at Leeds, I had raced up to Christmas and then began a hard six weeks period in which even my worst total was 118, and that was when I was injured. That was surrounded by five weeks in which I varied by only 1 mile a week, covering 125 or 126 miles of steady running each week. Then I had three weeks which included two fartlek sessions a week, and that was my only speed work.

It was a fast race, and I had trouble hanging on to Ian Stewart for some way, but I was stronger than I'd ever been before, and I'm the type of runner who, when I'm strong, I'm fast – or what I call fast, relatively speaking! The training had been steady, monotonous, boring running, but it was just getting it in for that length of time which counted.

I normally put the miles in by running the 10 miles to and from work, and 15 or 20 on a Sunday morning. On the Monday I take enough clothes in to last me the week, because I've got a locker and shower at work, and that day I'd do 10 miles in the lunch hour, and then 10 home in the evening. I run to and from work, for the rest of the week, and then on Friday I run at lunchtime again, and take the clothes home in the evening.

There is a slight detour I can take which goes along the towpath by the Thames and makes it 12 miles. I start out at 7.00 a.m., after a bowl of cereal and cup of tea, and even in the winter it's beginning to get light by the time I reach the river. I get to work, shower, and have a couple of rolls for breakfast in the canteen, because by then I'm ravenous. In winter evenings I can't go along the towpath home, but in the summer I can get two 12 mile runs plus a day's work done and still be finished by 5.30 p.m.

Running to and from work, like Black and Ford, is fine as long as you don't normally commute 50 miles by train. Yet another international runner, Graham Tuck, even manages to combine running with a rail journey. He runs for 2½ miles to Woking Station in Surrey every morning, catches a train to Walton, and then runs 9 miles along the bank of the River Thames to his work in a sports shop at Teddington.

Then in the evenings he runs 4 miles to Esher Station, takes a train to Woking, and then runs 4 miles home: a total of around 20 miles a day. Once, during a rail strike, he even ran the whole 22 miles to work, while all the other commuters were stranded on the platform. So when he isn't training for a race, he is racing for a train.

Having a sympathetic employer, like Tuck has, obviously helps because not every firm supplies changing facilities for its employees at work, and to commute by foot does involve some degree of organization with clothes, which Ford has also overcome. But when Brendan Foster was a student he used to run from his digs in Brighton to Sussex University, and one day arrived at his college to find that his organization had failed: all his clothes were at home, and he only had yesterday's damp tracksuit to change into.

These days Foster has a winter regime of around 100–120 miles a week of steady running, with no fartlek and few races.

I do 20 miles on a Sunday morning, then 5 to 10 miles most other mornings, with another 10 in the evenings, and an easy day on Friday. It doesn't change much in the summer, except that I do three sessions a week of interval track work.

I don't compete much in the winter now, but I wouldn't recommend that to youngsters. You've got to go through a learning process which can only occur through regular racing. The years of experience gained through such racing is one of the reasons we have got so many good internationals, and they all have a strong background.

Tony Simmons runs a twelve-month season:

I compete all year round, and I reckon I must race more often than any of the other internationals. But I really enjoy it. I hate training on Saturdays, so if I don't race I tend to do nothing that day!

From November to January I'm on about 60–70 miles a week of quite fast running. I do 4–5 miles most lunchtimes, then on a Monday evening I do another 8. On Tuesday I go to Welwyn and join a group of about a dozen other athletes there doing repetition runs of 8 × 1000 metres or 4×2000 metres on a road circuit. We all end up in the bar afterwards for a good old booze up, and I would say that without that bar I wouldn't still be running now.

On a Wednesday I do 5 miles at lunchtime and 6 in the evenings, on Thursday the same 5 and then perhaps another set of repetitions in the evening. I just run 5 on Friday, and usually race on Saturday. Then Sunday I go to the Luton Sports Centre, and a group of us run together on the country for anything from 10 to 20 miles. It's peaceful and quiet, with no cars hooting at you, and very relaxing.

From January to March, when the big cross country events are approaching, I step it up to 80–90 miles a week, training every day, and putting much more attack into the training.

Nowadays life has to be arranged solely around running at the highest levels. Running really has to come first and work second. I used to be a painter, working until eight o'clock at night, but it was upsetting my running so it had to go. Now I've got a light, non-physical job as a teacher, which is good for my career and good for my running. But it doesn't just happen by accident. You've got to work things your way. At international level a runner has to be very selfish. It's a lonely sport, and the further along you get, the more independent you have to become.

John Treacy, who now lives in the USA but won the World Cross Country title for Eire in 1978 and 1979, believes very much in peaking for that one race each winter, after building up very thoroughly for it:

Between October and December I put in around 110 miles a week, going up to a maximum of 125, and then in January and February it drops down to around 100, but includes a few speed sessions on an indoor track. At that time of the year the temperature may be 10 or 20 degrees below zero where I am in Rhode Island, and I have to go out wearing three tracksuits.

I include four or five indoor races as part of my speedwork for the World Championships, but I don't run in many cross country races. I'm sure that some athletes race too often so that they have nothing left when the biggest races come round.

A typical winter training week would include two runs a day, six days a week, with an average of 18 miles a day. I run on my own in the morning, getting out about 8.45 a.m., after a bowl of cereal, and then I meet up with a group of other runners in the afternoon for the second session. In March, when the championships are near, I ease down to 40 miles a week.

Treacy's biggest concern, after his surprise World championship win at Glasgow and then his storybook defence of his title at Limerick, where his Irish countrymen almost caused the race to be abandoned as they spilt all over the course in jubilation, is that he should not become known simply as a mud runner, although both his victories were achieved in very soggy conditions. 'A fit man,' he says, 'can run anywhere.'

Although Nick Rose is mainly known as a track runner, he has given hints of great potential on the road and in the country, and many people forget that he was the 1971 Junior International Cross Country Champion:

I'm happy if I'm doing around 100 miles a week in winter, or 15–16 miles a day, and I like to include one session of fartlek and one of hills each week. I do about 5 miles in the morning at around 9.30 a.m. when I'm always very stiff, and then I run again around 4.00 p.m. But I find I've got to get nine to ten hours' sleep a night, and if I only have seven then I feel as if I haven't slept at all.

When I'm doing hills, I start with about 12 the first week, building it up to 16, running 200 to 400 metres up and over the top, rather than simply stopping at the top. I always do that, because otherwise your body looks for a rest at the top of a hill in a race.

The fartlek sessions are usually repetition runs of ¾ mile or 1 mile, sometimes on a track, which other people might not consider fartlek at all. If I haven't got a race coming up, then I do hills on a Monday and fartlek on a Thursday. If there is a race, then I make it Monday and Wednesday so I can ease up for it.

How fast I do the steady running depends on how fit I am. If I'm going well, it may be 5 minutes 30 seconds or 6 minutes 40 seconds miling pace. At other times I may only be running 7 minute miles.

Nat Muir, the young Scot who made a big impression in international cross country competition at both Junior and Senior level as well as winning the 1977 European Junior 5000 metres track title, trains twice a day all year round, running for about 35 minutes at 10.00 a.m., and 1 hour or more at 5.00 p.m., unless he is doing a track session, which starts at 7.00 p.m.

He begins his yearly build-up in August, with four months of mileage and just one track session per week. On a Sunday he totals 15 miles, Monday 13 miles, Tuesday the track session of 8×600 metres or something similar, Wednesday 13 miles, Thursday 10 miles, Friday 5 miles and Saturday a race or 10 miles.

Then from Christmas he has six weeks including hill work three times a week, using a steep 150 metres slope, followed by six to eight weeks with more speed work, up to the end of the cross country season, where the most important races come. Muir dislikes training on the road and is fortunate that he can climb the garden fence of his home in the Lanarkshire village of Salsburgh to be right into suitable cross country facilities.

A great many club runners, of course, train in high volume with no illusions about their ability but just a desire to lower their best road times, improve their best cross country places, and perhaps one day to have a go at the marathon. They prefer LSD running for the most part, and do very little, if any, speedwork because, although they realize that it can help them become faster runners if applied properly, they simply do not enjoy it or want to risk injury to legs which are quite comfortably churning out 7 minute miles in training, and 6 minute miles in races.

A regular level of around 70 miles a week of steady running, even without speedwork, should still be enough to place most runners quite respectably in club races.

But if you are looking for a weekly mileage of 70, how should you break it down? Theoretically, it averages 10 miles a day, but actually doing a 10 mile run every single day would not only be monotonous but would probably have less conditioning effect than this possible schedule:

Sunday	15 to 18 miles
Monday	8 miles
Tuesday	12 miles
Wednesday	two runs of 5 miles each
Thursday	12 miles
Friday	3 to 4 miles easy
Saturday	race, or 10 miles

That would give you a chance to run for the best part of 2 hours on Sunday, still leaving the rest of the day free, although you could always tack on a few extra miles in the evening if you wished.

Doing two runs on a Wednesday might mean getting up early, or squeezing one into the lunch hour, but it would still keep most of the evening free and allow you to run a little faster because of the shorter length of runs. Friday would give you a chance to relax with just a jog to get any stiffness out of your legs (or could even be a complete rest) before Saturday, where a low-key race could become the speed session of the week. By adopting this sort of approach, you would give yourself a varied programme, leave yourself some time for social activities, and still get in your 70 miles a week.

But seventy miles a week takes a fair bit of time, and it is by no means the minimum amount of training. Some runners regularly cover 20 miles or less a week, and enjoy a club race at the weekend, where they may even fare better than a rival who covers 30–50 miles a week for a few weeks, then stops altogether for a couple of weeks.

Obviously results and improvement are subject to an imaginary sliding scale and, if you run only 20 miles a week, you cannot expect to finish near the front in 10 or 15 miles road races. But it would still be possible to improve your own best time for a particular course from year to year on such a distance if it was carried out consistently. A 20 mile week might break down like this:

Sunday	5 to 6 miles steady
Monday	rest
Tuesday	4 miles steady, including several hills if possible
Wednesday	2 to 3 miles a little faster, or 12×200 metres fast strides, with 200 metres jog in between
Thursday	3 miles steady
Friday	rest
Saturday	5 mile club race on road or in country

In planning your own individual target you simply have to decide how much time and effort you are willing to put into your running, be realistic about the sort of results you can expect for that input, and then stick to it.

Women

The first tip one could give any ambitious girl distance runner is to re-read the section on men's training, and then to work out in her mind how *she* would fit two or three sessions a day into her routine. For, at the highest levels, women must accept that they need to train more and more like their male counterparts and, if they cannot hope to match the actual pace, then at least they can attempt to put in the same volume and intensity of work.

In cross country events, the distances may be shorter than the men's races, but the competition is equally fierce and well-prepared. There is less time to correct errors in tactics or pace and

the battle is on from the starting gun. In international races there
are very few second chances.

In the UK some people have perhaps become conditioned to the
rather irrational thought that there will always be someone else
with a better training set-up, probably state-aided, and ready to
run the legs off our girl athletes. In certain women's track and
field events it may even be true that we are not competing on an
equal footing, and perhaps never will. But in distance running the
limitations are inside the head of the athlete, not imposed by the
finance department of a state-controlled sports federation.

What better, more encouraging, proof could you wish than
the fact that in the late seventies the greatest female cross-country
and road runner in the world came from an athletically under-
developed country in Scandinavia, where she received no sponsorship or grant-aid but worked full-time as a schoolteacher, trained
throughout the winter before dawn in sub-zero temperatures over
ice-covered streets, and yet could still dominate a World Cross
Country Championships field as though they were second raters?

Grete Waitz from Norway did not have success handed to her
on a plate. She had to work for it, and she has done so in a country
where the competitors in the National Women's Cross Country
Championships normally reach barely into double figures, while
often she has to run against just two or three other girls. All the
logic might say that there was no chance for a runner, and certainly
a woman runner, to succeed internationally in Norway's bitter
winter. But, because Grete refused to believe it, she overcame the
obstacles.

Her training is dedicated and aggressive. She runs hard always,
and when she has trained on tour with some of the greatest male
distance runners in the world, they have declined to join her for a
pre-breakfast run because they simply could not match her speed
at that time of day. Her strength comes from her determination
never to let up, and she keeps herself close to top physical condition
all year round, rather than peaking for a few specific races. In
turn, that builds from year to year and has taken her on to new
levels while others have fallen back.

To match her particular intensity would need a very special
mental approach for any runner, male or female. And there are
times, she admits, when even she is tired of training in the snow
and ice and feels like 'throwing my running shoes out of the
window'. But she doesn't. Instead, she goes on piling up a string

of World Championship and other international victories on road, track and, especially, cross country.

'There is no pressure of records and lap times, and the scenery is always changing. It's much more fun running cross country,' she says.

At home in Oslo she suffers all the pressures of being a national sports star, expected always to do well, with little real appreciation of what she achieves, because in general the Norwegians do not understand just how tough the world opposition which she defeats can be. But to those in Britain she should be, and is, a shining example of what can be achieved against all the odds:

I get up about 5.30, and start running at 6.00 a.m., after having done a little housework or read the paper, but I don't eat until I've run. In the winter it is dark and very, very cold – usually 10 or 15 degrees below freezing. I run for about 50 minutes, covering 13 or 14 kilometres (8–9 miles) and then I go to my work as a schoolteacher about eight o'clock. I'm home again about 2.30 in the afternoon, do some shopping and some preparation for next day, and about five o'clock I do my second training session, which may include shorter or faster runs over 300 or 500 metres if the weather is not too bad, or could be another long run.

In a week I normally cover a total of 120–130 kilometres (75–80 miles), although several years ago I was covering 160–170 kilometres (100–105 miles). But I think now that it was too much. I was always tired and, when I wanted to run hard, I couldn't because of the fatigue.

The worst of the weather is between the end of November and late March. I have to train on the roads then, dodging the cars, because they clear the roads but not the pavements! It is impossible to run in the woods because the snow is usually 4–5 feet deep. On the roads I sometimes fall over, and it is easy to get leg injuries because when you are running on snow and ice, your muscles are always tense.

When the snow goes I train much more in the woods and forests, and I think that is what helps me in cross country competition. I'm primarily a cross-country runner, not a track runner.

I don't do any special hill training any more, but then we now live on hills so I often have to run up them. I have used fartlek sessions in the past too, jogging for 10 minutes, then running 200 or 300 metres very fast, jogging 1 minute, then another stride out for 100 metres followed by a hard 600 metres. It totals about 12 kilometres, with the last 10 or 15 minutes just jogging.

I have been resting more in recent seasons too. Many middle-distance and long-distance runners are afraid to rest, because they think they may lose their form. I used to be like that. I always had to train, and I was always exhausted. But, to run a good race, you mustn't feel tired. To ease down, I train just once a day for five days before the race.

I go to bed at 9·00 or 9·30 p.m. in order to be able to get up early. I very rarely miss the morning session, and I make it a good one because, if in the evening the weather is very bad, or I'm very tired, then I have at least one good training session behind me that day.

For an athlete who sought no specific peak, it is easy to see why Grete would have become frustrated with the inevitable fatigue produced by a very high mileage, especially as she likes to train and race at a high quality all year round.

For the runner who does want to peak, however, a period of high mileage and the possibility of its accompanying tiredness at an unimportant time of the year is by no means unusual. And by high mileage, the leading senior female runners must be thinking in terms of building up to 80–100 miles or more in some weeks, similar to the men.

Several senior international girls in my own group have topped that level during their winter build-up period. One of them, Gillian Adams, subsequently set a UK marathon best in 1979 and for that event one would expect a high number of miles; in the USA female marathoners have been touching 140–150 miles a week on occasions.

But another schoolteacher, Hilary Hollick, a middle distance track specialist, reached 120 miles a week during 1977–78. The winter competition was less important to her, and although she was Welsh Women's Cross Country Champion the real aim was to build up a good background of strength for the summer peak.

Whatever your event, though, such training mileages have to be built up to over a period of years, and even then I favour the 'two steps forward and one step back' approach, which increases the total only on alternate weeks to try to reduce the risk of over-use or fatigue injuries. Building up from a track season level of 50 miles a week, over a four-month period to 100 miles a week, could go something like this: 50–55–60–55–65–60–70–60–75–65–85–70–90–70–100–75.

An example of an individual week of 120 miles, which in Hilary Hollick's case started on a Saturday, broke down as follows:

Saturday	10.00 a.m.	6 miles	
	4.30 p.m.	10 miles	
	8.30 p.m.	6 miles	*Total* 22
Sunday	11.00 a.m.	5 miles	
	3.30 p.m.	10 miles	
	8.00 p.m.	5 miles	*Total* 20
Monday	8.00 a.m.	4 miles	
	3.00 p.m.	2 miles at school	
	4 p.m.	7 miles home from school	
	7.30 p.m.	6 miles	*Total* 19
Tuesday	8.00 a.m.	3 miles	
	3.30 p.m.	7 miles home from school	
	7.30 p.m.	6 miles	*Total* 16
Wednesday	8.00 a.m.	3 miles	
	3.30 p.m.	2 miles at school	
	4.30 p.m.	7 miles home from school	
	7.30 p.m.	5 miles	*Total* 17
Thursday	8.00 a.m.	4 miles	
	3.30 p.m.	7 miles from school	
	6.30 p.m.	5 miles	*Total* 16
Friday	8.00 a.m.	2 miles	
	3.00 p.m.	2 miles at school	
	4.30 p.m.	7 miles home from school	*Total* 11
			Total 121

She says:

Obviously I did feel pretty tired, and I went to bed early most nights, but by spreading the load out evenly through the week, with just a couple of extra miles early on to provide a mental boost, it was not too difficult.

I hasten to add, in case anyone is tempted to try, that this level of training is suitable only for senior athletes with a solid background of running behind them, and not for trying to turn a thirteen-year-old athlete into a world-class runner. It would be more likely to turn them into a thirteen-year-old ex-athlete.

Sadly, the drop-out rate among young athletes in general, and girls in particular, is already too high for the sport's own good. The particular problems of young athletes are considered more fully in the next section, but basically the tremendous enthusiasm of junior girls sometimes wanes a fair bit in the Intermediate age group (over 15 and under 17) for reasons which are not all that difficult to understand. Leaving school, starting work, meeting with a wider social circle, subsequent pressure from friends outside the sport to give up running and do something else on a Saturday, and even a mistaken belief that running is 'only for kids', all contribute in their varying ways to the dropout rate. No one can blame them, because there *are* other things in life, and it must be admitted that training hard to become a top-class athlete can be a time-consuming, tiring, restricting pursuit, albeit a rewarding one in its own way.

But where the biggest vacuum occurs is at club level, because there are small numbers of female counterparts to the 'run for fun' club men. Of course, there are girls who compete and train at a modest level, and are content to do so, but too often the view seems to be that 'if I can't be a star, I might as well give up'. Consequently the Intermediate and Senior fields for cross country races are frequently just a fraction of the size of the Minor and Junior girls events.

Also, because running needs a regular training regime of some description to be a comfortably enjoyable pastime, even if only two or three times a week, while other activities like recreational swimming or badminton can be picked up and put down at will, some drift towards the latter.

Making the switch from school life to working life is discussed more fully in the section on young athletes, but girls seem to find it even harder than boys to make the transition. Because, unlike boys, for most teenage girls sport is still fairly low on the list of priorities. In a *Sunday Times* survey in 1976 more than half of 185 female students questioned admitted that they rarely or never took any exercise. Thus a female runner, when she leaves school, may find herself not just the only athlete at her place of work, but also the only female participant in any type of competitive sport. And that situation can occur whatever the age of the runner. Thus, she is likely to keep her sporting interest well separated from her work, and in her spare time, of which she will now have less anyway.

In fairness, some bigger firms do organize sports and social clubs, and a few even have specialist athletics sections, but very many do not, and even the opportunity to run to and from work as part of training presents itself less to a girl than a boy, with its accompanying problems of showers and changing. A male runner can cope with a quick change and a wash-down in the gents' toilet if necessary, but although the same should theoretically be possible for the girls (in the ladies', not the gents'!), few seem to do so because 'it's just not done'.

Some are in the apparently ideal job of a physical education teacher, with access to showers and changing rooms. But against that must be set the tiring effect of spending most of the day on your feet, organizing physical activity, so that by the evening it takes some extra determination to go out training.

If you look for them, there are 101 different reasons why training for distance running is difficult for a girl once she has left school. But few of them can be more of a problem than having to run at 6.00 a.m. on snow and ice in dark, sub-zero Norwegian winters. And, even if you have not got that particular degree of dedication and determination, there is probably no absolute reason why you could not still train regularly at some stage of the week, and put up very reasonable performances in open races. If you can train at least two, or preferably three, nights during the week, and use the weekend as well, then it should be possible to maintain a degree of fitness which will see you comfortably through cross country and the shorter road races.

Suppose you are an athlete whose training has become erratic and without specific direction at the moment. You may have been training only when the mood takes you, and consequently your fitness has suffered, which in turn makes you feel even less like training. Can you pull together the threads and get yourself back into racing shape? Of course you can, but the first essential is to make a training plan and stick to it. Too many runners, particularly girls, still expect results to follow a haphazard training pattern in which they only train when they feel like it, and only do what they feel like. If that is the way in which you are satisfied to approach your running, then that is fine, as long as you do not believe that consistent improvement will automatically result from it. Haphazard training produces haphazard results, and some runners are quite content to accept that fact.

But the point is that, just because you do not commit your life to becoming a world class runner, you do not have to accept the 'haphazard' approach to training as the only possible alternative. It just needs a methodical way of training, a framework on which to build the rest of your weekly activities, to be able to enjoy both your running and your life outside running.

Say you start the week on a Sunday. Most people can find some spare time to run on that day, so let us establish it as your regular 'long run' day, as it is for thousands of others already. 'Long' is only relative to what you have done before, of course, so if 2 miles is the furthest you have ever run then a 3 mile run will seem long. Whatever the distance, it should be covered just at a steady pace, not a flat-out effort, and you should finish feeling you could have gone just a little bit further. Then the next week you could try to go that little bit further, but again keeping the pace down so that you do not finish exhausted.

If you do feel that the first run you undertake is about your current limit, then just repeat it the following week instead of increasing it, and perhaps take it a little easier this time. Gradually it should become more comfortable anyway.

If you intend to run on Saturdays too, then we can call Monday a rest day, and spread your other training days over the midweek: Tuesdays and Thursdays, if you intend to train twice during the week, or Tuesday, Wednesday and Thursday if three times is possible.

The Tuesday sessions could be a shorter, faster run than Sunday, perhaps even broken up into two sections with a short recovery phase in between – medium-paced runs of about $\frac{3}{4}$ mile each, with $\frac{1}{4}$ mile jog in between, for instance. When you can handle that comfortably, you could increase the number of runs to three, or the length of the runs to a mile, or amend the session to any combination which allows a gradual progression in distance, speed or volume.

Thursdays could be earmarked as the interval session day, with perhaps 10 runs of about 100 metres at a fast stride, with a walk/jog back between each run as recovery. Again, as the weeks pass and you can handle the session comfortably, you can gradually increase the number of runs, or the individual distances, or cut down the recovery slightly – though not all at the same time. When you reach a combination which you feel is pretty close to the limit, then do not make it harder until you can manage it comfortably.

Assuming that you are normally going to train quite hard on Tuesdays and Thursdays, then the Wednesday session should be a light one, with perhaps just a couple of miles at a very steady pace being sufficient.

With Friday as another rest day, Saturday will either be a race or another longish run, perhaps with a complete change of scenery. A form of gentle fartlek (see page 71) might make a good alternative to just running at a steady pace again, and the length of time can be gradually increased over the weeks.

By establishing some sort of routine like this, you are far more likely to appreciate that there is an overall meaning and progression to the training and perhaps will be more inclined to get out and run than if your normal decisions about if and what come only when you poke your nose out of the front door to see whether it has stopped raining yet. The sort of routine outlined here will not make too much of a dent in your social life and, if it will not guarantee that you win the National Cross Country title either, it should at least ensure that you run reasonably well.

But, in turn, encouraging results in races will help you out of that front door more quickly, and your thoughts may turn to ways of eventually increasing your training still further, rather than which excuse to use to avoid going out tonight.

Graduation over a period of weeks or months is very much a personal thing, and your body will tell you whether you are ready to increase the load or not. But the sort of progression shown on the table overleaf over a ten week period might not be unreasonable.

The problem of monthly periods affects some female runners more than others. In one questionnaire given to women athletes, 20 per cent felt that their performance was worse during a period, while 10 per cent actually thought it was better and 70 per cent noticed little difference. Another survey, carried out during the Olympic Games of 1964, revealed that gold medals were won by athletes at all stages of the menstrual cycle.

In recent years some female competitors, particularly those who suffered badly from severe period pains which forced them to stop training for a day or so, have used the contraceptive pill to regulate their periods and ensure that one did not coincide with a major championship race.

Other physical disadvantages appear to be a slight increase in weight and a bloated feeling, due to the greater water retention which occurs during a period, and the risk of anaemia caused by blood loss. In the latter case, a simple iron supplement will help to offset the loss.

Some years ago, the very idea of a pregnant woman running would have been rejected out of hand, and brought forth a flurry of old wives' tales about such exertions being liable to induce a miscarriage or at least jar the foetus. Now, though, greater medical

Day	Type of Training	Week 1	Week 2	Week 3	Week 4	Week 5	Week 6	Week 7	Week 8	Week 9	Week 10
Sun.	Steady run	3 miles	3½ miles	4 miles	4 miles	4½ miles	4½ miles	5 miles	5 miles	5½ miles	6 miles
Mon.	Rest	Rest	Rest	Rest	Rest	Rest	Rest	Rest	Rest	Rest	Rest
Tues.	Medium-paced runs with ¼-mile jog	2 × ½ mile	2 × ½ mile	3 × ½ mile	3 × ¾ mile	2 × 1 mile	3 × ¾ mile	2 × 1 mile	4 × ¾ mile	3 × 1 mile	4 × ¾ mile
Wed.	Easy, relaxed run	1½ miles	1½ miles	2 miles	2 miles	2½ miles	2½ miles	2½ miles	2½ miles	3 miles	3 miles
Thurs.	Interval fast strides	10 × 100 metres	10 × 100 metres	12 × 100 metres	10 × 120 metres	8 × 150 metres	12 × 120 metres	15 × 100 metres	10 × 150 metres	12 × 120 metres	10 × 150 metres
Fri.	Rest	Rest	Rest	Rest	Rest	Rest	Rest	Rest	Rest	Rest	Rest
Sat.	Race, or fartlek for time	15 mins fartlek	20 mins fartlek	25 mins fartlek	Race	30 mins fartlek	Race	35 mins fartlek	Race	40 mins fartlek	Race

A ten week progressive training plan for a female club-level runner.

research has indicated that not only is easy running during pregnancy not harmful, but it can actually contribute to the health of mother and baby.

The limitations are not the pregnancy itself, but rather the discomfort of running with an increasingly large bulge in front of you! The foetus is well protected in the early days by the muscles and bones of the mother's pelvis, and in later stages of pregnancy by the sea of amniotic fluid which cushions it from shock.

With the agreement of the doctor (whose main problem with expectant mothers may well be persuading them to take any exercise, not stopping them), it should be possible to run for five or six months into the pregnancy, or even longer if there are no complications, and if it is not too uncomfortable. In the USA at least one woman athlete continued running right up until the day before the birth of her fine, healthy son, although by that stage alternate 100 yard walks and jogs were about her limit.

My own wife, a county-level runner with no burning ambition but a love of running, kept jogging into the fourth month of her first pregnancy and even took part in a 1½ miles fun run at Gateshead. She only stopped running when it became too uncomfortable to do so, but kept up an exercise programme and surprised the doctors with the speed and ease of the delivery of our first son. Within six weeks of the birth she was running again.

Some doctors are convinced that a mother can actually become a better runner than she was before giving birth, but the practical demands of motherhood often result in female athletes ending their competitive careers when they first become pregnant.

Joyce Smith is an example of what can be achieved by a mother who manages to look after a family, run a home and still train. In 1959 she first won the National Women's Cross Country title; in 1968 she gave birth to Lisa; and in 1972 won the International Women's Cross Country title, and set a UK 1500 metres record on the track.

The following year she finished second in the International Cross Country Championship behind the Italian Paola Cacchi, who herself had interrupted her athletics career to become a mother, and in 1974 Joyce became the first British woman to break 9 minutes for 3000 metres on the track. In 1976 her second daughter, Lia, was born, and within three months Joyce was competing again in the National road relays. During 1979 she set

British best performances on the road at 10 miles, 20 miles and the marathon. Joyce says:

> In 1974, when Lisa was six, I was running 60 miles a week, about twelve sessions in all. At 8.45 a.m. I would take Lisa to school in my tracksuit, then do a 4½ mile road run, have a bath, do some housework, then leave at 10.30 to go to my part-time job as a wages clerk. I'd be home by three to collect Lisa, have tea, then Bryan would come home for tea, and at 5.00 p.m. I'd do my second session of the day, consisting of faster repetition runs on the track or path.

As her aims moved away from the track and towards the marathon in late 1978, the distance to be covered increased, and on Sunday mornings Joyce would run with some boys who were coached, like Joyce herself, by her husband Bryan. The athletes would run from the Smiths' Watford home, via a slight detour, to Copthall Stadium, Hendon, for a total distance of 14 miles.

Meanwhile, Bryan would leave home by car some 20 or 30 minutes later with their two young daughters, and pass Joyce and the others midway through the run, ensuring that all was well before driving on to Copthall to conduct a track session with some more athletes, and await Joyce's arrival.

Her preparation for the 1979 Avon International Marathon at Waldniel, which she won, included some much longer runs, with two at 25 miles each, around a one-lap country lane circuit, with Joyce running on her own and Bryan accompanying her on a cycle.

But her whole racing and training programme, involving the highest mileages of her career, were always fitted in around family life and the demands of the children. In itself it was an example to any mature woman athlete that it is possible to be both a mother and an athlete, and successful at both.

Young athletes

The huge expansion of events for youngsters in recent years has reflected the growth of interest in cross country and road running among school-age children, and fields of several hundred boys or girls are now commonplace all over the country on a winter Saturday.

Few seniors throw as much undiluted energy into their events as these young runners, whose main tactic often seems to be to run as fast as possible for as long as possible, then slow down and hope they can make it to the finish! It is refreshing to watch such un-bridled enthusiasm as they charge across the fields, a waist-high swarm of colour, all running like there was no tomorrow.

It would be satisfying to think that they are all just running for fun, gradually learning about the sport, and not worrying about winning or losing. Many older runners, asked for advice, often tell such youngsters, boys and girls alike, just to play around with run-ning and not get caught up with a preoccupation over success or failure. Between the ages of eleven and sixteen, sport should be basically nothing more than recreation. But the reality can be slightly different.

For few areas of athletics generate the amount of emotion which sometimes surrounds young athletes' races. At women's cross country meetings, a vast number of parents, coaches and club officials often swarm round the Minor and Junior Girls fields as they line up for the start, collecting tracksuits, issuing last minute instructions, encouragement and threats, before galloping off to vantage points around the course. By the time the Intermediate and Senior athletes are lining up, the spectators have thinned out dramatically and some of them are already in their cars heading home and holding a post-mortem with little Sally on today's race.

The similarly large fields which turn out for Boys and Colts cross country and road events again attract this big following of adults who sometimes become as involved in the race, if not more so, than the athletes they have come to support.

Undoubtedly, such a healthy sport as running is ideal in itself for youngsters who are overflowing with energy and who are so often being accused of being part of a generation of overweight telly addicts. But unfortunately it sometimes seems difficult, by the nature of the activity, to promote any sort of low-key running event for them. Competitions involving young athletes rarely have the same relaxed atmosphere of some senior inter-club meetings, and I frequently feel that this is not due to the over-enthusiasm of the athletes themselves, but that it owes more to the constant worrying and fussing of the parents and coaches of the youngsters. They are the people who spend a lot of time and money in the preparation and transportation of the athletes, and in some cases they are the same people who have created the very competitions for which they are now urging little Jimmy to run himself into the ground.

There are extremes, of course, and it is the extremes which

irritate me, rather than the many reasonable parents and coaches. But there are parents so obsessed with their son/daughter obtaining success as a runner that it spoils the whole week for them if little Jimmy/Sally performs below the high standard sometimes unreasonably expected of them. But then are they any worse than the parents who take absolutely no interest at all in their son or daughter's sport, and rarely even ask them how they got on when they get back from a race on Saturday evening?

It is a very complex situation, but the ones who eventually suffer most are the youngsters themselves, who are being made to believe by the tune of the surrounding adults (who are usually right about everything else, after all) that it really matters whether they win or lose, when it patently does not matter. The youngsters will simply not possess the mature reasoning powers to work out that in many cases it matters only to the parent or coach because of their own frustrations or lack of success in sport or elsewhere, and that in broad terms it does not actually matter to the future of civilization whether they finish first or fiftieth.

If I feel that any of my own young athletes are beginning to come under some pressure over a particular race, I just point out to them that 54 million people in the UK will not even know that the race took place, never mind where he or she finished. I try to throw it back to the athlete: never mind what anybody else wants or thinks, what do *you* want to do? How well do *you* want to run? By letting them set their own targets, even if sometimes they are too high or too low, I believe the athlete can develop a much better judgement value than by simply relying on someone else to tell them whether or not they have done well. In dealing with young athletes especially, I feel sure that their whole long term commitment to the sport could be favourably affected if parents and coaches associated with these impressionable youngsters used variations on just three short phrases: *Good luck. Well done. Never mind.*

It could be worse, of course. In the USA, where there are four-year-olds running marathons and eight-year-olds covering 100 miles a week in training, surveys have shown that very few of the prodigious runners ever made the transition to success even in their teenage years. And adults must take the blame for that because no four-year-old sets out to run a marathon, or eight-year-old to run 100 miles a week, on their own and without a good deal of adult prompting and supervision.

Fortunately in Britain a four-year-old, or even a nineteen-year-old, cannot race a marathon, and in general the rules governing age and distance limits for young athletes are based on common-sense and protect the athletes from themselves, or at least ambitious adults.

But if I now start to talk on the next page about the sort of training young athletes could do to improve their performances, am I not setting myself up as just another 'pushy adult coach'? I hope not, but I acknowledge the possibility and answer it as follows.

Thousands of boys and girls all over the UK enjoy taking part in cross country and road running races. That is healthy. Like everyone else, they would like to improve and to run faster and to do better next time. That too is natural and healthy and to be encouraged.

My reservations come when, instead of simply letting nature take its course, adults expect constant success, often without considering what is involved in obtaining it. In a field of fourteen-year-old boys, are they really all equal? Will that skinny little lad have a chance against that well-built boy showing the first signs of a moustache? In a field of fourteen-year-old girls, how will the runner with the slim boyish figure fare against her close rival of last season, who has put on over half a stone in a few months?

In the school years, running should be just a sport to be mixed in as part of life, together with exams, TV, discos and other recreations, and not an end in itself. Some adult runners may decide to abandon everything for athletics, to work only part-time, refuse promotion or even remain unemployed in order that they may train longer and harder. They may deliberately go to live at altitude, or follow the sun to the other side of the world in winter, just to help them eventually run faster in competition. They may devote a period of some years just to running, and if they do then they have the right to decide whether the result of a particular race at the end of it was a success or a total disaster, in view of their sacrifices.

But no one is likely to win an Olympic gold medal for distance running under the age of sixteen, whatever happens in swimming or women's gymnastics. They are different sports, with separate specific physical demands, in which a youthful body may be a distinct advantage, and in which consequently serious training has to start very much younger than athletics. Few swimmers or girl gymnasts compete internationally in their late twenties – a time when runners are usually reaching their physical peak.

Training for distance running involves a gradually increasing work-load over a long period. To do too much too soon means it is unlikely that the full potential will ever be reached – like a car with just sufficient petrol for a particular journey which is then driven too quickly early on, burns up too much fuel and stops before its destination.

There are many different reasons why runners eventually drop out of the sport. Business reasons, family reasons, injury, lack of time, and so on. But the saddest of all is the athlete who showed promise early on but was simply ground down by constant demands for more records, more victories and more titles, while receiving scant praise for winning and only loud criticism for losing. It is sad, because with a little thought and consideration it could have been avoided and that same athlete might have carried on to achieve performances which would be remembered much longer and further afield than his or her youthful activities which will probably be forgotten as soon as the next wonder child comes along.

Statistics show that an athlete who displays tremendous ability as a runner in early teens will be less likely to make an eventual impact as a senior than the less talented runner who works away regularly at a gradual improvement on performance over a period of some years. Runners like Brendan Foster and Bernie Ford, both of whom were destined to become English National Cross Country Champions as Seniors, never even qualified for their county team at the English Schools Cross Country Championships when they were teenagers.

But how does the young athlete start in the first place? What do you do if you are a boy or girl around twelve years of age, and you think you want to become a distance runner?

The first step, if it has not already been taken, is to get in touch with the local athletics club. Often, if there is a running track or sports centre nearby, the club will be based there for at least part of the year. If the youngster is new to the sport, it is the best way to find out about competitions in the area, to receive on-the-spot coaching advice, and to meet others of their own age group who also enjoy running and with whom they will be able to train.

Training sessions are often held three times a week, with Sunday mornings and Tuesday and Thursday evening the popular, but not arbitrary, choice of many clubs. With races usually held on Saturdays (although there are now an increasing number of Sunday events too), that spreads the activity out over the whole week, and gives the runner a chance to recover on Mondays, Wednesdays and Fridays. As he or she gets older and fitter runs from home on Mondays and/or Wednesdays may become part of the training pattern too.

Many clubs organize coach travel to meetings outside their own locality, as well as fund-raising activities like discos and jumble sales, so there is often an active social side to club athletics too.

Attendance at every training session is not compulsory, but at least twice a week should be a minimum if possible. Athletes are usually organized in groups according to their age and ability, and the coach in charge of the group should be kept informed about the athlete's availability to compete, forthcoming holidays, colds, injuries or anything else relating to the long- and short-term planning. Each coach may have twenty to thirty separate athletes to keep tabs on, but each athlete only has the one coach, and it should be the athlete's responsibility to keep the coach informed.

The amount of actual training at each session will depend very much on the coach in charge, but no one will expect a newcomer to break any world records – in their first week, anyway! During the summer, most of the races available to the young distance runner will be on the track at 800 metres and 1500 metres, with the occasional 3000 metres for boys.

Don't ignore these events just because you want to be a cross country runner. Such track races are good background for the winter season, and a good start to competition.

For an athlete of eleven or twelve years of age, the two or three training sessions at the club, together with a race on Saturdays, should be quite sufficient to get him or her basically fit for running and able to cope with competition. There is no point trying to do more in the first year or so, and progress can be made by attempting to do the same training faster rather than increasing the volume.

The advantages of training with a club group is that the coach can introduce some activities into training like the caterpillar or shuttle relays, which gets the athletes running hard and having fun at the same time. In the caterpillar, for instance, a single file of any number of runners jogs around the track or the outside of a field, and when the coach gives the word the runner at the back of the line sprints to the front, joins on, and resumes jogging. Then the next runner does the same, and so on. It is a gentle introduction to interval training, and could possibly be described as 10×60 metres sprint, with 200 metres jog between. But to the participants it is virtually a running game and not a hard training exercise.

The same applies to the shuttle relay, in which teams of roughly equal ability are divided into two halves, facing each other about 50 metres apart, and then race, one runner at a time, in a continuous relay backwards and forwards across the 50 metres. It could be reduced clinically to something like '12×50 metres, with 90 seconds rest in between', but it will be remembered by the young runners as another enjoyable running game. At the same time, though, it is developing their ability to cope with harder sessions later in their athletics career.

As time passes, a gradual increase in the training load must be made because the body adapts to the stresses placed on it by training and needs a new level of work to continue the adaptation process. The extra runs on Mondays or Wednesdays can be introduced in the second or third year of training, and the amount of work at the club should be slowly increased. But there is no need to reduce the fun element too much. By this time the athlete will probably appreciate the benefits which training produces, and if they are keen to progress they will work hard anyway, but an exercise like the shuttle relay can be as fast as you want to make it and still provide a refreshing break.

Sometimes the need to increase the training load is overlooked, and a young athlete may find their form has tended to stagnate. In one case I came across, a girl who had been an outstanding Minor in her county when she was eleven and twelve seemed to be making very heavy weather as she moved in to the Intermediate age group. Some of the girls she had beaten easily as a Minor were now finishing ahead of her.

Examination of her training diary revealed that she was doing virtually the same training as four years previously, and had reached a level of fitness at which that amount of work no longer stretched her. Thus her progress had stopped.

She had beaten the other girls in the early days by having more natural talent, and in the Minor Girls and Colts age groups success frequently comes down to natural talent because few of the runners have been training long enough to have significantly improved otherwise. Her natural talent plus a light training load was eventually not enough to hold off the girls who had less talent but trained harder over a long period. Yet by gradually increasing her own training she was eventually able to get back close to where she had been in the county as a Minor.

The schedules shown overleaf are provided purely as an example of how the training of an eleven-year-old boy or girl can be graduated over a period of seven years, from three days a week training to six, with relevant increases in the amount of work. I am not a great advocate of vast amounts of mileage in this age range, not because I do not think that youngsters could cope with it – I am sure even the youngest could, physically, if asked – but because of the races in which they are competing, which are all relatively short and sharp. Consequently, the training, while allowing for overall strength increase, must give them a chance to run at or above their racing pace several times during the week.

There are a large number of cases where an athlete has just not been able to adapt to a higher training load after achieving a fair amount of success on natural ability plus light training. It is not that the athlete is physically incapable of hard training, but mentally it is something which is alien to them, not through arrogance but simply because it was not a necessity for success.

A few athletes in that situation are able to change course in midstream, and reorganize their training to a higher volume, but the majority, experience seems to tell us, are not. They tend either to carry on at the same rate, or drop out of the sport altogether. For that reason it is probably fair to say that the majority of those most physically capable of becoming top-class runners as seniors in the UK do not reach their potential.

And, while that is frustrating for the sport in many respects, it also offers great encouragement to those who do not excel in their first season or two as runners. They are the athletes who realize very early on that the only way they will achieve great improvement is by consistent training. The realization itself may even put a few off, but it steels the rest to their task and their long-term prospects are in consequence relatively high.

Which comes back to the problem of striking the right balance between too much pressure to succeed in the early days, and the need to graduate training over a long term. Let me put a hypothetical question. Suppose you had three young athletes of the same age, but in different situations:

	11–12 years	13 years	14 years	15 years	16 years	17 years	18 years
Sunday	Club session or 2 to 3 miles steady	3 to 4 miles steady	4 to 5 miles steady	5 to 6 miles steady	6 to 7 miles steady	7 to 8 miles steady	(a.m.) 7 to 10 miles steady (p.m.) 3 to 4 miles steady
Monday	Rest	Rest	Rest, or 2½ miles easy	2 miles warm up, then 10 × 120 metres on hills. Warm down	3 to 4 miles easy	40 minutes fartlek, including hills	60 minutes fartlek, including hills
Tuesday	1½ miles fast on road circuit	2 miles fast on road circuit	Warm up, then 'up the clock' session: 100, 200, 300, 200, 100 metres	3 miles road circuit fast	5 miles on road or country, with 4 × 300 metres efforts	3 × 1 mile hard effort, 10 minutes walk/jog between	3 miles steady then 6 × 600 metres on grass, jog 400 metres between
Wednesday	Rest	2½ miles steady on road	3 miles steady on road	30 minutes fartlek (in woods if possible)	2 × 1½ miles road circuit hard. 8 minutes recovery	4 miles road circuit hard	6 miles road run, including hills

Thursday	10 × 150 metres fast, on grass, jog between runs	10 × 200 metres on grass, jog between runs	4 × 600 metres approx., on grass. 4 minutes rest between runs	'Up the clock' session: 100 up to 500 metres, back to 100 metres	12 × 200 metres jog 60 seconds between	8 × 300 metres approx. on grass, 90 seconds recovery	15 × 200 metres on grass or track, jog 200 metres in between
Friday	Rest	Rest	Rest	Rest	Rest	Rest	Rest
Saturday	Race or rest	Race or 2½ miles fast on country	Race or 3 miles fast on country	Race, or 4 miles fast on road or grass	Race, or 4 miles fast on road or grass	Race, or 5 miles fast on road or grass	Race, or 6 miles fast on road or grass

A sample training plan for a young athlete, aiming to build up volume and ability over a period of years.

Athlete A is a natural runner, who wins everything at school sports days, trains only lightly but seems unbeatable.

Athlete B is less talented but is under great pressure from home to train flat out every day with the express intention of beating athlete A next winter.

Athlete C also has limited talent, but enjoys training and has gradually increased it season by season. The performances of Athletes A and B are, he knows, irrelevant as long as he keeps improving.

Of those three, which would you think was the most likely to still be around and running well in five years' time?

A hurdle which has to be tackled at some time by both boys and girls in the Intermediate and Senior age groups and boys in the Youths or Junior age groups, concerns leaving school. Quite a few coaches and athletes barely even consider this giant step when planning future races and training, but the fact is that the major upheaval which can result may be enough to throw some athletes off course for some time.

Again it all depends on the individual and the circumstances, but the potential hazards must at least be acknowledged. Even if the school-leaver gets a job which is enjoyable and not physically taxing, the new experience of working longer hours with fewer holidays, and having greater responsibility, will be somewhat tiring at first. It may mean getting up earlier and it will almost certainly mean getting home later. It could involve a journey of some length and, instead of being home by 4.30 p.m. and finished training by 6.00 p.m. with the whole evening free, he or she may not arrive home until 6.00 p.m. or even later, perhaps very tired.

Possibilities of training during school hours, such as in PE or games periods, will no longer exist, holidays will be much shorter, and training will have to be fitted into reduced leisure time.

The problems are not insurmountable if the spirit is willing, and the body and mind will adjust to the different situation (and the new financial opportunities . . . new running shoes . . . a new tracksuit . . .). But some form of allowance for fatigue has to be made in the first few weeks of work. Training should be reduced and competition results not taken too seriously until the adjustment is made. A reassessment of sleep and diet may be necessary after a couple of weeks. Does the new way of life need more hours of sustained sleep? Is there any skimping of meals now that school lunches are no longer being eaten?

Many thousands of runners do work full-time, often commuting some distance every day, then train in the evenings and still compete at weekends. It just needs some time to make the adjustment from school life to working life, and it only has to happen once.

Of course some jobs are more suitable than others for distance runners. Anything involving a lot of hard physical activity, like labouring or bricklaying, is not going to allow the athlete to feel very fresh or inclined to run a long distance in the evening, although it has been done. Likewise, anything which involves standing for long periods, such as working in a shop, will leave the athlete thinking only about an arm chair when he or she gets home. Naturally, it is not impossible for someone in one of these jobs to become a successful distance runner, but it would need a lot of dedication because their daily occupation will hinder rather than help.

A sedentary job, perhaps at a desk, could be more suitable and a large number of runners choose to work in insurance, banking or the civil service, all of which have very active athletics sections, including annual cross country championships, and are sometimes more helpful with time off for competition than other employers.

In some areas of the country there is little choice, or indeed very little employment unfortunately, and to talk of desk jobs may seem ridiculous. But the determined athlete generally gets what he or she is after eventually, even if it takes a little while and other work has to be accepted temporarily in between.

One problem which seems to affect girls in particular when they take on sedentary jobs is sometimes an increase in weight. At school they may have been active all the time but, once seated at an office desk, particularly if the job is not very interesting and breaks for coffee and buns come round every couple of hours, they may put on half a stone or a stone, much of it around their hips and bottom. This will do nothing for their running except slow it down, and attempts to crash diet it away may result in a loss of energy, or even anaemia. The best cure is really prevention by recognizing the dangers of this adjustment in daily life, and taking it easy with the calories in the first place.

A period of transition in which running has to take a back seat for a while must also be allowed for the new student athlete who is attending college or university for the first time. It particularly applies if he or she is living away from home for the first time, which can be a very difficult transitional period because not only is the educational establishment a new world to which they have to become accustomed, but normal everyday chores like shopping, washing and cooking are new energy-consuming challenges to the student on their own for the first time.

Again, some individuals will cope better than others, and some will find their running actually improves while others will note, temporarily anyway, a slight decline. In itself, that doesn't matter.

What does matter is that every one of us who at some time puts any degree of pressure on a young athlete, either as a parent, coach or club official, must remember that in producing good results there are a lot more factors to take into account than simply the right training schedule.

Dos and Don'ts for Young Athletes

Do remember to warm up well before your race, with at least 1 mile of steady jogging and a few fast strides covering 80–100 metres as the very minimum. Keep on the move and keep warm right up to the time you are called for your race.

Don't stand around talking before the start, getting cold and losing the value of the warm-up.

Do make sure your spikes are tied firmly with a double knot so they don't come undone in the race, or get pulled off in the mud.

Don't warm up or warm down in your spikes; warm up in flat shoes at a cross country race, and then change into your spikes before doing your strides.

Do make sure you are wearing your number securely pinned at both sides (not top and bottom, because it folds over and officials can't read it). Make sure that it is the right way up and that you really are number 66 on the programme, not number 99.

Don't eat crisps, Mars bars, sandwiches, chips, or indeed anything for at least two to three hours before the start of your race. You won't have time to digest it, it will just feel heavy in your stomach and could even make you sick.

Do hand your disc quickly in to your team manager at the end of a big race if the disc system is in operation. Don't take it home to show Mum.

Don't collapse in a heap on the ground at the end of a race. You really aren't as exhausted as that (it is amazing how quickly 'dead bodies' recover and are soon chasing around watching the other races). More importantly, it will cause a bottleneck at the finishing funnel which may wreck the whole results system, stop other runners from getting an accurate time, and anyway

give officials another problem they could do without.
Do take a complete change of clothing to races with you, including underwear, plus a towel, even if you travel to the event in your
running kit and tracksuit. There might be torrential rain and
ankle deep mud when you get there, and it won't be much fun
travelling home in that kit then.

Importance of tetanus injections for cross country runners

The honorary medical officer of the English Cross Country
Union, Frank Newton, wrote to *Athletics Weekly* concerning
the importance of tetanus injections:

I write to draw competitors' attention to the fact that it is very
much in their best interest that they have full protection against
tetanus infection. . . . During last year's National and Inter-
Counties Championships I had occasion to stitch quite severe
foot injuries sustained from spike wounds. Such wounds frequently
become infected since they are often ragged and contain mud, and
with the feet cold from snow and frosty ground they are often not
noticed by the runner until he has finished his race.

When such wounds do become infected it is on the cards that
the athlete may lose several weeks of the most important and
competitive part of his season. Almost without exception those
who were stitched had not had tetanus injections. Most were
about to climb on to team coaches for the long journey back home.
They were tired and in some cases, I felt, not in a fit state to
receive a tetanus injection, which in some cases can cause some
reaction.

The normal routine for protection against tetanus is to have
two injections into the arm with a six week interval, followed by
a booster six months to a year later, and thereafter one injection
every five years. Asthmatic sufferers are not usually given this
injection.

I should like to advise all cross country runners to ensure that
they commence a course of treatment or update their present
protection as soon as possible. One further point: wounds from
spikes frequently require stitching. Competitors may not know
that stitching should be done quite soon after the injury and that
a delay of 12 hours often means stitching will not be carried out.
Healing is then significantly delayed, and the resultant scar and
discomfort is often significantly larger. Competitors are therefore
urged to seek medical attention for such injuries as soon after the
race as possible, even if a coach of impatient team-mates is
waiting to make the long journey home.

6

Other Aspects

Although the right quantity and type of training are of paramount importance to any distance runner, there are some other aspects of preparation which, if not given sufficient thought and attention, can undermine the best training plans. Uncomfortable or ill-fitting kit, particularly shoes, or a poor diet, insufficient sleep, or failure to adjust to temperature extremes are just a few of these fringe areas worth examining more closely to avoid unnecessary pitfalls.

Clothing

Shoes

When you consider that your running shoes are the only contact between your feet and the ground for nearly a thousand strides a mile, it is quite surprising that some runners are content to spend the absolute minimum amount of time shopping for them. If they rub or distort your feet on one stride, then they will do so on every stride, and that adds up to many thousands of miserable strides perhaps millions, during the lifetime of the average running shoe. It also means a lot of rubbing and a lot of distortion, which in turn can lead to blisters and injury. It is obviously illogical to spend many hours training, and only 5 minutes in deciding on a pair of shoes which may injure you and undo a lot of the good work you have put in.

There is now a very wide range of shoes on the market, both in make and model, and each different shoe is probably just right for someone. But which is perfect for *you*? Unless you spend some time looking, examining and comparing, you may never find out. Two athletes may have the same length of feet, but one might have broad feet and the other narrow feet. In that case, the same model of shoe will not suit both, unless it is one of those now being made in different width fittings, or in a special ladies' version.

While you might get away with ill-fitting shoes for everyday wear, running shoes need to be just right, as you will know halfway through a long run if they do not fit properly. 'The last pair of running shoes I bought fitted like a glove,' said one runner. 'Next time I'm going to get some that fit like shoes.'

In Chapter 2 I discussed the type of grip needed for cross country running, so this section is confined to road shoes of the type the majority of runners probably wear for 90 per cent or more of their total running activity. But a lot of the points apply equally to selection of racing spikes.

The first essential whenever you are buying a pair of running shoes is that you should try both of them on, properly laced and tied. Only then can you tell what they really feel like on your feet. Sitting on a chair in the shop, trying on just one without even fully lacing it tells you very little about where the shoes could possibly rub or restrict your feet on a long run. Obviously, you may not be able to go out and run a couple of miles down the road in them before you buy them, but you can walk or even jog around the shop in them first.

If they seem at all tight, try half a size larger until you are satisfied. There are now a good many sports shops set up by active runners who understand your needs and can offer sound advice from their own experience. Ask them what shoes *they* wear, and why. But there are also a larger number of general sports shops where the assistants serving you may only be interested in getting a quick sale before their tea break. If the shop is 'waiting for your size to come in', don't settle for the wrong size in the right shoe, or the right size in the wrong shoe. Either hold off buying them until your size does come in, look for another suitable model of shoe, or go somewhere else.

If the shoe feels tight in one place (say, over the arch) or has too much room somewhere else (perhaps in the toes), then forget that particular model altogether because the chances are that no size will fit you properly. Don't be embarrassed if you have to try on a dozen pairs of shoes and then don't want to buy any of them. Remember that the onus is on the shop to find shoes suitable for your feet, not the other way round.

And, above all, never forget that you are trying to find shoes which have virtually to become part of your feet for many miles of running. If the shoes you buy are going to try to alter nature by cramping and distorting your feet, there can only be trouble ahead.

Don't be overwhelmed or distracted by the colour or flashiness of the shoes. A pair of vivid purple, green and orange shoes may be a wow at the club and help people to spot you easily in a fog, but if they give you blisters after 2 miles you are much better off without them. Don't be like the girl athlete who tried on two pairs of road shoes, one of which fitted and one of which didn't, and then bought the pair which didn't 'because the colour goes better with my new tracksuit'.

Examine all aspects of the shoes closely, and particularly the thickness of the heel. The distance runner lands heavily on the heel on practically every stride taken, and it has to be substantial enough to cushion the shock of around 80 per cent of the body weight landing on an unyielding surface like pavement or road. Many shoes have a heel wedge – an extra layer of rubber between the midsole and sole – but the overall thickness of the heel must not be so great that the weight is thrown too far forward, making it feel as though you are constantly running downhill.

To have too thick a heel also reduces the force exerted by the Achilles tendon on each stride. So a happy medium is usually the answer; personally I prefer shoes with a heel about $\frac{3}{4}$ inch thick.

The heel also has to be wide enough to prevent instability, and some road shoes now have a 'flared' heel, in which the sole actually widens towards the ground. This also helps to spread the load of shock, but some runners with a particular gait complain that the edge of a flared sole can cause cuts on the opposite leg if the foot knocks it.

A heel counter is the reinforced section curving around the ankle and often covered with suede, which stabilizes the heel on landing. But the heel tab above it is a controversial aspect on many running shoes. It is the hump which rises on the back of the shoe, above the heel counter, and exists ostensibly to protect the Achilles tendon, and also to assist in pulling on the shoe. Some doctors, however, insist that a rigid heel tab can itself cause Achilles tendon problems by digging into the vulnerable base of the tendon on every stride. Built-in arch supports are another point of debate. Theoretically, they should help, but evidence from the USA has suggested that, although they may feel comfortable, they actually offer no bio-mechanical assistance for most runners. Remember that the

One of the most spectacular sights in sport, as the English Senior National Cross Country Championship field pours over the first hill

Nearly every runner begins in schools events like this one, putting down foundations for the future and gaining invaluable experience

The 1978 English Women's National Cross Country Championship with the eventual winner Mary Stewart, (Number 36), among the leaders at the stream crossing

Aftermath. The 1978 World Championships at Glasgow were not short of mud, as these runners lining up in the finishing funnel show

Grete Waitz of Norway, (Number 125), has set new standards for women's road and cross country running, and here leads the 1979 World Championship

Enthusiasm among young runners is high but coaches and parents have to be careful not to put too much pressure on them

Above left: A typical takeover in a girls' relay race

Above right: No batons are used in road or cross country relays. A touch of hands is sufficient

Barry Watson (Number 1) and Dave Cannon (Number 18) help to push the pace along in the 1977 AAA Marathon.

Ian Thompson often covers 30 miles in training

Ron Hill has been the marathon's greatest innovator

Colin Moxsom (left) and Don Macgregor (right) take advantage of the sponges offered during the Harlow Marathon to help cool the skin surface

Exercises before training can help prevent injury. Demonstrating the Wall Push-up, Tim Race leans against a wall (left) and then bends his arms (right) while keeping his feet flat

The Astride Stretch, to loosen the hip, hamstring and groin and repeated on alternate legs

The Quarter-Squat (below). This position held for twenty seconds stretches the quadriceps and relaxes the hamstrings

The relaxation in 1975 on limitations of the distance British female road runners could tackle, enabled men and women to run side by side in races for the first time

The Kerb Stretch (above) can be performed on a step, stair or kerb. The Achilles tendons are gently stretched by lowering and raising the heels

The Bent Leg Sit-Up, of specific benefit to the abdomen and back as the feet are kept firmly on the ground

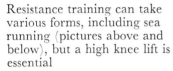

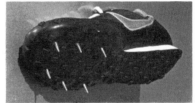

Resistance training can take various forms, including sea running (pictures above and below), but a high knee lift is essential

Grip is essential for confident cross country running. Conventional spiked shoes (top), and waffle soles (middle) are used on most surfaces. Perhaps the greatest stability is gained by the amalgamation of spikes and waffles (below)

Two of the author's athletes
David Bean (left) and Julie
Rose demonstrate the vigorous
arm action and high knee lift
developed by sandhill running

Right: The legendary Ethiopian Abebe Bikila, seen here on his way to becoming the first man to successfully defend the Olympic Marathon crown at Tokyo in 1964, where he set a world best of 2 hours 12 minutes

Below: Mass 'Fun Runs' are becoming increasingly popular with their deliberate avoidance of competition and emphasis instead on simply getting round. This one, organized by the author on the sea front at Folkestone, attracted three hundred and fifty fun runners who all received certificates for finishing

Left: Tim Race and Lois Adams join David and Julie in a session of sandhill training at New Romney

Overleaf: The author at the 23 mile mark during the 1978 Goldenlay Polytechnic Harriers Marathon Race at Windsor where he was placed 101 of the 220 finishers

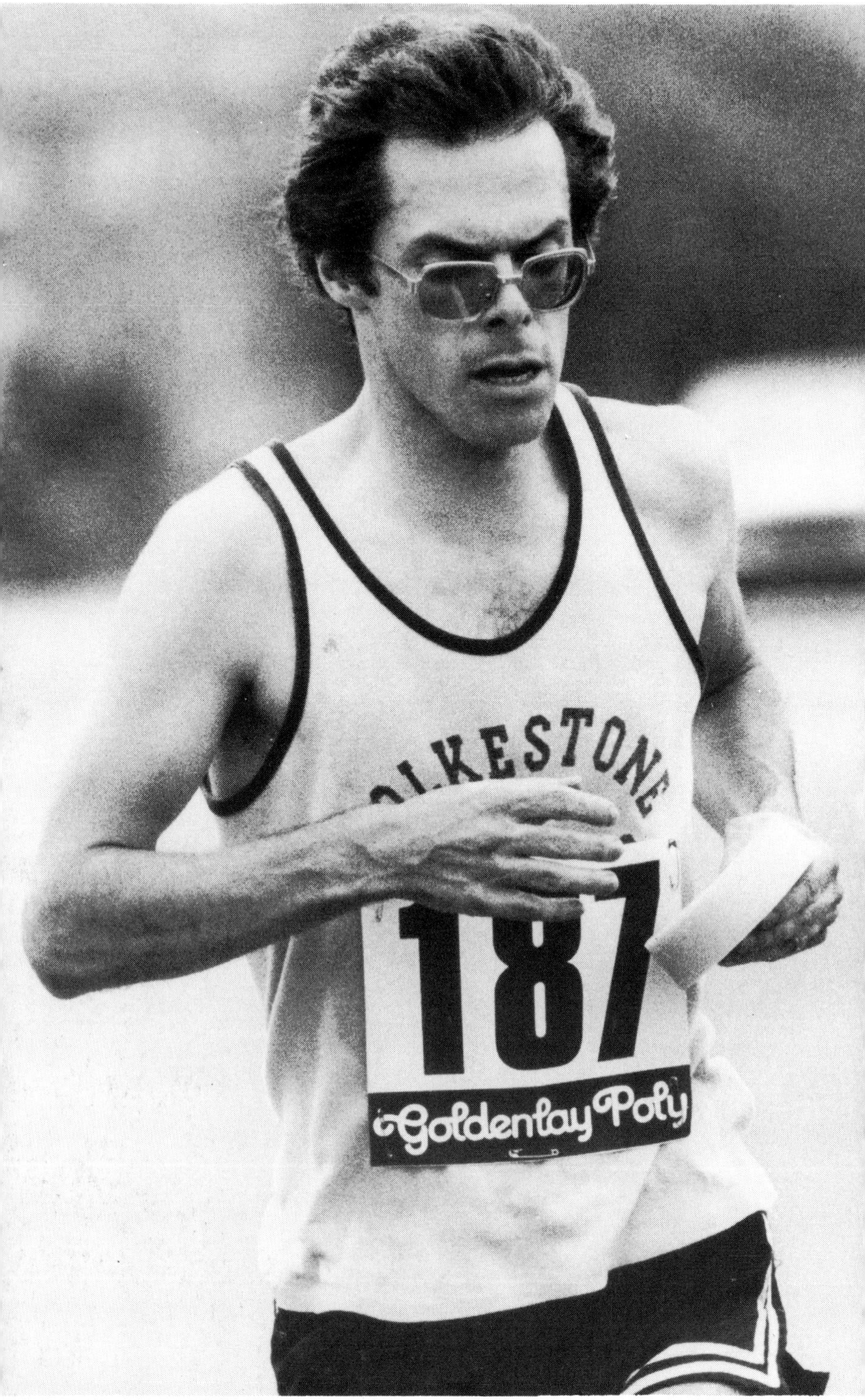
187
Goldenlay Poly

manufacturers are turning out millions of pairs of running shoes made on lasts which are designed to represent the average foot. In fact, relatively few people actually have an 'average' foot. Most feet are as different as our fingerprints, and one estimation is that arch-supports actually suit no more than ten per cent of the buyers of running shoes, and the rest are better off without them. In the USA the trend is towards orthotics, which are plastic shoe inserts, often custom-made, to correct any foot problems.

The sole of a running shoe needs the best of both worlds. It must be reasonably well cushioned to protect the forefoot against too much shock, but flexible enough to allow natural foot movement, particularly at the point of maximum bend, where the toe pushes off from the ground on each stride.

The toe-box, at the front of the shoe, should provide sufficient height and width to prevent the toes being cramped even when the feet expand, as they do when hot. (One authority suggests it is better to buy running shoes in late afternoon rather than the morning, because the feet are slightly bigger at that time of day!) Allow ¼ inch of room in front of the toes, especially if you have Morton's Foot, a condition in which the second toe is longer than the big toe. Running in shoes which are too tight, particularly going downhill, is like kicking a brick wall.

The eyelets for lacing should be reinforced with several thicknesses of material; anything less could result in the fabric being torn. There are three types of lacing. By far the most common is the U-throat, on the top of the foot, but the laces should be taken out and re-threaded every week or so to help spread the wear on the laces themselves. Although not an expensive item, a lace always seems to break at an inconvenient time, such as just before a race or when your available training time is very limited. Because the laces often become snagged on the material eyelets of the uppers, the lacing nearer the toes becomes slacker, and you end up each time just tightening up the two or three eyelets at the top of the shoes, and so the shoe is not fastened most efficiently.

The second type of lacing is speed lacing, where the laces pass through plastic or metal rings, and are easy to tighten all the way down. They can also be adjusted better for those runners with a high instep. The third lacing pattern, and the rarest, is the vamp, with the eyelets situated on the instep area of the foot, and not down toward the toes.

Spare laces should be taken everywhere by the runner, and

fitted as soon as possible after a lace has snapped. Sometimes, in the absence of spares, it is possible, indeed, necessary, to manage by missing out a couple of eyelets and using the short broken lace. But in that case a new lace should still be inserted afterwards. I have known some runners repair their shoes that way in an emergency, and then carry on running with the make-do lace still in place for months. Then they wonder how they had come to be injured, despite the fact that the unequal lacing in their shoes had been forcing them to run out of balance.

Padding around the ankle, the cushioned rim featured by some shoes, helps to prevent those blisters which are often caused in cheaper shoes by having little more than the thickness of the shoe material (and sometimes an irritating seam) around the ankle.

The shoe uppers, usually made of nylon, leather or suede, should have the minimum of inner seams. Leather provides more stability in the shoes but takes longer to break in and dry while nylon is light, easy to break in and dries quickly.

'Breaking in' is an important process, even for shoes that fit well. They need to adapt to the exact movements of the joints in your feet, and the best way is to wear them around the house for a few days, and perhaps jog a mile or so in them, before using them for training or racing – and even then start off using them only for shorter distances. Never wear brand new shoes in a race or on a long training run.

The weight of shoes is again a matter of personal preference. Very light road racing shoes are on the market, but to attempt to do high training mileages in such shoes would probably lead to injury. They are not substantial enough to protect the feet from the constant pounding every day. In fact, the American podiatrist Dr Steven Subotnick suggests that marathon runners who clock 2 hours 25 minutes or slower should wear training shoes rather than light racing shoes even in competition. He says:

I think that unless you are going to run a marathon at a speed faster than 5 minutes 30 seconds per mile (2 hours 24 minutes 12 seconds pace), then you should be wearing a good training shoe. It won't increase your time because during the last 8–10 miles of the marathon your body starts to fatigue and you are not running with as good a form as normal. This increases stress upon the joints and muscles in your body because they absorb more shock. As your form gets sloppier your skeleton absorbs more stress, and you need a shoe that's going to absorb a lot of shock and helps to maintain your foot in a good position. Racing flats have a tendency not to provide the protection training shoes do.

An innovation in recent years has been the increase of shoes with a rounded heel, known as the roll-heel. This enables a more natural foot plant for those who land fairly heavily on their heels. Before such shoes were available, and runners had to make do with flat-heeled shoes, I was never able to run comfortably and relaxed until I had worn the heels down a little way. Before that stage I always seemed to be running on flat feet. Roll-heels were ideal for me, but by contrast my wife, who runs more on her toes, prefers a flat training shoe and feels unsteady on a roll-heel.

But, just as certain shoes were not comfortable to me until they were slightly worn down, the problem can swing the other way, and continuing to run on shoes which are so badly worn down that they are over-stretching your Achilles tendon can bring on injury. Indeed, you should buy your next pair of training shoes well before your current ones have worn down. That way you will have time to break in the new ones and still overlap the dying days of the previous pair. To wait until your shoes are so worn down that they are practically injuring you before thinking about your next pair could leave you between the devil and the deep blue sea if you wish to continue high-level training. Do you continue in your old shoes and risk injury which will stop you running altogether for a while, or run straight away in the new ones and risk blisters which may also stop your running for a while?

Many international runners have three, four or even more pairs of shoes in operation at any one time, partly to avoid the problems just mentioned but also because when training two or three times a day, as many of them do, a switch in shoes from session to session give their legs and feet a chance to work slightly differently each time. No two pairs of shoes are exactly the same, even when worn by the same feet.

Some international runners, of course, have a big advantage in this direction over the club runner, because they are given their shoes free by the manufacturers, who in return are grateful for their particular brand to be seen on television and in newspapers and magazines being worn by the winner of a big race. In return, most internationals stay faithful to one brand of shoe, and wear their spikes, training shoes, tracksuits, tee-shirts, and even everyday leisure wear. One company even sends handkerchiefs bearing their crest to athletes!

The theory, of course, is that, if you see a top athlete wearing a particular type of shoe, you may want to emulate them and so buy the same shoe. If it gives you a mental lift, then there is no harm in it as long as you remember that, while the best shoes in the world may help a little, they will not in themselves make you run faster without the right training first. And which are the best shoes in the world? Like everything else in shoe selection, only you and your feet have the answer to that.

Vests

Although the choice of vest in a race is often dependent upon the rules concerning team colours, an equally important aspect is comfort and the vest should not be too tight or constricting. The weather is also a consideration and the AAA Rules have been modified recently, now stating that, 'For use in races of 20 kilometres or over, clubs may nominate alternative light coloured vests, including white, with a club badge.' This modification came into operation because it was accepted that light colours reflect the sun's rays while dark colours absorb more of them. Thus, in a long race on a hot day, an athlete compelled to compete in his club's dark colours would be at a disadvantage over another whose club had light colours.

White mesh or string vests have become almost standard wear among the leading marathon runners now, allowing as they do for easier dissipation of body heat. But one resultant problem has been the increase of 'runner's nipple', a soreness of the nipples caused by the constant rubbing of the uneven material. Some runners now cover their nipples with sticking plaster before a race, or smear them with vaseline.

A compromise solution for men, and an acceptable version of the mesh vest for women, has come with a new design of unisex vest from the USA, which has a nylon tricot upper half and a mesh lower half.

For women, foundation wear manufacturers are now producing special seam-free bras, specifically designed for sports activity, providing good support without chafing.

Shorts

Men's shorts should be brief cut but airy, not tight at the waist but not so loose that they are in danger of falling down every time you breathe in. Although cotton is more absorbent, nylon seems equally popular material for men, being light in weight and quick to dry, and the style designed by marathon runner Ron Hill, known as 'freedom shorts', are very popular, giving the minimum restriction in movement. Ordinary pants perform suitably the task for which the jock-strap was once thought an essential piece of wear, and the use of vaseline can prevent chafing between the thighs and around the crotch.

For girls the close-fitting towelling shorts are now replacing nylon shorts for popularity because of their comfort, especially when worn in long distance races and training runs. They are more absorbent too, and for the same reason pants worn under them should be cotton, not nylon. In the USA a style of shorts similar to the men's is very popular now, but has yet to catch on in Britain.

Socks

Socks cut down the friction between the foot and the inside of the shoe, reducing the chance of blistering, and help to absorb shock and moisture; again cotton is far better than nylon in this respect. The socks should be clean, with no inner seams to cause irritation, and no darns. If a running sock has a hole in it, throw it away!

Some runners prefer to run without socks, finding it cooler, especially in road races. Vaseline rubbed over the toes can cut down the friction which causes blisters, and sticking plaster applied before you run to any parts of the feet normally vulnerable to blisters can also help to keep down any trouble spots. Some runners put pieces of sponge in between their heels (a prime blister area) and the back of their shoe before a long race.

Tracksuits

The purpose of the tracksuit is to provide warmth both before and after running and, while many of the smartest tracksuits on the market are nylon or other man-made materials, they do not absorb moisture as well as cotton. Therefore at least a tee-shirt or fleecy-lined cotton 'slopp-shirt' is advisable between your running kit and tracksuit. Hooded slopp-shirts, although more expensive, are another good way of keeping in essential warmth, particularly after a race, when you are cooling down rapidly.

All pockets on tracksuits should have zips, because if you try to

run with a key or pound note in your pocket it may jump out
without your noticing it, and you could have to walk a long way
back afterwards looking for it.

Tracksuit trousers with flared legs were obviously designed by
someone who had never run more than 100 yards in their life, and
may be fine for standing around in, but not so good for actually
running in – especially in a high wind! The straight or tapered
leg, with or without side zip, is far more practical.

Sometimes on cold days wearing two tracksuits may be necessary
and, even if you do run round feeling like a Michelin man, the
important thing is to keep warm. And, if you actually train in a
tracksuit, always have another one to put on afterwards, unless
you are showering or bathing straight away.

Keeping the body temperature as level as possible is the aim.
Before you start running, you may need several layers to keep
warm. As you start running, your body temperature rises and you
can then discard some layers without discomfort. But, almost as
soon as you stop, you begin to get cold and the extra layers have
to go back on to maintain the temperature and prevent chills or
muscle stiffness.

Rain suits

These suits are also known as wetsuits, and that is what they
usually end up as, either inside or out. They consist of a lightweight showerproof jacket and trousers which are big enough to
go over several tracksuits if necessary. They prevent you from
absorbing too much rain into your tracksuit, and are very useful
on many occasions – especially going shopping! But their disadvantage can be that, if you warm up for too long in them, they
can become like mini Turkish baths and you end up almost as
damp as you would have done in the rain. However, a rain suit
is still an essential part of every runner's kit, and it takes up very
little space when folded up in your bag. It is often also overlooked
for its value in keeping off the type of driving wind which blows
right through many layers of cotton, wool and nylon.

Diet

Many thousands of words have been written in recent years about
the dietary needs of the athlete, while the level of concern among
athletes themselves ranges from the youngster who, on race days
anyway, seems to exist on a combination of crisps, lemonade and

Mars bars, to the more cautious international who arrives at the airport with small packets of different substances, all carefully weighed and measured, to sustain him through the following days in case the local diet is unsuitable.

You can read in various publications about the absolutely irreplaceable need for meat in the diet, and an impassioned defence of the vegetarian diet for runners. One nutritionist will insist that you keep your body stoked up for activity at all times another will recite the apparently revolutionary endurance achievements by long distance runners who fasted for 24 hours beforehand.

Eventually your head is spinning with the conflicting lists of Dos and Don'ts, as you are urged to eat haricot beans by the sackful, or avoid them like the plague. The runner may be left even more confused, trying to sort the wheat from the chaff ('Eat chaff in great quantities to increase you leg speed . . .'!).

The best answer I have heard to questions about whether long distance runners need special diets probably came from Brendan Foster. 'I eat exactly the same as my wife,' he said, 'only more of it.'

It has been estimated that an adult distance runner may burn up in excess of 4000 calories a day during hard training and, if he is fit and at his best racing weight, he will not want to lose any more weight. Consequently, he will eat sufficient food to provide the fuel, and a table of sample calorific values appears on page 138, but in the main his eating habits will be a response to the messages from his body.

Obviously, it would be undesirable, as well as excessively boring, to supply all the calories from one type of food, and the aim should be for a varied diet which ensures a good intake of proteins (milk, meat, cheese etc.), vitamins, minerals and carbohydrates. Such a mixed diet will help to maintain health, assist recovery, repair damaged tissues and, in the case of younger athletes, ensure natural growth. As long as a runner is eating well and regularly, dietary problems should be at a minimum.

But one problem which sometimes affects distance runners, particularly females, is iron deficiency anaemia. This often turns out to be the cause of an otherwise unexplainable drop in form of a runner who has been training hard and should be racing well. The symptoms, in addition to poor form, are a constant tiredness even after resting, headaches, occasional giddiness (especially when standing up suddenly) and general lethargy.

This form of anaemia is caused by a lack of iron, which helps transport the oxygen around the blood, and in many cases it can be cured by a course of iron tablets within a couple of weeks of diagnosis. In more serious cases, injections of iron may be needed. Your family doctor can perform a simple blood test to confirm whether or not you are anaemic and, if you are, prescribe the tablets.

The best precaution, of course, is simply to ensure that your diet includes plenty of iron-rich foods, like corned beef, dates and liver. In the case of female runners, anaemia may be caused or aggravated by blood loss during the menstrual periods, and during that time it may be wise to take an iron supplement if your doctor recommends it.

Athletes living on their own, or working or studying away from home, should take a special look at their weekly diet pattern. Does it consist of a wide variety of foods including fresh fruit and vegetables, or is it a constant succession of supermarket tins and fish and chips? Brendan Foster was an unwitting victim of anaemia for a long time when first going to university and living in a flat away from home for the first time. He trained hard, but existed on the simplest, most convenient foods to prepare, whose value he judged not nutritionally but simply on the amount of washing up they created, and subsequently his form at the time dropped off badly. Once diagnosed, though, the problem was soon corrected with iron tablets, and he began to pay more careful attention to his diet.

Some runners, particularly girls, are actually motivated chiefly by the weight control effects of running, and even experienced runners may sometimes be faced with having to shed a few surplus pounds after several weeks of injury, or a deliberate lay-off at the end of the season. Such runners tend to go on eating at the same rate during their non-active period as when they are training hard, but as they are not burning up the same amount of calories a surplus develops and is stored in the body as fat. In men this is usually seen on the stomach and around the waist (the 'spare tyre'), while girls tend to put it on around their hips and bottom.

The surplus soon disappears once a reasonable volume of training is undertaken again, and the key to losing weight is simply to ensure that the expenditure of calories (through exercise) is greater each day than the intake. But not by too much, because crash diets can make you feel weak or faint.

If you think a few extra pounds do not matter, just imagine carrying that weight as a bag of potatoes when you run. A distance runner wants the minimum percentage of fat in his body to allow it to work with maximum efficiency and excess weight means having to work harder for the same results.

Joggers are sometimes disappointed if they do not lose at least 2 stones in their first week and in fact they may lose very little weight, if any, at first. But they are burning up calories, lowering the level of fats in their blood, strengthening the cardiovascular system, and in general preparing the body to be able to do the work which will eventually lead to weight loss, as long as they also restrict their intake of calories.

Like a swan crossing a lake, all the action is below the surface at that stage, but they are getting there nonetheless. The motivation could be the knowledge that the fit distance runner, who trains hard six days a week, can usually afford to eat what he or she likes without putting on weight, and that in itself must be a tempting target for those people who cannot pass a biscuit tin without finding their hand inside it.

The question of how much to eat before a race, and when, is always a matter of personal preference, but generally it should be something light, easily digestible, and consumed no less than 3 hours before the race. Because the digestive process is a long one, the food you eat the day before will have more bearing on your performance than that eaten on the day itself. You have to satisfy your natural hunger without lining up for the race with a stomach full of undigested food.

Soccer teams may have steak for lunch before a match, but it will help them through the next game, not this one. There is no time for the body to make use of it. One of the boys I coach used to suffer from a mysterious stitch in some of his most important races. He was a good runner, a county champion at cross country, but he sometimes almost had to come to a halt because of mid-race stitch. Then I discovered that his father had been surreptitiously giving him a Mars bar to eat just before races 'for extra energy'!

Of course, it had just the opposite effect, because when food arrives in the stomach the body sends extra blood to help the digestive process. If you then start taking vigorous exercise as well, with the muscles also calling urgently for extra blood, the body simply cannot cope efficiently with the demands of both.

Trying to run a race with a stomach full of food is uncomfortable anyway, and if a race is important enough you may be too nervous to eat anything for some hours before. Nervousness is a natural feeling before any race, often characterized by frequent yawning (an involuntary method of dragging in extra oxygen), and an increased number of visits to the toilet beforehand. The body is merely 'clearing the decks for action' and to empty the bowels and bladder should be a part of every runner's pre-training or pre-racing routine, particularly when a long distance is involved. Races on cold days are notorious for the higher percentage of runners disappearing into nearby bushes, which may be free but costs a lot of ground in the race, and is often avoidable.

Calorie values

This table, giving approximate calorie values for some everyday foods, is only designed as a guide. Obviously, varying brands and sizes will make a difference, but it can be seen which foods provide many calories and which provide very few. Many of the foods also supply, in varying quantities, vital proteins, minerals and vitamins too, of course.

Food	Calories
Apple	40–50 per 4 oz apple
Bacon	100 for grilled back rasher (1 oz)
Baked beans	25 per oz
Beer (lager)	100 per half pint
Banana	50 for 4 oz banana
Beef	70 per oz cooked lean meat
Beefburger	140–180 each
Biscuits	100 for 2 small plain or 1 small sweet
Bread	70 per oz, white or brown
Brussels sprouts	negligible
Cereals	80–100 per oz
Buns	170 per 2 oz bun
Butter	226 per oz
Cake	100–150 per oz, without icing or filling
Carrots	6 per oz
Cauliflower	negligible when raw
Celery	negligible
Cheese	120 per oz
Chicken	50–60 per oz cooked
Chips	68 per oz
Chocolate	130–150 per oz
Cider	110 per half pint
Coca-Cola	130 per half pint

Food	Calories
Cod	40 per oz fried
Coffee	negligible
Corned beef	60 per oz lean
Cress	negligible
Crisps	100 per small packet
Cucumber	negligible
Dates	70 per oz
Doughnut	200 per 2 oz doughnut
Dumplings	120 per oz
Eggs	80–90 per oz poached or boiled; 160 scrambled
Fish	25–30 per oz if steamed, grilled or poached; frying may double the amount
Fruit juice	40–50 per small glass unsweetened (grapefruit and tomato juice – negligible)
Glucose	120 per oz
Grapefruit	without sugar, negligible
Ham	100 per 1½ oz lean
Honey	80 per oz
Ice cream	100 per 2 oz
Ice lolly	50–60 per lolly
Kit-kat	146 per oz
Liver	35 per oz, grilled, steamed or casseroled
Luncheon meat	95 per oz
Meat	approx. 100 per oz, depending on leanness
Milk	19 per fluid oz
Mineral water	none
Nuts	from 100–180 per oz, apart from chestnuts (40 per oz)
Onions, fried	100 per oz. Negligible otherwise
Orange squash	25 per fluid oz
Puff pastry	120 per oz
Peaches	35–40 per fresh peach
Peanuts	170 per oz
Peanut butter	184 per oz
Peas	14 per oz, fresh or frozen
Pork	90 per oz roasted
Potatoes	20 per oz boiled
Raisins	70 per oz
Rhubarb	without sugar, negligible
Sardines	84 per oz
Sausages	approx. 100 per oz raw
Sausage rolls	112 per oz
Scones	105 per oz
Steak	86 per oz grilled
Strawberries	7 per oz
Syrup	70 per oz
Toast	70 per oz

Food	Calories
Trifle	43 per oz
Water	none
Yoghurt	12 per oz plain. 130–200 per carton, fruit
Yorkshire pudding	63 per oz

Heat

Heat is the enemy of the long distance road runner, and extreme heat is not only uncomfortable and has a detrimental effect on performance, but can actually be dangerous. A runner in the 1912 Olympic Games Marathon collapsed from heat stroke at 19 miles and died the next day. The sad scenes of Jim Peters' collapse within sight of the finish of the 1954 Empire Games Marathon in Vancouver (in which only six of the sixteen starters finished) remain on film as a vivid reminder of what can happen to the human body under the stress of running a marathon in high temperatures. Yet long distance races are still staged in hot weather, and in a recent South African marathon one runner became aggressive, lost consciousness and suffered multiple convulsions as a result of heat stroke.

As the body produces heat through hard exercise, the internal (core) temperature rises and nearly three-quarters of the total energy generated by exercise may be released simply as heat rather than actually powering the muscles. To avoid heat storage, and a subsequent rise in temperature, cooling the body obviously becomes of major importance. But on a hot day this process is hampered, especially if there is a high humidity (which hinders the evaporation of sweat), or a light following wind which, unlike a headwind, offers no relief of convection to the runner.

Convection is one of the three mechanisms on which the runner relies to help him lose excess heat, and is simply the cooling of the skin by the air. Simple heat radiation is another mechanism, while the third is sweating, which is not a method of heat loss in itself. Rather, the fluid released on to the skin by the sweat glands evaporates, thus lowering the skin temperature. But, if the air is humid, the sweat does not evaporate so easily, and its efficiency as a heat loss agent diminishes, while the athlete becomes more dehydrated from the sweat loss.

Dehydration in turn raises the body temperature, and the

athlete may find himself in a vicious circle, as the flow of blood to the skin surface (which transports the heat from the muscles) is reduced and diverted as reinforcement *to* the muscles themselves. This vicious circle, known as the hyperthermic spiral, will continue until heat stroke unless the runner either reduces the amount of heat being produced by easing off the pace, or stopping altogether.

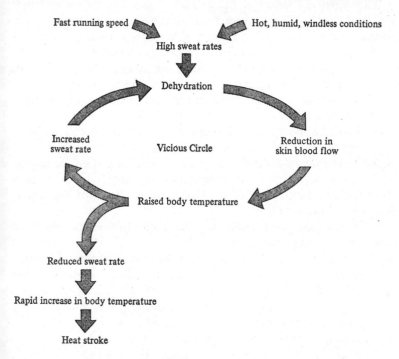

Therefore, the runner needs to take certain precautions before and during any long race in hot weather. Running kit should be light in texture and colour, allowing maximum skin contact with the air. Mesh or string vests are ideal, and even women's models with mesh panels are available now too.

Plenty of fluid should be drunk before the race, and taken at every opportunity during it, without waiting to feel thirsty. Runners can lose between 1 and 2 litres of sweat per hour, and as much of it as possible must be quickly replaced because a fluid loss of more than 3 per cent of the total body weight brings on the first stages of dehydration. Cold water is rapidly absorbed, but adding large amounts of glucose to it, as some runners do, actually reduces the speed of absorption and thus its effectiveness in preventing dehydration. Solids taken during a run (other than in ultra-long-distance events) should also be avoided because they can delay the absorption of liquids too, and use up valuable energy in being absorbed themselves. They cannot quickly provide any additional calories anyway.

The warm-up before a race on a hot day should be minimal and undertaken without a tracksuit. Some runners stay completely in the shade before such a race, and keep their racing vest somewhere cool until a couple of minutes before the start, then discard their warm-up vest and change into the cooler one. Every little helps in keeping body temperature down on such a day.

Make due allowance for the temperature in assessing the pace to run. If in doubt, err on the side of caution in the early stages, and make the most of every sponging point on the course, for a few extra seconds spent there may save you minutes later on – or could even make the difference between finishing the race or not. Sponge well over the head, shoulders and thighs; the latter produce a large proportion of heat because of the hard work performed by the muscle groups situated there.

If, despite all precautions, you do begin to feel the effects of heat, which may include shivering, or a confusion of thoughts similar to drunkenness, you should slow down considerably, and if that does not improve matters, stop altogether. Lie down in the shade, with the feet raised if possible. A good intake of liquid and sponging down should aid recovery, although in more serious cases, such as nausea, sickness, dizziness, headaches and disorientation, medical help will probably be needed.

Cold

If keeping body temperature down is the main problem in hot weather running, then the opposite applies to the cold weather. But the task is not such a difficult one, because extra layers of clothing, including a woollen hat and gloves if necessary, can be worn to maintain body warmth. And even the slowest running speeds of 10 to 12 minutes per mile are still sufficient in terms of energy expenditure to help this process in sub-zero temperatures without the need for ridiculous amounts of extra clothes.

What to wear in very cold weather is a matter of personal preference and common sense, and in the British Isles we very rarely experience temperatures anywhere near as low as those with which runners in other countries regularly have to cope. In Minnesota, for example, runners often train in winter temperatures of 30 degrees below freezing. In Oslo, Grete Waitz has become the best female cross country runner in the world despite having to train in the winter on snow and ice in similarly bitter conditions. She says:

When I'm going out to run in very low temperatures, I wear two pairs of trousers, one thin and one thick, plus long woollen stockings, a polo neck jersey, a sweater, a thick tracksuit top, gloves and a cap.

Brendan Foster, who well knows the bite of winter in north-east England, says:

There is no benefit in training in very cold weather wearing just shorts and a vest. Some runners seem to think that to adopt such a Spartan approach adds some value to the session, but the opposite is true. Your body functions far better if it is warm, and I often wear two tracksuits, a hat and gloves on a really cold day. It's not soft to do so, just good sense. Sometimes it's difficult enough to force yourself out training on a cold day without having to freeze to death as well!

Wearing several layers of lightweight absorbent clothing is preferable to donning bulky garments, as the thin layers of trapped air between them help to insulate against loss of body heat.

At the lowest temperatures, the 'wind-chill factor' can aggravate the actual temperature shown on the thermometer. Even a 10 m.p.h. wind blowing at 32 degrees fahrenheit (freezing point) will cool the face twice as quickly as still air at the same temperature, while the same wind on a day when the thermometer shows zero will produce a wind-chill factor of minus 24 degrees.

The table on page 144, produced by J. Karr Taylor, a Montana doctor with a lot of experience of running in very low temperatures, indicates the effect of the wind in lowering temperature.

Karr Taylor says:

Wind direction is critical because a side wind has only a fraction of the impact of a headwind. The trailing wind is important only if you have to return into it. It is worth noting, too, that to run into the wind at, say, 5 m.p.h., increases the wind chill appreciably.

Running in soft, fresh snow can be an exhilarating experience and provides the legs with some cushioning and resistance at the

Estimated wind speed (m.p.h.)	Actual thermometer reading (°F)						
	50	40	30	20	10	0	−10
	Equivalent temperature (°F)						
calm	50	40	30	20	10	0	−10
5	48	37	27	16	6	−5	−15
10	40	28	16	4	−9	−24	−33
15	36	22	9	−5	−18	−32	−45
20	32	18	4	−10	−25	−39	−53
25	30	16	0	−15	−29	−44	−59
30	28	13	−2	−18	−33	−48	−63
35	27	11	−4	−20	−35	−51	−67
40	26	10	−6	−21	−37	−53	−69

same time. What is less fun for the runner is the time when the snow starts to melt by day and then freezes over again at night, turning roads and pavements into a giant ice rink. If possible, you should try to find somewhere which has escaped the snow through being covered. Some shopping precincts, subways or station approaches may fit the bill; anything with some form of roof which gives you a non-slippery surface on which to run. I have used the stands of Folkestone cricket ground, running up and down between the rows of seats, which was less boring than you might imagine, given the alternative of skidding around the local roads.

But if you do have to run on snow and ice, try to stick to known routes, because otherwise your ankles may discover unknown pot-holes and steps which have been covered by the snow. And, if you should approach a group of children who all suddenly stand back to watch you coming, beware! You are probably about to set foot on their sliding patch, and you may cover the next 20 yards a good deal faster than you expect!

Glasses

Those of us who wear glasses know all about the problems of running in them, and to those who don't it doesn't matter anyway. They may never know the frustrations of having to keep pushing them back on your nose as they slide down, or of having to de-steam them, or keep wiping the rain off them!

Most problems can be overcome, however, and adjustable elastic spectacle holders can now be bought in some sports shops. An ordinary piece of elastic can be adapted to serve the purpose anyway, going around the back of your head and looping over the ear pieces of the glasses. In heavy rain, a peaked cap can keep the worst of the water off. But several leading runners, including Bernie Ford, use contact lenses with success.

Ford first discovered he needed glasses when he ran off course three times during a Surrey Cross Country League race at Croydon in 1973:

The marker flags were red, there were lots of horse chestnut trees around the course, and it was autumn. The leaves on the ground just made a red blur, and I realized after that I needed to visit the optician.

But I switched to contact lenses after a very muddy cross-country race in San Sebastian. The conditions were the worst I have ever run in. The mud and water were literally knee-deep in places, and after about $\frac{1}{4}$ mile I couldn't see a thing through my glasses. So I chucked them to the team manager, and ran the rest of the race blind.

Fortunately my eyes are not that sensitive, so I was able to wear contact lenses straight away. The only problem is grit, which if you run on the road a lot can occasionally get caught behind the lens. Once I scratched my eye and had to go back to wearing glasses for a fortnight, and that brought home to me just how inconvenient they can be. They steam up, slip down and get rain and mud on them. I'd never go back to glasses for running, or any sport, now.

Training diary

Every runner, whether a first-year Colt, a top international, a seasoned Veteran, or just a keep-fit jogger, should have a running diary in which they can record their daily training. The degree of detail could vary from a single figure indicating the number of miles covered that day to a complete breakdown of the length of the run, course, time taken, weather, what you wore, who you ran with, how you felt, and so forth.

By committing your running to paper, you provide the opportunity to look back in some years' time to compare your progress and training. If you want to recapture the form of a previous season, you can always look back to see what training you were doing in the months before your peak. You can keep a record of your fastest times on each training course you use regularly, and in each race. You can note your weight as it rose and fell, and your resting pulse rate (best taken first thing each morning) as it too rose and fell over the years when your fitness increased and declined, as everyone's does from time to time.

In short, with the expenditure of just a few moments of effort every day, you can put between the covers the definitive You, recording one aspect of your daily life more accurately than a photograph album.

An ordinary diary will do, though the more information you want to record the bigger it will have to be. Several specifically designed athlete's diaries are now on the market, but another alternative is a large loose-leaf file into which can be inserted the result sheets of races in which you have competed as well as the training sheets.

Some runners cannot be bothered with such things as diaries, but I still find some kind of fascination in being able to look back and read what training I was doing twenty years ago.

Sleep, rest and relaxation

Although runners are always looking for more ways to pile on extra training loads, they sometimes overlook the corresponding need to increase their sleeping and resting hours to counterbalance the extra fatigue. Some athletes only think specifically about sleep the night before a race, then have an early night only to spend two or three hours restlessly tossing and turning and thinking about the event. Then in the morning they sometimes get up more tired than when they went to bed.

In general terms, an athlete could often be encouraged even to have a relatively late night before a race with beneficial results, unless a lot of travelling is involved. Assuming the athlete has been easing down on training in the days before the race, he or she will probably be feeling livelier and more awake than usual. So to go to bed earlier than when fatigued has the opposite effect to that intended.

Instead, a relatively quiet social night and going to bed half an hour later than usual can ensure a good night's sleep, especially if the athlete has the chance of an extra hour in bed next morning. Obviously, the athlete has to act responsibly, and attending an all-night orgy will probably not help them through the latter stages of a marathon the next day! But the resulting mental benefit of a change of scene and routine just before a race can have beneficial effects on race performance. Having said that, though, all the training in the world will be undermined without adequate sleep during the rest of the week, giving the body a chance to recover from the previous day's training and preparing it for the next session. To cut back on sleep, or burn the candle at both ends, will inevitably catch up with you, especially during a high mileage period. Remember the formula: hard work plus rest equals success.

The runners who try to fit in an extra run before breakfast to add to their training mileage should always weigh up whether they are going to be in bed early enough the night before to undertake such a regime. If not, they will either have to make a conscious effort to go to bed earlier, or forget the early morning run if an extra hour in bed will have a more beneficial effect. That is not laziness – it is common sense.

Grete Waitz gets up most mornings at 5.30 to train, but to do so she goes to bed at 8.30 or 9 o'clock the previous evening. By getting up that early she gives herself a chance to 'come to', by spending half an hour on odd jobs around the house before actually beginning to run. This seems a sensible precaution, because doctors report a higher proportion of injuries among those who go out training first thing in the morning, when the body is stiff and barely awake, than among those who train later in the day.

Usually your body tells you how much sleep you need, and it varies from runner to runner, but most hard training athletes probably need a minimum of 8 hours. More would perhaps be beneficial, but most runners have to work for a living too, which often means travel, and thus the body is up against a perpetual time limit from the moment it starts running, which can lead to tension.

The pre-breakfast trainer has to allow time for showering, dressing, having an often rushed breakfast, then dashing to catch a bus or train to work. I am second to none in my admiration for athletes who can do that nearly every day of the week, then train at lunchtime and again in the evening, fitting a full day's work and travel around the training sessions.

But it seems probable that, however well athletes ran on that regime, they would run even better with less rush and tension during the day. Ignoring for one moment the obvious financial aspects, the ideal situation might be for the runner to have a job with a late start, to allow an early morning session or lie-in, and an early finish, to give time for a good evening session with at least some of it in daylight during the depressing winter months, and an early night. The job should be a sedentary one, close to home, or even *at* home, and involve the minimum of stress.

To have no job at all might seem attractive on the surface, but in practice athletes who have put themselves in that situation admit that there is a tendency just to sit around waiting to train, and worrying about every little ache and pain. To have at least a part-time job provides a mental break, away from running.

Of course, for the vast majority of runners such a utopian existence is impossible as they have to earn a living and have families to support. To others it might not seem a very attractive proposition anyway, especially those to whom running is merely a recreational activity. And that is how it should be.

But I am convinced that in the future the potentially successful runner, both male and female, at international level will have little choice but to devote their lives, temporarily at least, completely to running. Some already do. But as the training loads necessary for international success increase, not just in volume but intensity, greater consideration will have to be given to the extra rest and relaxation needed to counteract it and avoid injury or mental breakdown.

There will come a time when there are clearly three pegs – work, training and rest – which will have to be fitted into just two holes. The international gold medallist in the 1980s and 1990s will not be an amateur in the original sense, although one hopes that the rules concerning amateurism will have been radically altered or totally abolished within a few years.

Instead, everything will revolve around physical and mental state, as sauna baths, massage and yoga will have become as important a part of the training routine as the 10 mile run, as the athlete tries to relax his or her body between the constant demands of training. To what extent this is already normal in some Eastern European countries is impossible to say, but it would be foolish to close our eyes to the way the sport is generally progressing at its highest competitive level.

Fortunately, whatever the trends in the international field, there will always be club competition of the type which has changed little in the last century. If that ever ceased, the sport would be in trouble, the foundations would crumble, and there would be no peak for the ambitious to climb.

7

Injuries

Any activity which pushes the body to the limit, as distance running does, is bound to produce a breakdown of some sort from time to time. Injury is the runner's nightmare, because it restricts him or her from doing the one thing they want to do: run. Occasionally, even seeking medical advice can produce a somewhat unsympathetic response, 'You run 100 miles a week and you say your leg hurts? Well, stop running 100 miles a week and the pain will probably go away. Next, please.'! However, in fairness to the medical profession, the problems of the sportsman are being recognized more widely and there now exist a number of sports clinics around the country which specialize in treating athletes and their particular ailments.

In the distance runner's case these centre mainly around the lower leg – the knee, shin, Achilles tendon, ankle and foot – and tend to be injuries caused by over-use.

There are now generally acknowledged to be three types of sporting injuries. The *direct* injury, such as a fracture or concussion, which results from some form of physical contact, such as a hard tackle in soccer. The *indirect* injury, which is caused by violent forces not involving physical contact, such as sprains and muscle tears, perhaps caused by treading on a stone or down a hole. And there is the *over-use* injury, which is brought about by excessive repetitive movements in training and competition.

The direct injury is not seen in distance running at all, unless we count road accidents or the very rare collision in a track race which results in a fall; limbs have been broken that way. The indirect injury is more common and equally unpredictable. But the vast majority of running injuries stem from over-use, and it is not hard to understand why. Even a runner covering only 20–30 miles a week would still be taking well over 2 million strides a year, and the runner reaching 100 miles a week would take around 9 million strides a year, on top of other everyday activities, with every step involving some thirty different muscles working together to produce the movement.

Much of that running will probably take place on hard surfaces, like roads, and on every one of the strides a great amount of force bears down on the legs. This has been estimated as being up to three or four times the runner's bodyweight – say 500 pounds or more in a 10 stone runner. Normally the body is able to absorb this huge pressure, but only if everything is in balance. If undue stress is placed on one part of the leg for whatever reason – a blister on one foot, or a worn-down running shoe – then the abnormal force, together with the repetition of the action over a long period, can cause injury.

Sheer repetition in itself, without sufficient recovery in between, can also produce the same over-use symptoms. In the chapter on training methods, the essential formula of hard work plus rest equals success was referred to. In direct contrast, hard work plus insufficient rest can equal injury.

Whenever athletes meet at races they usually spend a good deal of time discussing their injuries with other runners, comparing notes and symptoms. To have had a stress fracture of a metatarsal or chondromalacia patellae is almost like a battle decoration, while someone who has actually had an operation on their Achilles tendon has really reached the heights, especially if they had to go to Sweden for it!

But, while one can joke about it afterwards, there are few more miserable, irritable creatures than the injured athlete. They are like caged tigers with withdrawal symptoms, brimming with all that excess energy and the frustration of not being able to use it for running. But I am convinced from my own experience that the worst part of being injured is not the pain of the injury, nor the frustration of not being able to train or race, nor even the despair of feeling that you are losing fitness with every day that passes. Instead, it is the absolute uncertainty of not knowing *how long* the injury is going to last. A few days or all season? You cannot plan training, racing or even social activities with confidence when all the time you are worrying about the pain in your leg. At such times, runners can be very introspective.

If someone could only look into a crystal ball and say categorically, 'You are not going to be able to run for four days, and then it will improve and you will be able to start training again', or, 'The problem will need long term treatment, so you can safely take your holidays now without worrying about missing the Digglesbury 6 mile road race – you're going to miss it anyway', then the injury would be so much more bearable.

But running injuries are awkward things which can sometimes come on suddenly and disappear just as quickly for no apparent reason. Or they may linger with you, despite every known treatment, for months. You end up, while at work during the day or lying in bed at night, constantly stretching and prodding the injury, testing it to see whether the ailment has upped and left within the last few minutes. It rarely has, and instead, just sends back extra sharp mocking pains.

Sooner or later, though, it does heal and then you immediately have to curb your own enthusiasm to rush out and run 20 miles a day to make up for lost time. Instead, you just have to face the fact that to be sidelined through injury will inevitably have cost you some degree of fitness, and the longer you have been unable to train, the more fitness you will have lost. A loss of two or three days will probably make little difference, and may even do you good if you are one of those runners who is normally loth to rest (which is why you may be injured in the first place; your body was trying to tell you something). But after three days of inactivity you will start to lose a little condition, so when you start training again you must do so gradually and make due allowance for your time off. Training is like trying to run up a down escalator. If you work hard, you will make progress, but if you have to stop you will be gently taken down again. So don't expect to pick it up exactly where you left off before the injury. And don't push the training beyond a point where the injury starts to hurt again. Stop short, for nature has its own way of letting you know when enough is enough – through pain.

Catching an injury early is half the battle, so take note of your body if it starts to hurt. Try to diagnose what the problem is, and how it could have been caused. Have you made any changes in your training routine recently? Are you suddenly running up hills a lot, or in spikes for the first time this year? Have you suddenly increased your mileage by a large percentage? If the answer is no, then look at your running shoes. Are they worn down at the heels, making you run awkwardly and stretching the Achilles tendons too much? Is the sole of one shoe worn more than the other? If so, you are running out of balance, but why? Do you run on a road with a camber, for instance?

If there is no apparent cause, consider the over-use possibility. Have you been giving yourself enough rest? If not, take it a little easier or even stop training for a couple of days. A few days off now are preferable to several months off later.

Trevor Wright had a successful career as an international cross-country and marathon runner interrupted when he continued to train with a foot injury:

> This caused me to run off balance and, although the injury cleared up, the achilles tendon on my other leg broke down. I had intensive treatment, but it was finally necessary for me to have an operation in May 1973, and it was not until January 1974 that I was able to train normally again.

Although you can often work out for yourself why a particular injury has been caused, prevention is obviously far better than cure, and the use of stretching and strengthening exercises before a run, as described on page 85, will lessen your chance of injury. When increasing the total weekly training mileage, any step up of more than 10 per cent per week often invites trouble, while putting foam rubber padding in the shoe will help to reduce jarring effects for the high mileage road runner.

Eventually, though, despite everything, you may find yourself on the injury list, and the following section outlines some of the most prevalent injuries and ailments among distance runners, their cause and treatment. It is meant only as a self-help guide, but in some situations it may be enough. With more severe cases, and some other injuries, nothing can replace on-the-spot medical expertise.

Achilles tendon

The Achilles tendon, or heel cord, connects the calf muscle and the heel bone, and is one of the commonest areas of injury among distance runners. The severity may range from the inflammation known as tendinitis to complete rupture, although the latter is rare in distance running, involving as it does a sudden load being thrust upon the tendon, which is far more likely to occur in sprinting or jumping events.

The usual tendinitis, consisting of a thickening of the actual body of the tendon, is very painful and tender when pinched, but nearly always clears up of its own accord eventually after a modification of training to a bearable amount. This form of tendinitis is quite separate from the condition in which pain is felt at the insertion of the tendon into the heel bone. In this case, there is no swelling of the tendon itself, little or none at the site of the pain, and often it does not clear up on its own, perhaps eventually needing an operation.

The cause of the pain is usually traceable either to a sudden change in training routine, whether it be to hill running or sand-dune running (involving extra stretching of the tendon), or to putting on spikes after a winter spent mainly in heavy training flats, or to an increase in interval work, with recovery jogs in spiked shoes with little heel support. Other causes include running in road shoes with worn-down heels, and general overload of training.

One key to prevention is to graduate any change. In hill running, for example, the tendon has to stretch considerably more than it does on the flat to touch the ground even briefly. To run a long session of hills with no similar type of work in recent months is to invite Achilles problems, which are usually discovered not at the time but when the athlete gets out of bed next day and tries to walk; pains above the back of each ankle will tell him that he has overdone it.

A high mileage during winter months will probably have been accomplished in training shoes with a substantial heel to reduce jarring. But the tendon may shorten during that time, as its range of movement is curtailed, and a sudden switch to heavy track work in the spring could produce severe tendinitis if the spikes initially worn on the track did not have a similarly built-up heel.

Many spiked shoes have very little support under the heel, which may help to keep the shoe light in weight, but means that the tendon is repeatedly stretched beyond the limits to which it has become used in road shoes. In this respect, the 'recovery jogs' in between hard runs on the track may be worse than the runs themselves. In running fast, the athlete gets on to his toes more. When he jogs, his heel lands first, again overstretching the tendon and placing a great pressure on it. Thus, more and more athletes are now using 'interval shoes', which have built-up heels like road shoes, but spikes in the sole.

A similar cause, not immediately related to sport, is our everyday shoes – a particular problem with female runners. During the day most people wear shoes with some sort of built-up heel, and in the case of girls it may be several inches of heel. The tendon duly adapts to the very limited range of movement required of it during walking. To go out running then in shoes with much less heel means that the tendon is suddenly stretched beyond its 'normal' limit again.

So, in many cases, prevention is possible by removal or avoidance of the cause. Once the cause has been attended to, the pain should disappear, although the volume of training should be reduced until it does. Other activities, like cycling and swimming, can be added or substituted as a means of keeping the cardiovascular system exercised and reducing the amount of conditioning lost through the lesser training. In severe cases, where all other treatment has failed, surgery may be necessary.

Ankle

Ankle injuries tend to be more prevalent in other athletics events, but some distance runners do suffer from them, usually as a result of an outside element, such as tripping over a kerb or a rut. A sprain (a tear or rupture of ligaments) of varying seriousness may result, and the American podiatrist Dr Steven Subotnick in his book *The Running Foot Doctor* divided them into four degrees, described below.

The first degree sprain is just tender, with little damage done and, after application of ice to the affected area, the ankle might be bandaged. If it is stable, the athlete can resume training almost immediately, as the sprain will clear up in two or three days.

A second degree sprain involves more damage to the ligaments and causes the runner to limp slightly, but it responds well to application of ice and if it is well bandaged it may be no more serious than a first degree sprain.

The third degree sprain is a more serious one, which needs careful examination to rule out the possibility of any bone fracture or complete rupture of ligaments. It is impossible to run and difficult to walk, and the ankle needs to be elevated when possible, and treated with ice. Crutches may be needed until the athlete can walk without pain, and even light training must be approached cautiously after the injury appears to have healed.

The most severe sprain, the fourth degree on Subotnick's list, is the one in which ligaments are completely ruptured. Examination is made more difficult 20 minutes after it has happened because swelling takes place and makes it difficult to estimate the damage. Sometimes a plaster cast is needed for 4–6 weeks, and occasionally surgery is performed after the injury has been sustained to repair the ruptured ligaments.

The more severe ankle sprains are, fortunately, rare among distance runners, but often badly worn shoes (the culprit for a whole range of injuries) are the prime factor in ankle injuries. If the runner's foot is continually thrown on to the outside throughout a series of training runs in old shoes, the tendons of the outer ankle will become strained.

Sometimes the ankle is the victim of an imbalance injury, in which the runner throws more weight on to one leg than the other, and the imbalance causes a strain in one ankle only. However, in subconsciously trying to protect that ankle and get back into balance, the runner may over-compensate and end up injuring the knee on the opposite leg, which has to absorb most of the re-distributed weight.

Backache

Backache is by no means an ailment exclusive to the elderly. A high percentage of the adult population suffers from some form of intermittent back pain, and the distance runner is no exception. It can be caused by a high intensity of training on the road, with the consequent absorption of a large amount of shock in the small of the back. A switch to softer surfaces, and increased padding in the shoes, or at least a switch to shoes with a more substantial shock-absorbing heel, should alleviate the problem, together with regular mobility exercises. Strong abdominal muscles are also helpful in prevention of back ailments, and exercises like sit-ups and leg raising when lying on the ground can help develop these.

Blisters

Every distance runner gets a blister at some time, and the most common causes are shoes that fit badly, or ones that have inner seams which rub against the foot or have not been properly broken in. Beginners and runners stepping up their training mileage or returning from a lay-off are the most likely sufferers, as their skin is softer than on a hard-training runner's foot, but no one is immune. Friction causes the blister, as the outer layer of skin (epidermis) separates from the layer below it (dermis) and the body sends a watery component of the blood, called serum, to fill the space in between and to provide a cushion against the friction.

Sometimes, if the damage is more serious, the blister will fill with blood, and this type should be treated very carefully as infection is a danger if the skin is broken, even minutely.

An ordinary clear blister, however, can be drained quite simply, once the skin has been sterilized with meths, using a needle which has been sterilized (by heating it red-hot in a flame and allowing it to cool) and piercing the outer skin of the blister. This is a virtually painless operation, and you can then squeeze out the clear fluid and mop it up with cotton wool. The operation may need to be repeated two or three times to drain all the fluid, then the area should be cleaned again with a disinfectant and covered with Elastoplast or similar protection for several days. Leave the outer skin in place, as this helps the healing process, and studies by US Army doctors showed that in 90 per cent of the cases of drained blisters they examined, the outer skin re-attached within four days.

Draining simple blisters not only reduces pain, it also allows you to continue training. To carry on running with blisters is to risk a sub-conscious, or even conscious, alteration of the running action, perhaps favouring the affected foot and causing a compensatory muscle injury in the leg or foot.

Prevention of blisters is, of course, preferable. Shoes that are too tight or too big are always going to present problems, so care must be taken when buying shoes to ensure they are comfortable.

In these days of nylon uppers, breaking in shoes is much less of a task than it used to be with leather uppers, but nevertheless wearing new shoes around the house for a few days will help to adapt them to your feet.

Running socks should be clean and comfortable. Sweaty socks dry hard and create folds and crinkles which can cause blisters rather than protect your feet against them. Dusting the feet liberally with talcum powder, sprinkling it inside your socks and shoes, will also help to absorb sweat, for wet feet are particularly prone to blisters; soldiers who have marched long distances in wet boots, or hikers, can confirm this. Use of vaseline over the toes or any other area liable to blistering is a good precaution as it reduces friction almost to a minimum.

Elastoplast, or gauze covered with sticking plaster, can help protect any spots liable to blistering if firmly applied before a race or long training run. If you have consistent problems with a particular pair of shoes, throw them away, and if one pair of shoes which are normally comfortable causes a blister problem (perhaps through being wet) don't wear them again until the blisters have cleared.

Runner's knee

Runner's knee, or *Chondromalacia patellae*, is still something of a mystery in medical circles, but knee problems figure very highly on any list of the distance runner's All Time Most Popular Injuries. Chondromalacia is a softening of the cartilage of the undersurface of the kneecap (patella), which normally moves smoothly over the end of the thigh bone (femur). This softening may be caused by excessive rotation of the knee as the foot hits the ground, possibly due to the athlete being slightly knock-kneed, bow-legged or having a foot imbalance. One American doctor, who is also a runner, suffered from chondromalacia in his left knee and found that, when he ran on the right-hand side of the road, where the camber forced him to run on the inside of his left foot, the pain vanished. From this experience, he and a number of his runner-patients used specially designed arch-supports in their shoes, which had a high success rate in clearing up the problem.

The knee is the shock absorber of the body, and the Clapham Junction of the leg, with bones, muscles, tendons and ligaments being anchored at this joint. Torn cartilage and strained ligaments are other causes of knee pain and, if it is persistent, medical help should be sought.

Shin soreness

Shin soreness, or shin splints, is suffered by some runners during or after prolonged exercise, and consists of a sharp pain and tightness on the outside of the shin. The problem arises because the anterior tibial (shin) muscles, which also support the arch mechanism of the foot, have little room to expand, as they do during sustained exercise. This causes a build-up of pressure within the restraining sheath, which restricts proper circulation of the blood.

Heavy mileage on the road or other hard surfaces, and even inflexible shoes, have been cited as further contributory factors; if a shoe has a hard sole, it does not bend when the foot strikes the ground and an unusually large amount of shock is then absorbed by the shin muscles. Inflexibility of the ankles and an imbalance of strength between the shin and calf muscles are other possibilities which have been suggested as causes in a somewhat controversial area. In 1970 a *Sunday Times* investigation into the specific shin soreness experienced among race walkers, conducted at the Royal Free Medical School in London, blamed a condition called ischaemia (a lack of oxygen) in the shin muscle, but this appeared to be caused mainly by the strict rules governing the race walking action.

Treatment of shin soreness includes a switch to running on softer surfaces while it persists and the application of ice or cold packs to the muscles on the outside of the shins two or three times a day, for 5–10 minutes at a time. Wearing different training shoes for each session, rotating several pairs to alter foot balance, helps, and any adjustment of the running action so that less strain is placed upon the anterior tibial muscles, by ensuring that the feet do not turn significantly outwards, should reduce the aggravation.

Attention must be paid to the shoes and condition of the feet, for any shoe wear or feet problems, like corns or callouses, can result in a faulty running action which places extra strain on the shin muscles. And, although it may be tempting to bind the legs in an effort to reduce pain, this could actually make the problem worse, and anything which grips tightly around the lower leg, like knee-length socks, should be avoided. If all else fails, rest may be the only answer. To continue to run bravely on despite shin soreness could even produce a stress fracture, and indeed great care must be taken not to confuse the two.

Stitch

The unpredictable onset of 'stitch' can affect anyone from the beginner to the Olympic athlete, and no one has yet come up with an indisputable theory about the cause or, more important, a quick cure. Stitch is generally accepted as being that sharp pain in the side, or sometimes in the shoulder, during a run, and in its most widely accepted sense it is probably caused by a spasm of the diaphragm. This often gives the runner great difficulty in breathing deeply and almost inevitably leads to a slowing of pace, voluntarily or not. W. G. George, the world record holder for the mile from 1880, wrote on the subject of stitch in his book *Training for Athletics and Kindred Sports,* published in 1902:

Never stop when this distressing trouble overtakes you. Slow up, even walk, but *never* stop. Immediately it becomes less painful, increase pace, and keep running until it is quite gone. It is probable that the next time the trouble attacks you, it will be less severe, and if the suggested remedy is persisted in, stitch will soon be a thing of the past.

Which was a roundabout way of saying that he had no solution to offer, and now, nearly eighty years later, we are still little the wiser. But what causes the spasm in the first place? Again, there is no hard and fast answer.

A poor physical condition is one possible reason, but then that does not apply to Olympic runners who have been struck by the pain. Running too soon after a meal, and thus asking your body to digest food and efficiently to perform a vigorous exercise efficiently and simultaneously sometimes produces the same effect, but no experienced athlete would do that anyway. Running straight after emptying the bladder seems to cause stitch in some athletes; running *without* emptying the bladder causes it in others!

Certainly it is extremely frustrating to have to watch rivals in a race pull away from you simply because stitch is slowing you, and not the limitations of your muscles. Personally, and on no other grounds than practical experience, I agree with the theory that poor running form, perhaps lolling slightly to one side, may cause stitch; and my own solution, which has met with a reasonable success rate, is to try to correct it by running as upright as possible, lifting the body from the waist and trying to stretch the area in spasm, in the same way as you would stretch a cramped muscle.

Stress fractures

The stress fracture is another common injury among distance runners, particularly those churning out a large amount of mileage on the road, and usually occurs either in the metatarsal bones in the foot or the tibia or fibula of the lower leg. It is not quite as dramatic as it sounds, for there is no sudden and apparent snap of a bone cracking and usually the runner has no idea that a stress fracture has occurred until they notice a recurrent pain in the foot or lower leg. The latter may at first seem to be shin soreness, sometimes accompanied by local swelling and tenderness. In fact, it is a classic case of an over-use injury, where repetitive stresses across a long bone have produced a minute crack which does not always show up on X-rays.

Obviously, complete rest would allow the bone to mend, but runners hate having to stop completely unless it is unavoidable, and a carefully thought-out exercise programme will allow some activity to continue while still enabling the bone to mend. The essential thing is to cut down immediately on heavy mileage, avoid all competition and to keep off roads and other hard surfaces during this period. Steady running or jogging on soft grass is often possible, as long as it is not carried to extremes, and the measure of how much actual running can be undertaken will be made by signs coming from the injured area itself.

Other aerobic exercises, like swimming and cycling, will help to keep the cardiovascular system ticking over without putting any pressure on to the affected area, and thus help to minimize the inevitable slight loss in running condition while the bone heals.

A period of three to six weeks is usually needed to complete this process, but much will depend on the severity of the fracture and how quickly it was diagnosed; to have continued to train hard on a stress fracture will obviously have aggravated it, perhaps even to the point where complete immobilization and a plaster cast are required. Once the healing process is complete, the return to full training should be gradual, and accomplished in well-padded shoes with particular avoidance of too much road work in the early days.

8

The Marathon

Surrounded as it is by mystique and legend, the marathon has an aura about it unequalled by any other athletic event and by few in other sports. Indeed the very word 'marathon' often conjures up associations with exhausted, disorientated athletes weaving unsteadily towards the finishing line, or of weary runners sitting at the roadside, having abandoned their attempt at the distance, and slowly taking dusty shoes off their blistered feet.

The fascination of simply beating the distance looms more intensely to the potential marathon runner than of beating their rivals. Once you know you can run the distance, then you can think about running it faster.

Sometimes, though, it is necessary to reduce the marathon clinically to what it is: simply a long road race, whose exact distance lies not in Greek history but within this century, and whose origins as a sporting event barely stretch into the last. Only what it symbolizes goes much further back.

The race commemorates a run supposed to have been made by a Greek messenger named Pheidippides in 490 B.C., from the village of Marathon, some 23½ miles north-east of Athens. The Athenians had defeated the Persians in a battle there, and Pheidippides is said to have run all the way to Athens with the news; around the latter stages of a modern marathon, most competitors probably wish he had just sent a telegram instead.

However, on arrival in Athens, Pheidippides gasped out the news of the victory to the city elders, and then collapsed dead (at which point I always envisage the elders looking at each other and asking, '*What* did he say?').

Something which tends to keep Pheidippides firmly in the area of legend rather than fact is that his run was not mentioned by historians until nearly 600 years after the battle, although a courier named Pheidippides is said to have run from Athens to

Sparta, covering 120 miles in two days, to request military help *before* the battle.

One theory is that the Roman historian and storyteller Plutarch created Pheidippides' run from Marathon to Athens simply as a means of transferring his tale from the battlefield to the city, instead of resorting to whatever was the Roman equivalent of: 'Meanwhile, back in Athens . . . .' Another theory is that Pheidippides' run is not mentioned at all by contemporary Greek historians because he was a deserter.

Whatever the truth, and we shall never know, what is certain is that the distance from Marathon to Athens is not the classic 26 miles 385 yards (42,195 metres) which the race has now become. As a sporting event, its roots are relatively recent, springing from the preparations which were being made by Baron Pierre de Coubertin for the staging of the first modern Olympic Games at Athens in 1896.

A friend of de Coubertin, named Michel Breal, who was an historian, linguist and professor at the Sorbonne, suggested to the organizing committee the inclusion of two athletics events in the Games which would particularly reflect the glories of Ancient Greece. One was the discus throw, and the other was an endurance run along the original route supposedly taken by Pheidippides from Marathon. Both ideas were accepted and the endurance race, the marathon, eventually provided the highlight of those inaugural Games when the Greek shepherd Spiridon Louis gave the home nation its first and only victory of the Olympics in 2 hours 58 minutes 50 seconds. Greek runners also took second and third places on a course which was just under 25 miles.

The marathon quickly became an integral part of the Olympic Games, on courses around 25 miles, and it was only when the Games came to London in 1908 that the first race over the now standard distance of 26 miles 385 yards was held. The event was due to begin in Windsor and end at the White City Stadium, Shepherd's Bush, in West London, and the actual start was staged on the private lawns of Windsor Castle, because the children of the Royal Family wanted to see the runners. It was also decided that the race should end opposite the Royal Box at the stadium, so that Queen Alexandra could see the finish clearly.

The distance between the private lawns at Windsor and the Royal Box at White City was measured as 26 miles 385 yards and, although the 1912 and 1920 Olympic marathons were held over courses of slightly different length, from 1924 onwards the curious distance set in 1908 was adopted as the standard marathon length. The ultimate irony came many years later, when the 1969 European athletics championships were held for the first time in Athens and the marathon, along the classic route, had to include a detour of several miles in order to bring it up to the required standard length! Appropriately, in the circumstances, it was an Englishman, Ron Hill, who won that race.

But that 1908 Olympic event became widely known as 'Dorando's Marathon'. A diminutive Italian, Dorando Pietri, was first into the stadium at the end of the race, but collapsed several times and only crossed the finishing line with the help of some officials. Inevitably, he was disqualified for receiving assistance, and the race was awarded to the second runner home, Johnny Hayes of the USA.

Queen Alexandra was deeply impressed by Dorando's performance, however, and later awarded him a special gold cup, while the incident itself helped to establish the marathon well and truly as an event for the strong and the brave. Those scenes of Dorando's collapse are among the most famous in athletics history, and the opening ceremony of the 1974 European championships in Rome included a 're-creation' by the Italians of the finish of that race.

Following the exploits of Spiridon Louis and Dorando Pietri, the finish of the Olympic marathon has always had a specially dramatic quality, and the gold medallist has been guaranteed a special place in the sport's roll of honour, with names like Emil Zatopek and Abebe Bikila among the previous champions.

In the fifties and sixties, three British athletes helped to take the men's world best time for the distance towards the 2 hours 10 minutes mark. Jim Peters, from Essex, who set new standards of training mileage in the post-war years, clipped nearly 5½ minutes off the old world best with a run of 2 hours 20 minutes 42 seconds in 1952, and improved it three more times, down to 2 hours 17 minutes 39 seconds in 1954, the year of his retirement following his dramatic collapse in the sweltering Empire Games Marathon in Vancouver.

Brian Kilby ran a world best of 2 hours 14 minutes 43 seconds in 1963, a year after winning the European and Commonwealth Games titles (within six weeks) but this 'record' was taken by his own Coventry Godiva Harriers team-mate Basil Heatley in 1964 with a run of 2 hours 13 minutes 55 seconds from Windsor to Chiswick.

Heatley also finished second that year in the Tokyo Olympic Games race (in 2 hours 16 minutes 19 seconds), but his record was broken by the winner, the brilliant Ethiopian runner Abebe Bikila, whose performance of 2 hours 12 minutes 11 seconds was not only a world best but came just six weeks after an operation for appendicitis. Bikila thus became the first man ever to retain the Olympic marathon title, having won (barefoot) in 1960. His attempt to complete a hat-trick ended after 10 miles of the 1968 Olympic race where severe leg pains forced him to drop out. The following year he was badly injured in a car crash, receiving spinal damage which paralysed him from the waist down, and he died in 1973 at the tragically early age of forty-one.

The first man to average under 5 minutes a mile for the full distance was the Australian Derek Clayton, who clocked 2 hours 9 minutes 36 seconds in 1967 and, despite a series of leg injuries which required surgery, he improved his own world best to 2 hours 8 minutes 33.6 seconds at Antwerp in 1969.

Clayton, a native of Lancashire who emigrated to Australia in 1963, has the completely opposite build to the normally accepted marathon runner's light frame. He stands 6 feet 2 inches and weighs 11½ stones, and his heavy physique, together with his aggressive way of training – always hard, high quality and high quantity running – probably contributed to his frequent injury problems. These involved nine surgical operations altogether and partly led to his competitive retirement in 1974, although he still runs regularly and maintains his racing weight.

Women have now become regular competitors in the marathon too and the first major international Games to include a women's marathon is the 1982 European Championship meeting in, appropriately, Athens. There are moves afoot to try to have it included in the Olympic Games, alongside the men's race, in the not too distant future as well.

The earliest female marathon runner appears to be a French girl, Marie-Louise Ledru, who finished thirty-eighth in a men's marathon in 1918, although her time is unknown. And in 1926 there is a record of a Violet Piercey, who ran the Windsor to Chiswick course in 3 hours 40 minutes 22 seconds. Women began 'gatecrashing' men's marathons in the USA in 1963, while a Scottish girl, Dale Greig, set an unofficial world best of 3 hours 27 minutes 45 seconds on the Isle of Wight course in 1964.

From the early seventies, the marathon for women was recognized officially in the USA, with great progress being made as a result of the national running boom there. By 1975 women in Britain were finally allowed to race the distance, and from 1978 even had a Women's AAA National Championship. But the highspot of its short British history came when Joyce Smith won the 1979 Avon International race, an unofficial world championship, at Waldniel in West Germany, with Britain winning the team title. Joyce's winning time of 2 hours 36 minutes 27 seconds was the sixth fastest ever by a woman, and a Commonwealth best.

There are no official records for the marathon because of the varying types of course terrain. Some races involve a number of laps, others just one big lap, while a third alternative is the out-and-back course which follows a certain route for 13 miles, where the runners turn, and come back the same way. But the most suitable for producing fast times are the A-to-B courses, partly for the psychological reason that the runners feel they are getting somewhere, and partly for the beneficial effects of any following wind, which can be of considerable help in a race lasting well over 2 hours.

At the 1979 Mardi Gras Marathon in New Orleans, for example, a local police strike caused a last minute change of course to include a 24 mile long, flat, straight causeway over Lake Pontchartrain which provided a strong following breeze. The winner, John Dimick of the USA, improved his best time by over 4 minutes to 2 hours 11 minutes 53 seconds, while the women's winner, Gayle Olinke of Canada, improved hers by no less than 15 minutes to a Commonwealth best of 2 hours 38 minutes 12 seconds.

But when hurdles, sprints and jumping events are aided by following winds in excess of 2 metres per second (4.47 m.p.h.), they are not ratified as records, and as measuring the following wind on what may be a twisting marathon course is impossible, the statisticians are left with the problem of how to list the New Orleans performances. A wind-assisted marathon?

That a runner of Derek Clayton's size could set a world marathon best which would stand for more than a decade indicates that there can really be no more hard and fast rules about the necessary build for this event than for any other. After all, during the 1979 track season, middle-distance world records which had been set by the 6 foot 3 inch/13 stone 3 pound Alberto Juantorena and the 6 foot 1 inch/12 stone 2 pound John Walker, who had both

seemed to be opening up new ground in their events, were broken
by the 5 foot 7 inch/9 stone Sebastian Coe.

Although marathon runners do, in the main, tend to be light-
framed runners, in recent years the event has seen a few exceptions
among the fastest performers, and the following table of height and
weight indicates the range that can sometimes be found.

Men	Marathon achievements	Best time hrs mins secs			Height ft ins		Weight st lbs	
Ron Hill (UK)	1969 European champion; 1970 Commonwealth champion	2	09	28	5	6½	9	
Derek Clayton	First man to average under 5 minute miles for marathon	2	08	34	6	2	11	7
Frank Shorter (USA)	1972 Olympic champion; 1976 Olympic silver medallist	2	10	30	5	10½	9	4
Ian Thompson (UK)	1974 Commonwealth and European champion	2	09	12	5	6½	9	5
Bill Rodgers (USA)	Three times winner of Boston and four times winner of New York marathon	2	09	27	5	8½	9	2
Waldemar Cierpinski (East Germany)	1976 Olympic champion in Olympic record time	2	09	55	5	7	9	2
Women								
Miki Gorman (USA)	Former holder of world best for women	2	39	11	5	1	6	13
Christa Vahlensieck (West Germany)	Former holder of world best for women	2	34	48	5	3	7	12
Grete Waitz (Norway)	Broke world best for women by 2 minutes in her debut race	2	32	30	5	7¾	8	5
Joyce Smith (UK)	Winner of Avon international race 1979 in Commonwealth best	2	36	27	5	6½	8	0
Julie Brown (USA)	Former holder of US best of women	2	36	24	5	6	9	9

But, whatever your build, one inescapable fact constantly faces you when preparing for the marathon. You cannot realistically hope to run the distance at all, let alone well, unless you are willing to put in a considerable amount of training mileage beforehand. The event, after all, tests endurance to a high degree and, without running regularly in training, and including some long runs in that training, your level of aerobic fitness will not be sufficiently high for a confident approach to the race. Even allowing for the probability that most first-time marathon runners will be satisfied simply to finish, the point is that, unless some reasonable degree of preparation has been undertaken, the chances are that you will either not finish, or else do so in such a fatigued state that you may not wish ever to attempt it again.

This is one of the major differences between marathon running in the UK and in the USA, where the boom has resulted in many marathons being established in which walking or jogging the distance in 6 or 7 hours is not considered particularly unusual. Yet to 'run' a marathon in 7 hours involves an average pace of around 16 minutes a mile, which is actually walking pace, and in the UK a marathon runner taking even 5 hours (11½ minutes per mile pace) might find very few officials left at the finish.

The obsession with the marathon distance as a compulsive challenge to the ordinary jogger has not yet reached this side of the Atlantic and, while there may in the future be more marathons for such people here, in general the best advice for the fun-runner at present is to stick with the wide range of shorter road races available, and only attempt the marathon if they really feel capable of running the distance.

Another reason, of course, for the vast numbers taking part in marathons in the USA is the almost total lack of restriction on age and distance. Such American performances as the 4 hours 56 minutes 36 seconds marathon run by five-year-old Jennifer Amyx, and the 6 hours 3 minutes 35 seconds run by four-year-old Brent Bogle, are the sort of thing I hope never to see equalled in Britain.

To run a full marathon in this country, whether you are male or female, you have to be twenty years old and, although some slight reduction in that age limit (perhaps to voting age?) might not come amiss, I certainly would not want to see children running the 26 miles with, as likely as not, a parent or coach alongside consulting time schedules.

The marathon is not an event to tackle on the spur of the

moment. A graduated approach to it is essential and, even if you have been running shorter road races for years, some sort of stepping stones to the full 26 miles are advisable: several races at 10 miles or so, and at least one each of around 15 and 20 miles before the big day, just to assure yourself that you will be able to get within a reasonable reach of the full distance. If you cannot run 20 miles, or even 15, then you certainly will not be able to run 26.

But, having established that, the marathon offers more chance of success to those runners who are usually well down the field in shorter road races. It requires less speed, less skill and less technical ability than any other event. But what it does need is a great deal of preparation through sufficient steady-paced running, a graduated race programme, and long-term overall planning if you are to get full satisfaction and success out of it.

So how much training is sufficient? The real answer is that there is no real answer. Some top international runners may train 140–160 miles a week, others may achieve reasonable results on 70–80 miles a week, and there will always be a few who will tell you that they got by in a marathon on 30 miles a week. Perhaps, but such people usually have a much longer history of running over a period of years which helped them through, and in any case such a modest preparation is not to be recommended.

In general, I am against the application of rigid formulae and equations in working out potential, because such things cannot take into account so many minor yet relevant factors (sleep, diet, injury, illness etc.). But one rule of thumb which often seems to work is an American theory that a distance runner's 'collapse point' is three times his average daily mileage for the past two months. In these terms, collapse point does not refer to literally collapsing, nor is it exactly the same as 'hitting the wall' in a marathon, which is discussed later in this chapter.

Instead, it refers to the point at which the life and bounce leave a runner's legs in a steady-paced race. For example, if your average daily training for two months has been 4 miles, then by this theory you should be able to run 12 miles in a race reasonably comfortably before reaching the collapse point, after which running becomes a much harder physical effort for less result. From this it can be seen that someone who had only averaged 4 miles a day for two months would have a hard time in the marathon, because the life will have left their legs before even the halfway mark.

Yet joggers and runners who do average less than 4 miles a

day – sometimes considerably less – are entering marathons in the USA, and they are the ones who are taking 16 minutes per mile to complete the course.

Using the same theory, therefore, a potential marathoner should average at least 9 miles a day (or 63 miles a week) for the two months before the marathon to be reasonably confident of being able to run the distance ($3 \times 9 = 27$ miles).

9 miles a day may not sound too much, just an hour or so of steady running each day. But remember it is an *average*, based on seven days a week for eight consecutive weeks. In practice, few runners will run literally 9 miles a day like that (nor would they necessarily be advised to) but, in order to allow for the occasional rest day, the odd ache and pain, or the unavoidable social occasion the daily total must often be higher than that. And, to make up for any below-par weeks, the total mileage on other weeks may have to be bumped up a little to ensure an average of 63 miles plus and, since the runner will want to ease down on training before the actual race, some extra miles will have to be allowed for in the early weeks to maintain the average all the way through. Remember, too, that the 63 miles a week is the *minimum* recommended amount to be reasonably confident of being able to run the whole distance at a steady pace. Theoretically, it allows very little margin for error, such as misjudging the starting pace of the race and going off too fast.

Obviously, there will be people who have run marathons on less and lived to tell the tale. But, if you intend to tackle the marathon, you should always be asking how you can fit in more training, not how little you can get away with.

At the 1978 AAA Marathon Championship in Sandbach, Don Shelley, the National Marathon Organizer for the British Amateur Athletic Board, conducted a training survey through questionnaires which were given to the competitors. Among the information he obtained was this insight into the average weekly mileages of those runners who were capable of breaking $2\frac{1}{2}$ hours for the distance:

60–70 miles per week	$17\frac{1}{2}$ per cent
70–80 miles per week	$12\frac{1}{2}$ per cent
80–90 miles per week	20 per cent
90–100 miles per week	25 per cent
100–110 miles per week	5 per cent
110–120 miles per week	20 per cent

To ask an under-conditioned body to run a marathon is like placing a huge load on a table with weak legs: it might just hold, but it won't be happy about doing so.

Whatever the level of training, the runner must aim to build up stamina, which is the single most important factor in marathon running. Long steady runs at a comfortable pace will help to build the foundations, and will strengthen the muscles for the constant repetition and increase the efficiency of the cardiovascular system in transporting oxygen economically to the muscles, while all the time adding the type of mental confidence to cope with the challenge which can only be accumulated by many hours of such running.

99 per cent of the marathoner's efforts are aerobic. In other words, the demand for oxygen should not exceed the supply at virtually any stage of the race, and if a marathon runner does get into oxygen debt he will have to reduce his pace until the debt is paid, and then concentrate on staying on that side. A pace which may seem ridiculously slow in the early miles of a marathon can become very difficult to maintain in the closing stages but, through training and performances in shorter races during the build-up for the marathon, the runner should have a rough idea of a target time at intermediate points in the race.

The charts on pages 171 and 172 show what average pace in miles and kilometres is needed, and the cumulative splits, on an even pace schedule for the final time in the right-hand column.

In terms of breaking down the training mileage into manageable units, one significant question would be: when does 20 miles not equal 20 miles? The answer is when it is made up of two tens or four fives. In other words, whatever your total training mileage for the week, it should include at least one long run, rather than consist entirely of a great many shorter runs.

I believe it was Bill Adcocks, another of Britain's best ever marathon men to hail from Coventry, who said that in some respects it was easier to run a 2 hours 10 minutes marathon than a 3 hours 10 minutes one 'because you're on your legs for an hour longer'.

A world class marathon man will be running hard for nearly $2\frac{1}{4}$ hours, and a top woman marathoner will take between $2\frac{1}{2}$ and $2\frac{3}{4}$ hours. Those are the minimum lengths of time; for most of us, it takes a lot longer, so the body needs to get used to running continuously for a long time. The Sunday morning 20 miler has

1 Mile	5 Miles	10 Miles	15 Miles	20 Miles	Marathon
4:50	24:10	48:20	1:12:30	1:36:40	2:07:44
5:00	25:00	50:00	1:15:00	1:40:00	2:11:06
5:10	25:50	51:40	1:17:30	1:43:20	2:15:28
5:20	26:40	53:20	1:20:00	1:46:50	2:19:50
5:30	27:30	55:00	1:22:30	1:50:00	2:24:12
5:40	28:20	56:40	1:25:00	1:53:20	2:28:34
5:50	29:10	58:20	1:27:30	1:56:40	2:32:56
6:00	30:00	1:00:00	1:30:00	2:00:00	2:37:19
6:10	30:50	1:01:40	1:32:30	2:03:20	2:41:41
6:20	31:40	1:03:20	1:35:00	2:06:40	2:46:03
6:30	32:30	1:05:00	1:37:30	2:10:00	2:50:25
6:40	33:20	1:06:40	1:40:00	2:13:20	2:54:47
6:50	34:10	1:08:20	1:42:30	2:16:40	2:59:09
7:00	35:00	1:10:00	1:45:00	2:20:00	3:03:33
7:10	35:50	1:11:40	1:47:30	2:23:20	3:07:55
7:20	36:40	1:13:20	1:50:00	2:26:40	3:12:17
7:30	37:30	1:15:00	1:52:30	2:30:00	3:16:39
7:40	38:20	1:16:40	1:55:00	2:33:20	3:21:01
7:50	39:10	1:18:20	1:57:30	2:36:40	3:25:23
8:00	40:00	1:20:00	2:00:00	2:40:00	3:29:45
8:10	40:50	1:21:40	2:02:30	2:43:20	3:34:07
8:20	41:40	1:23:20	2:05:00	2:46:40	3:38:29
8:30	42:30	1:25:00	2:07:30	2:50:00	3:42:51
8:40	43:20	1:26:40	2:10:00	2:53:20	3:47:13
8:50	44:10	1:28:20	2:12:30	2:56:40	3:51:35
9:00	45:00	1:30:00	2:15:00	3:00:00	3:56:00
9:10	45:50	1:31:40	2:17:30	3:03:20	4:00:22
9:20	46:40	1:33:20	2:20:00	3:06:40	4:04:44
9:30	47:30	1:35:00	2:22:30	3:10:00	4:09:06
9:40	48:20	1:36:40	2:25:00	3:13:20	4:13:28
9:50	49:10	1:38:20	2:27:30	3:16:40	4:17:50
10:00	50:00	1:40:00	2:30:00	3:20:00	4:22:13

Kilometre Splits

Average 400 metres pace	1 km	5 km	10 km	15 km	20 km	25 km	30 km	35 km	40 km	Marathon 42.195 km
1.12	3.00	15.00	30.00	45.00	1:00.00	1:15.00	1:30.00	1:45.00	2:00.00	2:06.05
1.14	3.05	15.25	30.50	46.15	1:01.40	1:17.05	1:32.30	1:47.55	2:03.20	2:09.58
1.16	3.10	15.50	31.40	47.30	1:03.20	1:19.10	1:35.00	1:50.50	2:06.40	2:13.35
1.18	3.15	16.15	32.30	48.45	1:05.00	1:21.15	1:37.30	1:53.45	2:10.00	2:17.08
1.20	3.20	16.40	33.20	50.00	1:06.40	1:23.20	1:40.00	1:56.40	2:13.20	2:20.39
1.22	3.25	17.05	34.10	51.15	1:08.20	1:25.25	1:42.30	1:59.35	2:16.40	2:24.10
1.24	3.30	17.30	35.00	52.30	1:10.00	1:27.30	1:45.00	2:02.30	2:20.00	2:27.41
1.26	3.35	17.55	35.50	53.45	1:11.40	1:29.35	1:47.30	2:05.25	2:23.20	2:31.19
1.28	3.40	18.20	36.40	55.00	1:13.20	1:31.40	1:50.00	2:08.20	2:26.40	2:34.43
1.30	3.45	18.45	37.30	56.15	1:15.00	1:33.45	1:52.30	2:11.15	2:30.00	2:38.14
1.32	3.50	19.10	38.20	57.30	1:16.40	1:35.50	1:55.00	2:14.10	2:33.20	2:41.45
1.34	3.55	19.35	39.10	58.45	1:18.20	1:37.55	1:57.30	2:17.05	2:36.40	2:45.16

long been part of the British distance runner's routine, especially for marathoners, and, apart from the benefits to the cardiovascular system, just being on your legs for several hours of easy paced running helps to build a special endurance which could not be equalled by four separate runs of 5 miles, nor two of 10.

Not that 20 miles is by any means the upper limit, and runners like Ian Thompson had covered 30 miles at a stretch in training several times before his dramatic breakthrough in the 1973 Harlow Marathon, which was in turn a springboard to his gold medals in the 1974 Commonwealth and European Marathons. There is no reason why such 'overdistance' training should not work as effectively for the marathon as it does when applied to the track events, but one would need to be very careful to avoid injury and to allow for the extra fatigue such runs would produce. The points about the need for additional rest and relaxation, made on pages 86 and 146, would have particular relevance here.

But to run regularly 30, or even 20, miles also needs a special type of mental toughness and dedication to the task which is frequently found in marathoners. Natural physical ability counts for less than the determination and willingness to churn out a high mileage day after day, when on some days things go well and some days not so well. We all have days when we don't feel like training, but the marathoner has to accept that his or her feelings may change maybe three or four times during the course of a single long run, as they might in a race. Successful marathon runners are not the ones who sometimes have to be goaded into training; they are the ones who sometimes have to be held back from over-training.

Remember the formula: hard work plus rest equals success. It applies to the marathon runner as much as anyone, yet because of the nature of the event, the training and the number of occasions on which you can race a marathon flat-out during one year, the preparation has to be viewed over a much longer time scale than shorter events. You have to think in terms of seasons and years rather than weeks and months if you are considering dramatic improvement.

Ian Thompson was never an 'instant' marathon success:

Before my first marathon I had ten years of background, including some very long runs, and an important part of my preparation is still the long run on a Sunday, which I try to build up week by week so that I go over the marathon distance, and do perhaps three or four runs of 30 miles. When you've got runs like that behind you, it gives you a lot of confidence that you should be able to get the full distance. You've got to know that you're going to make it.

When I start building up for a specific marathon now, I usually begin fourteen or fifteen weeks beforehand, when I step up my normal 'ticking over' mileage of 60–70 a week to about 140 miles a week within two or three weeks. It's the sort of big jump that you should never do but, perhaps because I've got the background for it, it doesn't seem to cause too many problems, although I wouldn't recommend it for others.

Having then established myself at 140 a week, the process is to refine it so that I'm doing that 140 faster and faster. I must have a lot of slow twitch muscle fibres, because sheer distance in itself doesn't represent too much trouble, but doing the distance fast is more of a problem.

An average week of 140 would start on Sunday with a 25–30 miler in the morning, then another 3–5 miles in the evening in order to stay loose and to help prevent me stiffening up overnight. Then for the rest of the week I average about 16–17 miles a day, often with 5 miles in the morning, 8 at lunchtime, and then another session in the evening, which might be interval running in the woods – 6 × 800 metres, or 4 × 1 mile, or something similar. On another evening I might do an hour's fartlek, including 12–15 × 50 to 100 metres sprints, while another night it could be 20 × 1 minute efforts, with a 1 minute jog in between.

On a Saturday I might do an easy 5 miles in the morning, and perhaps a short club race in the afternoon, but only as a means to an end. They're enjoyable, but I'm primarily a marathon runner.

Approaching a big race, I ease down on training for two to three weeks, and the other main considerations are getting enough rest and eating the right food. I sleep 9–10 hours a night normally, and when I'm training hard I sometimes also take an afternoon nap to get some freshness back into my system. Fortunately I work in an office close to my home, and they're very good to me.

But, looking back to my most successful years of 1973–74, I was only doing 6 hours a week studying for a teacher's certificate then, and not very demanding study either. There was all the time I needed to train and rest, and not much else to do to tire me out. But when you are working, whatever sort of work it is, it has some kind of stress element attached to it, and that all adds to the total stress of the day.

One of the reasons I often race well abroad now is that I can usually spend a week relaxing in a hotel before the race and so I feel rested. At home, one is still in the hurly-burly of everyday life, and the rest is not quite the same – especially if you've got children!

Bill Rodgers, the American multiple winner of both the Boston and New York marathons, would seem to have found an almost perfect training routine with the success of his own running gear business in Boston, which allows him to sleep late often, and train at 10.30 or 11.00 a.m., and again at 5.00 p.m. But Rodgers feels, like Thompson, that being a student would be an even better situation:

The student life produces less stress than business, and it's not the end of the world if you don't hand a paper in on time. With business there is more stress, and it is sometimes difficult to fit everything in. But I still have a pretty good training and racing situation, I must admit.

Rodgers covers a great deal of mileage in training, even for a top class marathoner, and in 1978 he averaged 125 miles a week throughout the year. Yet it actually dropped slightly from the 131 he averaged in 1977 and 130 in 1976:

In a typical week I train twice a day, covering about 10–13 miles in the morning, and 8–10 miles at night. On average it usually works out to about 130 miles a week, or 18 a day. Once a week I do a track session of interval $\frac{1}{4}$, $\frac{1}{2}$ or $\frac{3}{4}$ miles, with a 220 yards job, or perhaps 6 repetition miles at about 4 minutes 45 seconds. Then I do a long run of about 18–20 miles each week, at about 6 minutes 30 seconds pace, with another run at night of 5–10 miles, perhaps a little quicker.

What you really need is a well rounded programme, with the rest, the distance, and the speedwork all put together in the right combination. But I try to learn from my mistakes and see where my weaknesses are. I know some of them, but not all. And I watch other runners to learn their strengths and weaknesses.

It's always better to be in a giant-killing position, better to be unknown and an underdog. The runners who become well-known have to do interviews, attend parties, dinners and press conferences, and they feel the tension from those things. But once you've knocked off the high level competition, then you're in the boat yourself, and you've just got to maintain your position and put up with people who come up to you after a race when you were pleased to finish second and say 'too bad you lost'.

The Australian marathoner Dave Chettle, who clocked 2 hours 11 minutes 41 seconds in 1979 and has a best of 2 hours 10 minutes 20 seconds, also tends to go in for big mileages:

When I'm preparing for a marathon I usually build up to about 140 miles a week, but I wouldn't want to go above that level. I don't think I could handle much more, although I know some runners do cover 160–170 miles a week.

A typical week for me would include three long runs, starting with a 24 miler on Sundays. On Monday to Friday I'd do a 7 miler each morning, and on Monday evening 15 miles. Tuesday it would be 12 miles, including repetition hill work, then on Wednesdays 18 miles. On Thursday night I'd do track work – say, 12×400 metres in 62–63 seconds, with 200 metres jog in 45–50 seconds in between. On Friday it would just be an easy 10 miles if there was a race next day, and Saturday the race. It averages about 20 miles a day, but you get very tired doing it, and you need quite a bit of rest. You can't have a job that is too demanding, physically or timewise.

Barry Watson, a British Olympic representative in 1976 and a 2 hours 15 minutes 8 seconds runner, finds that his work sometimes tends to be both, and seldom tops more than 110 miles a week:

My job as a primary school teacher leaves me feeling pretty washed out at the end of the day. I am in charge of boys' discipline in an inner city school, and I absolutely deny that teaching is an easy option to allow one to spend a lot of time training. Recently I had to duck to avoid a flying chair, and as most of the aggro happens at lunch time there is no cushy 2 hours break and no opportunity to run at that time of the day.

So I am up for 5–6 miles at seven o'clock each weekday morning, and out for another 8–12 miles most evenings, with track work once or twice a week. Then I collapse in front of the television, while my wife talks about all the decorating that needs doing!

Instead of running more in the school holidays, I find I benefit from using the extra time to rest, and thus be ready for better quality training sessions.

I realize that I have my priorities a bit mixed up, and would only suggest that, however much time and energy one is prepared to give to the sport, it should be channelled to the best effect and a good, regular routine be established rather than 25 miles one day, then a few days' rest, followed by a 7 miler – and then a stress fracture!

These men are all experienced international marathon runners now, but even they had to run a first marathon at some point, and for many club runners that might in itself represent the ultimate challenge: simply to run the distance, to feel that, even if you could not cover it anywhere near as fast as the top men, you could still condition your body sufficiently well for it to be able to conquer the distance.

But, unless you are already doing a fairly high mileage, at least six months would be a reasonable minimum amount of time to allow yourself to prepare for a first marathon. Select the race in which you want to make your debut six months hence, and then spread out on a table some sheets of ruled paper, a calendar, your diary, your club's fixture list, the current Road Runners Club fixture list if you have it, some copies of *Athletics Weekly* containing advertisements for forthcoming races, or else some back number from last year which will give you an idea of what races there are to choose from; most events are held annually around the same weekend.

Suppose you are a keen club runner, whose longest ever run has been 11 miles and whose average training mileage is around 40 per week. You may decide that you want to run in the Poly-technic Harriers Marathon at Windsor, which is normally held in June. So working back from the actual date, you should try to find a 20 mile road race some 4–6 weeks beforehand, a 15 mile road race about 2–3 weeks before that, and then several 10 mile races spread over several months before that. These will then become your stepping stones to the Marathon, well-spaced to allow recovery, a return to hard training and an easing off in between. Some possibilities might be:

17 March: Bath 10 miles
31 March: Worthing 10 miles
13 April: Maidenhead 10 miles
5 May: Chichester to Portsmouth 25 kilometres (16¼ miles)
20 May: Pembroke 20 miles
16 June: Polytechnic Marathon

Next, mark in some other reasonably accessible road races between now and your planned marathon. These will be alternative events to help you across any voids, or to take the place of any race you have to miss unavoidably, even though you may not end up doing any of the alternatives unless you want to:

17 March: *Bath 10 miles*
24 March: Romford Half-marathon
31 March: *Worthing 10 miles*
7 April: Suffolk 10 miles
8 April: Chas Kendall 10 miles (Barrow)

13 April:	*Maidenhead 10 miles*
14 April:	Newport 10 miles
14 April:	Canterbury 6 miles
15 April:	Cambridge 10 miles
21 April:	Solihull 10 miles
28 April:	Herne Hill 10 miles
5 May:	*Chichester to Portsmouth 25 kilometres*
7 May:	Trowbridge 10 miles
12 May:	Croxdale 10 miles
19 May:	University 10 miles (Coventry)
20 May:	*Pembroke 20 miles*
26 May:	Newport 15 miles
28 May:	Faversham 17 kilometres (10½ miles)
3 June:	Michelin 10 miles
9 June:	Thanet 10 miles
16 June:	*Polytechnic Marathon*

The task is then to work out a training plan which will enable you to increase your mileage gradually over six months but will also allow you to ease off before the 'stepping stone' races so that you can judge the benefits of the training without feeling too tired, while still graduating by stages to your longest racing distance.

If your main ambition is to run a reasonable marathon in six months' time, then it is best to accept from the start that you may not necessarily be able to turn out your most sparkling performances at shorter distances week after week if you are also trying to build up to your highest ever training mileage. You cannot always produce your best when your body is still recovering from being pushed to its maximum load.

Thus is it a personal choice whether you will want to run in any or all of the other races you have listed. Almost certainly it will not hurt you, and it may well provide a mental break from the training efforts; some people thrive on racing and would wither without at least one race a fortnight. Others might prefer to race very sparingly and not risk any possible depression if they did run a slower time than the previous year despite their extra training. In many cases, it may even be considerably faster, but the overall plan cannot be judged on such intermediate races. A very practical alternative, of course, is that the athlete might prefer to use the Saturday for a long run, or several shorter sessions, thus totting up more miles than they might get in a race.

A further choice is to train on the morning of a race, or after a race, if travelling does not make it too difficult. It is a matter of personal preference, and there is no specific 'right way'; the right way is the one which suits you.

A simple but effective way of working out the overall training plan is to number the weeks between the present moment and the marathon, in this case from 1 to 24, and list the numbers down the side of a piece of ruled paper, together with the relevant dates, the stepping stone races, and the alternative races. Then with this framework, a pencil (and a rubber!) you can produce a training plan which might look something like the chart on pages 180-1.

It cannot be stressed too much that the figures are just a guide, and that some runners will want to do fewer miles and some will want to do more. But if, as in the imaginary example I have used, the runner was only averaging 40 miles a week before the build-up, with a longest run of 11 miles, then I feel the figures quoted may well be the maximum load he or she could attempt without very greatly increasing the chance of injury. The key is to build up gradually over a long period, going close to the border of break-down without actually stepping over it.

The training chart could apply equally to women marathoners too, if not all of the races (although some are open to female runners). The length of the marathon is exactly the same for women as it is for men, and so they need to train in the same volume, though their pace may be slower than that of a male counterpart. Some of the top American women marathon runners are covering 120-140 miles a week themselves now.

Another aspect of the chart should be particularly noted. After a few weeks of gradually increasing the load, the total occasionally drops back down for a week, either to accommodate an easing down period for a race, or simply to allow some slight recovery from the highest mileage weeks: mental as much as physical.

Some years ago a young distance runner showed me his planned weekly mileages for the forthcoming winter. He had never run more than 85 miles in a week before, and he intended to start, quite reasonably, with several weeks of 40-50, building up through 70 and 80 miles a week, but increasing the totals every single week until he planned to be doing 110, 120, 120, 130 and 130 in successive weeks. If he had been Ian Thompson or Bill Rodgers, then it would have been fine but, as I pointed out to him, he was planning to run at least five consecutive weeks at a load over 50

Week No.	Dates	Stepping Stone Races	Planned Total Weekly Mileage	Long Sunday Run	Alternative Races
1	31 Dec.–6 Jan.		40	10	
2	7–13 Jan.		45	11	13 Jan.: Cross country relay for club
3	14–20 Jan.		50	12	
4	21–27 Jan.		55	12	27 Jan.: Cross country league for club
5	28 Jan.–3 Feb.		50	12	
6	4–10 Feb.		60	14	Feb. 10: Southern Cross country Championship
7	11–17 Feb.		65	14	17 Feb.: Hillingdon 5 miles
8	18–24 Feb.	24 Feb.: Woking 10 miles	55 incl. race	15	
9	25 Feb.–3 Mar.		65	15	3 Mar.: National Cross country Championship
10	4–10 Mar.		70	16	
11	11–17 Mar.	17 Mar.: Bath 10 miles	65 incl. race	16	
12	18–24 Mar.		75	17	24 Mar.: Romford Half-marathon

Week	Dates		Miles		Races
13	25–31 Mar.	31 Mar.: Worthing 10 miles	65 incl. race	17	
14	1–7 Apr.		80	18	7 Apr.: Suffolk 10 miles
15	8–14 Apr.	13 Apr.: Maidenhead 10 miles	70 incl. race	18	8 Apr.: Chas Kendall 10 miles 14 Apr.: Newport 10 miles
16	15–21 Apr.		85	20	15 Apr.: Cambridge 10 miles 21 Apr.: Solihull 10 miles
17	22–28 Apr.		80	20	28 Apr.: Herne Hill 10 miles
18	29 Apr.–5 May	5 May: Chichester–Portsmouth 25 kilometres	75 incl. race	18	
19	6–12 May		90	22 (Sat. 12 May)	7 May: Trowbridge 10 miles 12 May: Croxdale 10 miles
20	13–19 May		60	18	19 May: University 10 miles
21	20–26 May	20 May: Pembroke 20 miles	70 incl. race	20	26 May: Newport 15 miles
22	27 May–2 Jun.		80	22–24	28 May: Faversham 17 kilometres
23	3–9 Jun.		50–60	15	3 Jun.: Michelin 10 miles 9 Jun.: Thanet 10 miles
24	10–16 Jun.	16 Jun.: Polytechnic Marathon	60 incl. race	—	

A sample twenty-four week build up to a first marathon (see page 179).

per cent in excess of the most he had ever run in a week before, straight after a string of consecutive weeks also well above his previous maximum. Could he imagine, I asked, going to bed exhausted on the final night of his second 120 miles week, then waking up next morning and having to start the first day of another two weeks at a still greater, and even more fatiguing, target?

By not considering such practical factors, he was setting himself a far too ambitious load, which was likely to end in physical breakdown or high mental fatigue. If he was going to attempt to increase his mileage drastically (admirable in itself, I hasten to add, and he is now a sub 2 hours 20 minutes marathoner), it would be far better to allow for breathing spaces in between, dropping the mileage down to a lower level every third week or so to allow the body a chance to recover, repair damaged tissues, and generally prepare to face another push forward, rather than force an already tired body to perform continually and reluctantly at a level currently beyond it.

These are principles which have to be considered. There is no foolproof guide to the point at which your body is being asked to do too much. Perhaps, if it was ever discovered to be, say $89\frac{7}{8}$ miles a week, then a lot of the fascination would go out of the sport.

But 'too much' is only relative to what you have done in the past and your current capabilities. Every runner is a separate case, with a different background, but by understanding the problems in general terms it is possible to work out a training programme which will most likely be of the greatest benefit to you *at the moment*.

There *are* marathon runners who can pile up 150 miles a week, week after week, but they have built up to it over a period of some years, not a few months. If you respect your body, its current capacity, and do not ask it to become a world class marathoner's body overnight, progress will be steady but relentless. Like the race itself, you will get there eventually, but not by sprinting the first 100 metres. The marathon runner who started his preparation last year may be ahead of you, but if you start now, you'll be ahead of the runner who is going to start next year.

The diet

An interesting point to come out of the 1978 AAA Marathon Championship Survey was that virtually two-thirds of the competitors (65 per cent) normally prepared for marathons by using the special carbohydrate-loading diet which has become popularized in the past decade. Yet among them there was still a lot of uncertainty about whether the advantages outweighed the disadvantages, and whether they would have been better off by using a modified version, or ignoring it altogether.

'The diet', as it is usually called, has little to do directly with weight loss; instead, it can lead to a slight weight gain. But it has become one of the most controversial, misunderstood, half-understood areas of athletics.

Briefly, the theory is this. To provide energy for endurance exercises like marathon running, the body burns up chiefly glycogen, which is stored in the muscle cells, and fats. But, while there is an almost inexhaustible supply of fats, the glycogen can only be stored in limited quantities, and research suggests that the depletion of these glycogen supplies is the main limiting factor in endurance events. When it has been used up in a marathon, there is a sudden and unavoidable decrease in pace, estimated at anything from 1 to 3 minutes per mile. Many runners experience this at around the 22 mile point, and the rapid deterioration in speed is known as 'hitting the wall'. It comes without warning; it just happens, often making the final miles a very hard slog at a much slower than average pace.

'Hitting the wall' is not specifically related to fitness, unlike the collapse point discussed earlier, because runners covering upwards of 100 miles a week are as likely to experience it as those on a lesser mileage. But, by using the carbohydrate-loading diet, physiologists claim, it is possible to increase artificially the glycogen stores (which come from carbohydrates) during the week before the race, in an effort to postpone this depletion.

In its original and most extreme form this is not simply a matter of stuffing yourself with cakes and buns. That comes later! Instead, the technique has three main components:

1. Seven days before the race for which you are aiming (say the Sunday before a Saturday race), you take a very long run, perhaps 20–22 miles or more, deliberately to deplete the glycogen currently in your muscles. You 'run to the wall', in fact.
2. After the run, and for the next three days, you take very few carbohydrates in your diet, but live mainly on fats and proteins, while continuing to train very lightly.

3. From the Wednesday lunchtime you switch to a high percentage carbohydrate diet (bread, cereals, cakes, doughnuts, chocolate etc.), while still taking in fats, proteins, vitamins and minerals.

What happens is that the original long run on Sunday (known as the 'glycogen bleed-out'), followed by the abstinence from carbohydrates, stimulates the body into producing extra glycogen-storing enzymes to compensate for the temporary lack, and these in turn will allow the body eventually to store more glycogen than it could before.

Thus, when the carbohydrates are reintroduced in the middle of the week, glycogen loading takes place to a degree which would not otherwise be possible. The method, used correctly, is said by some researchers to be capable of almost doubling the glycogen stores in the muscle cells, and can thus help the runner through the later stages of a marathon.

It sounds a perfect solution, you might say. But, if so, why does every runner not use it now, why have some stopped using it, and why are others still undecided? The answer is that there are a number of cautionary points associated with the technique, to which we will return in a moment. But first, how did this diet find its way into the marathon world anyway?

As with so many other marathon innovations, the link rests with former European and Commonwealth Champion Dr Ron Hill and his scientific approach to distance running. In 1969 he received a letter from his former international team colleague Martin Hyman outlining some research work being done at that time in Sweden with long distance cyclists riding bicycle ergo-meters, and then using the carbohydrate-loading principle with dramatically successful results.

Appreciating its value for the marathon, Hill tried the system out in the 1969 AAA Championship race in Manchester and beat the holder of the world best, Derek Clayton, by 2 minutes. He took the lead at 15 miles and went on to record his then best ever time of 2 hours 13 minutes 42 seconds, which was also the second fastest by a British runner.

Two months later he used it again at the European Champion-ship race in Athens and, although by 19 miles he was third, feeling tired, and had mentally settled for the bronze medal, in the last 7 miles he found himself steadily moving through to first place. To do so, he had turned a deficit of $1\frac{1}{2}$ minutes on Belgium's Gaston

Roelants into an advantage of ¾ minute by the time he crossed the finishing line, 'seemingly moving faster and faster as the end neared', as Mel Watman reported in *Athletics Weekly* at the time.

After the race, and to his later regret, Hill let the secret of the diet out of the bag in a newspaper interview. Even that might have been forgotten had he not then continued a string of notable racing successes, including victory in the Fukuoka classic in Japan in December 1969 in 2 hours 11 minutes 54 seconds, in the Boston marathon in a course record of 2 hours 10 minutes 30 seconds in April 1970, and the 1970 Commonwealth Games Marathon three months later in a European best of 2 hours 9 minutes 28 seconds.

He took the bronze medal at the 1971 European Championships, while his disappointing sixth place at the 1972 Munich Olympic race, for which he was favourite, probably had more to do with the unexpectedly adverse effects of pre-Games altitude training, referred to on page 82, than anything else. Hill had been an international marathon runner since 1962, and others inevitably associated his increased level of international success solely with his adoption of the carbohydrate-loading diet, and the word quickly spread.

Now the diet is very widely – and sometimes incorrectly – used all over the world. But two points must be clearly understood. Firstly, that the carbohydrate-loading diet does not seem to work for everybody, and if it is to be tried it should be before a low-key unimportant race first before it is risked on an important event.

Secondly, the diet in no way replaces training, or the need for it. For a start, it is no good going to the considerable trouble of boosting your stores of glycogen for use at 22 miles if you are not fit enough to run 22 miles in the first place. The extra glycogen merely allows a fit body to go on working efficiently longer than it might otherwise have done.

I mentioned the cautionary points associated with the diet, and it is important also to weigh these up when deciding whether or not to try it. For instance, it should not be attempted by anyone with a dietary problem such as diabetes, because it basically involves tampering with the biochemical processes of the body.

As details of the diet were not formulated until the mid-sixties, there is no research available yet on what the long-term effects, if any, of undertaking the diet regularly might be.

There is also a medically-backed feeling that it should not be used more than two or three times a year at the most, partly because of those unknown long-term effects and partly because of the great physical and mental strain on the runner. Another, more mundane, reason is simply that, if it is undertaken too often, it does not work effectively because it is thought that the body 'catches on' and adapts accordingly.

The first three days of the diet, with no carbohydrates, is also a very testing and tiring time for the runner; it is a time in which resistance to colds or other infection is very low, and this could adversely affect the race, as Barry Watson discovered at the Montreal Olympics:

I was superbly fit before the race, fitter than I had ever been. My training in Montreal emphasized this. It seemed to me at the time that I couldn't miss having a really good run. Not only was I physically fit, but also very confident and positive.

I did a very strict version of the diet, eating only proteins after a fast depletion run with Jeff Norman, my team-mate. But then I caught a flu bug. My body was *too* weakened during this phase of the diet, and the illness caused me to lose my appetite, so that carbohydrate loading was difficult. The result was one of my poorest ever races over the marathon distance.

Training during the first three days should only be of a very light level because the blood sugar, which supplies the fuel for mental and nervous energy at the rate of 2–4 grams per hour, will also be greatly reduced following the initial long run. To train hard at this time could reduce that level still further, to the point where hypoglycemic stress (loss of concentration, depression, loss of temper, impatience, irritability and migraine headache) can occur.

During the final, and more enjoyable, part of carbohydrate loading, care must be taken not to overeat, but rather to increase the *percentage* of carbohydrates in the diet, while still taking in minerals, proteins and vitamins. Additionally, a steady supply of liquids should be included because 3–4 pounds of water (1½–2 quarts) may be stored per pound of glycogen in the body and, if there is insufficient liquid in the diet, the body will extract water from elsewhere in the body, resulting in possible dehydration. When the glycogen is used up in the race, however, that excess water is sweated out, and can thus act as a temperature regulation boost as well.

Before the race athletes may feel bloated, heavy and lethargic, with a week of only light training in their legs and their weight up perhaps 3–4 pounds on normal racing level. It takes a lot of confidence in the diet to believe that you are going to race well. But, once the athlete feels it has worked, and that he did not hit the wall in a marathon, then he may be reluctant to tackle another one without using it. At the same time, there are those who feel that using it wrecked their chances in a particular race because they never felt right.

Ian Thompson is one of those athletes whose views on the diet have changed through experience:

I've had some good races with the diet and some bad ones. My early successes, including winning the Commonwealth and European golds, were achieved with the diet, but when I used it for the 1976 Olympic trial race, it didn't work, I just felt rough, and I didn't make the Olympic team.

Now I use a modified version, with three days of eating lots of meat, fish, cheese and dairy products, but also just a reduced carbohydrate intake, instead of cutting it out altogether. I cut down on potatoes, and on bread, for instance, but I don't cut them out. I have one potato instead of three or four, and half a dozen chips instead of the usual pile. Then I load for 1½ days, and that seems to work better. I don't get so tired now during the protein stage, and I sleep better instead of always dreaming of food!

When you push your body to that extent you risk putting it out of gear and perhaps wasting 3–4 months of training through trying to grab that extra little bit. You can never be quite sure how much it will help you, and I think that last 36 hours is the really important time, when you need plenty of carbohydrates, sweet drinks, cakes, pastry and spaghetti. I now actually do some loading the day before a 30 mile training run as well, to help me through 3 hours of hard running.

Tony Simmons, on his excursions into the marathon world, admits that he has not been too happy with the diet:

For the 1978 European Championships Marathon I didn't even go to Prague until three days before the race so that I could do the diet properly at home. But by the Wednesday before the race I was shivering. My body was crying out for starch, because I normally eat a lot of sugar, potatoes, bread, sweets and chocolate.

It took me until the day of the race to pull myself together, and I was finding even a session of short repetition runs very hard because I couldn't seem to use my arms. The danger is that for the 10 per cent you gain from the diet, you might lose 20 per cent in mental turmoil because you feel you're not running well. I think a lot of athletes are switching to just a very modified version of the diet now.

That is certainly true of Dave Chettle:

I stoke up on carbohydrates, but I don't do the depletion. It's more fun that way!

Bill Rodgers also has a modified approach:

I've never tried the whole diet, because I don't like the idea of putting that extra weight on at the end. But I always eat a lot of carbohydrates anyway, and I make sure that I eat pizza the night before the race.

This approach seems the more widely accepted now, and has medical backing from Dr David Costill, an American specialist, who feels that running a marathon is hard enough without beginning the agony a week beforehand. He believes that simply easing off training to a light amount three to four days before a race, together with a high carbohydrate intake, can still boost glycogen storage levels above normal, without the energy loss and psychological difficulties of the first stages.

Other researchers emphasize that the extra storage powers could never be as high as those achieved with the glycogen-depletion run. But then again, they may just be high enough. Barry Watson says:

It's not a magic formula, and there is no way that a guy who trains three times a week is going to do a world class performance because of the diet. I ran 2 hours 15 minutes 8 seconds with the diet, and 2 hours 15 minutes 27 seconds without it.

Little research has yet been done on women and glycogen depletion, although one theory which has a lot of support is that, because women have a higher percentage of body fat than men and can utilize it for energy production more efficiently, they seldom if ever use up all of their glycogen stores in a marathon and 'hit the wall'. When Grete Waitz set a women's world best of 2 hours 32 minutes 30 seconds in the 1978 New York Marathon she ran the second half of the race $3\frac{1}{2}$ minutes faster than the first, yet she had never even heard of the diet before the race. A year later, on the same course, she improved her time to 2 hours 27 minutes 33 seconds.

Another school of thought, however, suggests that women are

not yet running marathons fast enough to reach this level of depletion. One other likely cause of female runners fading drastically in the final miles (as well as a good many male club runners) could simply be put down to insufficient training mileage.

For, male or female, whatever your dietary preferences, if you have not covered enough miles in training before the race, then the sheer distance will usually win in the end.

9

Your Racing Programme

Competition is the thread weaving through all aspects of running, and to some people (though by no means all) the chance to test themselves regularly in races is the main incentive for them to run in the first place. Every week there is a wide selection of events on country and road for male and female runners at a whole range of distances. In fact, the selection throughout the winter is so great that to the newcomer it must appear positively bewildering, and certainly many people who have been in the sport for years are not always *au fait* with the entire racing programme.

Little wonder really, because both cross country and road running (and indeed athletics generally) have a plethora of organizations, associations and unions who each tend to concentrate on one area of the sport and often go their own way. In consequence, the winter fixture list can sometimes become a congestion of clashes of dates, and even venues. Once I attended a cross country race on a famous common near London, and found another, totally separate, race was using a slightly different course on the same common, with the result that the runners at one point crossed over each other's routes, and it looked very like a motorcycle figure-of-eight display where the riders miss each other by inches.

The following attempt to sort the major types of cross-country and road events into some semblance of order is intended not only for the novice who wonders what types of races are available to him or her, but also for the more experienced runner who is looking for new areas of challenge. The following pages may provide some ideas.

Cross-country (*Men*)

Club races

As a first step, every runner who intends to compete should join a club, although it is possible to enter open races individually as an 'unattached' competitor during your first year of competition, as long as your status conforms to the amateur definitions.

Each club draws up a fixture list of events to which it intends to send representatives and, depending upon the size, reputation and geographical situation of the club, the list will include inter-club fixtures, open races, relays and league events, as well as the main championship races of the season.

The inter-club matches, often held annually, bring together a number of clubs, usually from within the same area, and with an agreed number of runners to score (say six to run, and four to score) each club may field two, three, four or more teams, designated as their 'A' team, 'B' team, and so on, depending on how many of their members turn up on the day. The races are low-key, with the Senior and Junior men often running the same event over a course of 5–6 miles, while the Youths, Boys and Colts may compete together or separately on a course of $2\frac{1}{2}$–3 miles. The exact details will vary from race to race, but this is the friendliest, most informal, type of meeting and an ideal 'first step' for a newcomer.

Runners of all standards compete in unlimited numbers, while a variation on this is the inter-club race known as the 'mob match'. In this, each club tries to field as many runners as possible, and the result is worked out with the maximum number of scorers. For example, if one club has fifty-seven runners taking part and another fifty-three, then the scores of the first fifty-three runners home from both clubs will usually count.

The total scores in these mob matches often run into five figures, but the attraction is that many of the runners who regularly finish near the back of the field know that they are making as important a contribution to the total score as the club's star runners up front.

Another attraction of the relaxed attitude of inter-club matches is that they are nearly always 'one-off' meetings. There is no carry-over to another meeting, and nothing at stake. There are seldom prizes and, in many respects, they are the classic amateur races, for enjoyment only.

Open races

Open races are events organized by one particular club, advertised in the athletics press and which invite entries from anywhere, either teams or individuals. There are usually a series of races for different age groups, with prizes or medals for the leading individuals in each race, plus team prizes for each scoring runner in the leading teams.

The exact number and nature of the prizes depends on the size of the meeting and the generosity of the sponsor, if there is one, but the prizes are usually listed in the advertisements. Occasionally there are prizes for the first 'B' team to finish (as long as that club's 'A' team has finished in front of them; otherwise a club might be tempted to put all of its leading runners in their second team and go for the 'B' prize!) and, if there is no separate race for Veterans (runners over forty), then there may be one or more prizes for the leading Veterans in the Senior race.

The greater the number of prizes, the more attractive the meeting may become to other clubs, and a big turn-out of runners adds to the prestige of the meeting, and of the promoting club. There is often great rivalry between clubs to attract the greatest number of entries to their meeting, and often promotions which include races at all age groups for both men and women will do particularly well because clubs are willing to travel further if they can ensure filling a motor coach. The more athletes who can be involved in the meeting, the further the athletes are usually willing to travel.

Haywards Heath Harriers, in mid-Sussex, started such a cross country meeting based on a similar German promotion in 1968, and by 1979 it included twelve different races. Additionally, every entrant receives a free tracksuit badge and can purchase an official certificate showing their name and position in the race; for youngsters, that is always a great attraction.

At Bristol each November, there is a total entry in excess of 2000 runners for the nine separate races (four for women, five for men) comprising the Mike Sully Memorial Cross Country Meeting. It was established in 1960 to commemorate one of the local club's outstanding young runners, who was killed in a motorcycle accident that year at the age of twenty-one.

At Gateshead, also in November, a programme of open events has been developed around the international televised cross country races, which gives young athletes a chance to run on the same course as the stars and to watch their heroes in action at close range afterwards. This Tyneside town, which has built up such a rapport with the country's distance runners through the successes of Gateshead Harriers and their most famous son, Brendan Foster, hopes to be the scene of the 1983 World Championships.

League races

League races are really a development of the inter-club match, only providing a link of continuity and incentive for the clubs taking part. Each league will have a series of meetings at different venues through the winter, usually totalling around three or four altogether, although occasionally more.

Clubs which are eligible to take part under each league's constitution can affiliate at the start of the season, and it is then up to the club to field teams at each league meeting. Usually anyone can run, and league points are awarded for the team's finishing order after every meeting; these points are accumulated through the season to give a winning club at the end of the final meeting. Often that winning club may not be the pre-season favourite, but a team which is able to get out a full quota of fair standard runners regularly will finish ahead of a club which has some stars among its membership but cannot get them to compete regularly in the league races.

Leagues can help to build up club pride, organization and membership, and a good team manager who will organize and chase up his team efficiently is worth his weight in gold.

The leagues may cover a small or large geographical area for their membership, and some examples of leagues in operation during the 1978–79 winter season included: Gwent League, Metropolitan League, Birmingham League, Westward League, Scottish League, West Glamorgan League, Merseyside Colleges League, Lincs Services League, Avalon League, Scottish Services League, North-East Wednesday League, North Yorks & South Durham League, Mid-Lancs League, Kent League, North Wales League, Surrey League, Sussex League, Reebok Students League, Rugby & District Young Athletes League, North Eastern Harriers League, Hampshire League, Chiltern League, Escafield League, North-West London Young Athletes League, West Midlands Young Athletes League, West Yorkshire League, Gloucester

League, North Staffs League, Red Rose League, Manchester & District League, Sunday Young Athletes League, London Colleges League, East Anglian League, and Wilts & Border League.

Cross country relays

Another popular type of club event which gives a solid team a chance of beating a team containing several stars but some weak links is the cross country relay. In Senior events the number of stages is usually between four and six, with each runner normally covering the same course.

The aim is to balance your running order in such a way that you achieve the best result. There is little point in putting your slowest runner on the opening leg, for instance, if he is going to be left such a long way behind that the rest of your team will be demoralized. On a later leg he might be more effective.

Cross country relays like the Solihull event in October, or the Aaron Relay at Leeds, or the Redhill Priory Relay in November, with their short stages, provide a good stepping stone in the autumn for those track runners switching back to the country for the winter.

Unlike track relays, batons are not used and instead a touch of hands between incoming and outgoing runners in the takeover area is sufficient. In open cross country relays (which accounts for the vast majority) there are usually prizes for each member of the leading teams, and perhaps for the first 'B' team too. Often there are also awards for the individual athletes recording the fastest lap times, which gives an incentive to those runners who know that their own club will finish out of the leading places in the team race itself.

In Scotland, National Cross Country Relay Championships on a course of approximately $4 \times 2\frac{1}{2}$ miles are held in October, together with a race for young athletes, in which each member of a team comprising a junior Boy, a senior Boy and a Youth runs a 2 mile course. Similar Championships are held in the various districts a little earlier, but there is no English National Cross Country Relay.

County Championships

In England and Wales the County Championships for men are traditionally held on the first Saturday in January, and for many club runners this race is the highlight of the winter. A good performance in the 'county' is always something to look back on with pride, and to talk about at least until next year. Entry to these Championships is unlimited in numbers per club, as long as each runner has a qualification for that county. The qualification basically comes from being born within that county, having lived in the county continuously for nine months before the competition date, or having nine months of service in a unit of HM Forces stationed in the county. Most county committees have special scrutiny meetings to ensure that all entrants for their Championships have the correct qualifications.

The usual County Championship races are for Seniors, Juniors and Youths, although many counties now hold Championship races for the Boys age group, and quite a few have added separate Colts and Veterans Championships too. This reflects the growing age range of the sport, but can also make for a very crowded afternoon's racing at a time of the year when the daylight is at a premium. Regrettably, but inevitably, some counties have now had to split up their Championship programme. In Kent, for example, in the 1979–80 season, the Colts, Boys and Veterans County Championships were held in November, and the Seniors, Juniors and Youths on the traditional January date.

Team and individual awards are made at County Championships events, and selection for the Inter-Counties Championships is usually made on the basis of the results.

The Inter-Counties Championships

Although no longer perhaps holding quite the same magic for the top Seniors as it once did, the Inter-Counties Championships, usually staged in late January, remains one of the most important domestic events of the English cross country season. Organized by the Counties Athletic Union, it now brings together teams representing more than forty counties from all over England and Wales, and was first staged for Seniors at Beaconsfield on 3 April 1926, when Worcestershire won the title from fifteen other counties.

With a standard distance of $7\frac{1}{2}$ miles, it is $1\frac{1}{2}$ miles shorter than the English National Championships, much closer to the World Championships distance, and its field of 300 runners makes it considerably easier for the fastest men to get to the front than in the National, and there is a feeling in some quarters that this race might be a better selection event for the World Championships. However, problems might arise with individual counties and their team selection, and its position so early in the calendar might not make it an accurate reflection as to who would be in top form for the World Championships two months later.

With 300 'selected' athletes taking part in the Senior Inter-Counties race, for which nine athletes run for each county and six score, competing in the Inter-Counties can be a reasonable stepping stone, or even lifetime target, for the more serious runner in earning his county colours.

The CAU itself was formed after a meeting between a number of county representatives at the AAA offices on 4 February 1926. The Senior Cross Country Championship was held every year from 1926 to 1939, then from 1947 until the present time. From 1950 to 1969 the *Daily Telegraph* sponsored the Championships completely, having helped with part-sponsorship in previous years, but from 1970–77 the Championships continued without sponsorship. They are now sponsored by British Meat.

The first CAU Junior Inter-Counties Championship was staged at Solihull on 7 March 1964, with twenty-eight counties taking part, although an inter-county match had been organized by Derek Hayward of the CAU Council for the previous three years. In 1966 the first CAU Youths Inter-Counties Championships was held at Leicester, supported by twenty-three counties, with Tony Simmons (Bedfordshire and Huntingdonshire) winning the individual race. Again, the inauguration of these Championships followed several years of unofficial inter-county matches, this time organized by the Worcestershire AAA, and from 1966 to 1970 the CAU Youths and Junior Championships were held on the same day. In 1971 both races were absorbed into one championship programme with the Seniors. Both the Juniors, who run six miles, and the Youths, who run four, field six runners per country, with four to score.

A Boys and Colts Inter-Counties race has been staged by Derek Hayward at Shrewsbury for some years and, although it has no official championship 'status', it now attracts teams from almost as many counties as the official CAU meeting, and is often held on the same date.

Area Championships

The English Cross Country Union area is divided into the following four district associations, comprising the counties listed, and each district holds its own Area Championships in early February:

Eastern CCA: Bedfordshire, Cambridgeshire, Humberside south of the River Humber, Lincolnshire, Norfolk, Suffolk, and Essex north of the line of latitude 51.53 degrees including the town of Colchester.

Midland Counties CCA: Avon, Gloucestershire, Herefordshire, Leicestershire, Northamptonshire, Nottinghamshire, Salop, Staffordshire, Warwickshire, West Midlands, and Worcestershire.

Northern CCA: Northumberland, Durham, Tyne and Wear, Cleveland, North Yorkshire, West Yorkshire, South Yorkshire, Humberside north of the River Humber, Cumbria, Lancashire, Greater Manchester, Cheshire, Merseyside, the Isle of Man and Derbyshire.

Southern Counties CCA: Berkshire, Buckinghamshire, Cornwall, Devon, Dorset, Hampshire, Hertfordshire, Kent, Middlesex, Oxford, Somerset, Surrey, Sussex, Wilts, and Essex south of the line of latitude 51.53 degrees excluding the town of Colchester.

National Championships

The English National Championships, organized by the English Cross Country Union, normally take place on the first Saturday in March at venues within the areas covered by the Eastern, Midland, Northern and Southern Cross Country Associations in rotation. They are 'run for by teams of first-claim members of any British cross country club affiliated to the National cross country bodies'.

With nine athletes to run (and six to score) in the Senior nine miles, the field is always immense; in 1980, 245 different clubs fielded teams, or parts of teams, in the race, quite apart from the individual runners: a total of 1627 finishers out of 1710 starters.

There were 602 starters and 532 finishers in the Junior race over 6 miles, and 734 starters and 628 finishers in the Youths event of 4 miles. In the Junior and Youths races, teams field six runners from their original entry of twelve, with four to score.

Quite apart from the team and individual honours to be won at the National Championships, the goal for many of the top runners is to earn selection for the English team for the World Cross Country Championships a few weeks later. The selection is

delegated to a committee of four by the ECCU constitution – one
member from each of the four area associations, with the immediate past president of the ECCU as the committee chairman. On
the day of the National Championships they are not given any
other job, and their selection is usually announced at the end of
the awards ceremony on the day of the race.

One of their considerations may be to take into account
whether a particular athlete who may have had a poor race at
the National has performed well enough during the winter to earn
a place despite that poor performance, which could have been due
to flu or another temporary ailment.

For example, the form book was thrown out of the window at
the 1972 National Championships, held at Sutton Coldfield, and
still talked about in quaking tones by those who were there! An
icy blizzard, with bitter winds, descended during the middle of
the senior race, turning it into a survival test, and Trevor Wright,
who three weeks earlier had won the Northern Counties title for
a record fourth time in succession, was in the leading bunch when,
a few hundred yards from the finish, his limbs froze up, and he
dropped to twenty-third. The selectors still included him in the
nine-man England team anyway and a fortnight later he con-
firmed their judgement by leading the English squad to victory
in the International (now World) Championships.

The main problem in selecting the Junior team of six runners
for the World Championships is the difference in definition of a
Junior between the ECCU (whose rules stipulate a Junior as
being under twenty on 1 September preceding the competition)
and the IAAF (who specify a Junior for the World Championships
as being under twenty on 31 December in the year of the race).
This gap of fifteen months leaves a vacuum in which a promising
young runner may find himself. It happened to Nick Lees of Derby
at the 1978 National. Lees was born on 23 January 1958, so for
ECCU purposes that year he was a Junior, and not old enough to
contest the Senior National race, even if he had wanted to. He won
the National Junior title that year by nearly half a minute from
Mick Morton of Blackburn, but then could not be selected for the
World Championships because he was already twenty.

Morton, who was born on 14 November 1959 and was thus a
Junior in everyone's eyes, went on to win the World Junior title
easily. You can imagine what a frustrating winter it was for Lees –
he was running well, but was too young for the Seniors and too

old for the Juniors in the World Championships. 'It was like being trapped in a tunnel,' he recalls.

The other irony was that the England selectors had to go down to seventeenth place in their own Junior Championships, and brought in the Youths Champion as the sixth man (there being no World Youth Championships). Occasionally, it is true, the National Junior Champion has been included in the Senior team, and it was not the first or last time that the Youths Champion had been added to the Junior team. But it would make it much simpler and more satisfactory all round if the ECCU age groups were brought into line with the IAAF ages.

In Wales there are several records of cross country events being held prior to 1882, but in that year the first club, Roath Harriers, was formed. Their officials were responsible for the first ever Welsh Cross Country Championships, which took place at Ely Racecourse, Cardiff, on 7 March 1894, and were won by Fairlamb of Roath Harriers, who led his team to victory.

In 1896 the Welsh Cross Country Association was formed, a Welsh Junior Championship was inaugurated in 1907, and a Youth event in 1928.

Now the male events total five, with the addition of Boys and Colts Championships.

The Welsh Championships for all age groups, which now include the Boys and Colts events, as well as the women, are normally held in mid-February. The Senior men run approximately 7½ miles (12 kilometres), the Juniors 5 miles (8 kilometres), the Youths 4 miles (6½ kilometres), the Boys 3 miles (4.8 kilometres) and the Colts 2¼ miles (3.6 kilometres).

Additionally, a separate 10 kilometre championship event for male athletes over the age of eighteen on 1 September prior to the race is held on the second Saturday in November, and incorporates the Welsh Senior Inter-Counties and Welsh Veterans Championships, usually attracting a total field of around 120.

Originally, this race was a 7 mile event established in 1954 with barring clauses which prohibited Senior internationals and members of the winning team of the previous year from taking part. The distance was reduced to 6 miles in 1962, all barring clauses were removed after the 1968 race, and the distance was amended to 10 kilometres in 1972.

An Inter-Counties event for Youths, Boys and Colts is also held, usually on the third Saturday in November.

The Scottish Men's Cross Country Championships, usually held in early February, cover five age groups, with Seniors running $7\frac{1}{2}$ miles, Juniors 5 miles, Youths 4 miles, the Senior Boys 3 miles, and the Junior Boys 2 miles.

Although the Championship results undoubtedly weigh heavily, there is no set specification for selection for the Scottish team for the World Championships, and the selection committee examines performances throughout the season, up to and including the National Championships.

In Northern Ireland the National Championships are spread through the second half of the winter season, with the Senior $7\frac{1}{2}$ mile event being held 3–4 weeks before the World Championships, and used as a trial race to select the Northern Ireland team. A separate trial is staged to pick the Junior team, restricted to those eligible to run in the World Junior Championship race, but a 'Junior' Championship, by standard rather than age, is also held in which an athlete of any age who has neither won the race nor been in the winning team may compete.

This event is normally held at the same time as the Northern Ireland Boys Championship, while the remaining age groups, the Colts and the Youths, are often held in conjunction with the Mallusk International race on the second Saturday in January, with fields of 300–400 turning out for the Colts Championship alone.

The age groups used for the NI Championships are as set out on page 34, although for the rest of the season clubs are permitted to set their own age groups in promoting races.

World Cross Country Championships

Although they only came under the jurisdiction of the IAAF in 1973, an International Cross Country Championship has been held since 1903, when Alf Shrubb of England led his team to victory over Ireland, Scotland and Wales at Hamilton Park Racecourse. France first took part in 1907 and the Championships, held annually ever since, apart from the war years, grew slowly in both size and prestige. The organizers, the International Cross Country Union, handed over the reins to the IAAF in 1973 and the event became known as the World Team Cross Country Championships but, although the number of participating countries increased (twenty-one took part in 1979), it is still a surprisingly small percentage of the potential, as the IAAF has 162 member countries.

The Senior men, with nine runners per team and six to score, cover a course of approximately 12 kilometres (7 miles), and the immediately obvious difference to the English National Championships is that a much shorter circuit is used. The sheer numbers in the English National make three laps of 3 miles essential, and even then lapping takes place. But the World Championship race may consist of five or six laps of a circuit of around 2 kilometres (1¼ miles), which enables spectators and television viewers to watch the race far better than on a 3 mile lap in which the runners come past and then disappear for ¼ hour. The more manageable numbers in the World Championships make this possible, of course.

In the Junior Men's Championship, first introduced in 1961, the athletes run approximately 8 kilometres (5 miles), with six to take part and four to score. A Junior must be under twenty on 31 December in the year of competition, but a Senior, under IAAF Rules, can be any male over sixteen years on the day of the race. This could cover a situation where a country may have no full Junior team but would have a reasonable Senior team with the addition of their top Juniors.

Before 1978 only complete teams were allowed to enter the World Championships, although individuals were permitted to do so, experimentally, in 1978 and 1979. If individuals from countries with incomplete teams are regularly allowed to compete in future, as one would hope, then perhaps the Senior age limit will be amended accordingly.

The future of the individual participation of the UK countries in the World Championships has an element of uncertainty about it. Although England, Scotland, Wales and Northern Ireland compete as separate national teams at present, none of them are affiliated *as such* to the IAAF. Only the UK is affiliated, through the British Amateur Athletic Board.

The IAAF is known to be unhappy about this separation of the UK countries, which provides a potentially awkward precedent, and is keen to have just one UK team competing, which would technically be correct. However, each of the UK countries seems set against such forced amalgamation because it would mean just nine British runners taking part in the Senior men's race, for example, compared to the total of thirty-six participating in the current situation. A decision is expected to be made very soon.

Cross country (Women)

Club races and open races

Although straightforward inter-club matches are rarer in women's cross country racing than men's they do exist where the fixtures secretaries of a group of local clubs find themselves with a spare Saturday afternoon to fill. But league races, championship races and schools events take up a great deal of the winter programme now to the point where an increasing number of races are held on Sundays, and most active club runners can find themselves in action somewhere nearly every weekend.

For those with fewer racing opportunities, or who want a change of scenery, a growing number of open cross country events for women are being staged all over the country, and advertisements for them appear in the specialist athletics press during the autumn and winter months.

Leagues

The success of men's league races in the late 1950s and early 1960s prompted the formation in 1962 of the Greater London Women's Cross Country League to help cater for the female side of the sport, where only a handful of races existed at that time. Their first fixture, held at Brook Farm, Whetstone (the headquarters of Hampstead Harriers), in October 1962, attracted twelve clubs, and in the Senior 2½ mile race fifty-nine runners completed the course. The league only catered for Seniors, but a 'run' for girls under sixteen attracted seventy runners, and the following season the introduction of Intermediate and Junior competition saw the start of races within the league for these age groups.

Women's cross country racing grew so quickly in the sixties that, by the 1968–69 season, the League, established to fill a void, had to cut back its meetings from four to three a season because of fixture congestion! In the early days, runners from the north had travelled down to compete as guests in the Greater London League, but in 1965 a Northern Women's League was formed, and by 1967 an annual Inter-League fixture was established to give the girls who supported the Leagues some chance of representative honours. Prior to 1967, when the Women's International Cross Country Championships were re-instated, the last intercountry match in which any of the UK countries took part was an England *v*. Scotland match at Hornchurch in 1956.

The second Inter-League fixture was held in 1968 as a supporting race to the Women's International Championships, staged that year at Blackburn.

The Greater London League itself grew rapidly and, with clubs from as far away as Bournemouth, Peterborough and Southend among its members, it decided to change its title to the Southern Women's Cross Country League in 1975.

It now holds three fixtures in the autumn, attracting total fields of nearly 900 runners, from which it selects a team for the Inter-League match. This is now traditionally held just before Christmas and these days involves teams from Southern, Northern, Midland, Scottish and Gwent Leagues.

In Northern Ireland, where cross country is very much a provincial sport, but rapidly growing, the NIWAAA/USC League, sponsored by the Ulster Bank, is flourishing, with Minor and Junior fields of around 100 competitors in each of the four League meetings held before Christmas.

Cross country relays

These have had their place in the women's calendar since at least 1932, when Birchfield Harriers began their cross country relay and are usually well supported, particularly by the younger athletes, as clubs often enter a number of separate teams in open events. In the case of a club having one or two 'extra' runners, it is often possible, with the referee's permission, to make up a number of composite teams on the day, consisting of athletes from several different clubs. Although they are not eligible for team prizes, they are often eligible for fastest lap prizes, if there are any, although again this rests with the referee on the day.

If there are not enough athletes to make up full composite teams, the referee will sometimes allow individual athletes to run on the first stage, so that they at least receive a time, or even an incomplete team to start and drop out of the race when each available athlete has run; an athlete would not be allowed to run twice in the same relay. Generally speaking, race officials are usually sympathetic to finding ways of allowing athletes to run and receive a time rather than finding ways of preventing them from doing so.

Some organizers of women's cross country relays are finding, however, that they get a better response if the Senior age group

event is turned into a straightforward individual race rather than
a relay, because some clubs have difficulty in raising a full Senior
team and their athletes are not always willing to travel some
distance on the off-chance of being allowed to run individually or
in a composite team.

As in the men's races, no batons are used and a touch of hands
between ingoing and outgoing runner is sufficient for the 'take
over', as long as it is achieved within the designated box.

County Championships

The women's County Championships are organized by the respective county associations, and are usually held earlier than the
men's, in either late November or early December, and any
number of properly qualified athletes can be entered for the four
standard age group races. County qualification is virtually the
same as for the men: being born in that county, having lived in
the county continuously for nine months before the competition
date, or having nine months of service in a unit of HM Forces
stationed within the county.

Area Championships

The three district areas of the Women's Cross Country Association
– North, Midlands and South – hold their own area championships annually for all four women's age groups. The areas are
divided as follows:

Northern Counties WCC & RWA: Cheshire, Cleveland, Cumbria,
Derbyshire, Durham, Greater Manchester, Humberside, Isle of
Man, Lancashire, Lincolnshire, Merseyside, Northumberland,
North Yorkshire, South Yorkshire, Tyne & Wear, West Yorkshire.

Midland Counties WAAA: Avon, Gloucestershire, Herefordshire
and Worcestershire, Leicestershire, Northamptonshire, Nottinghamshire, Salop, Staffordshire, Warwickshire, West Midlands.

Southern WCC & RWA: Bedfordshire, Berkshire, Buckingham-
shire, Cambridgeshire, Cornwall, Devon, Dorset, East Sussex,
Essex, Greater London (including Middlesex), Hampshire (in-
cluding Channel Islands), Hertfordshire, Isle of Wight, Kent,
Norfolk, Oxfordshire, Somerset, Suffolk, Surrey, West Sussex,
Wiltshire.

Inter-Counties Championships

A National Inter-Counties Championship meeting for all four age groups is organized annually, usually in January, by one of the county associations affiliated to the WCCA 'at no expense to the National body', and counties can enter up to sixteen athletes, with eight to run and four to score in each age group. Counties can enter individuals if a full team cannot be raised, and awards are made to the first three individuals and the first three teams in each age group.

It was first held at Swindon in January 1969, with Midland and Northern teams 'guesting' in the Southern Inter-Counties meeting, which was a long established fixture on the calendar. Now, with the increasing importance of the National Inter-Counties, one feels that perhaps such a separate area Inter-Counties Championship is somewhat superfluous to a crowded fixture list, especially as there is no equivalent Northern or Midland fixture.

A Welsh Women's Inter-Counties Championships for Intermediates, Juniors and Girls is staged on the third Saturday in November.

National Championships

Although National Championships have been held in England since 1927, when A. Williams of Littlehampton AC won the inaugural Women's AAA cross country title from over 100 rivals at Luton, the current Championships now come under the auspices of the Women's CCA. This body came into being in September 1950, and was given responsibility by the Women's AAA for cross country and road running. The 1951 Cross Country Championship, held at Tadcaster and won by Phyllis Green of Ilford AC, was the first to be organized by the new governing body, which was known until 1980 as the Women's Cross Country and Race Walking Association.

The Championships are now held if possible on the last Saturday in February each year, and are competed for by 'teams of first-claim members, and by individual members, of any British cross country club affiliated to the national cross country body of either England, Northern Ireland, Scotland or Wales, and by any unattached competitor in her first year of competition only'.

As the younger element of the sport increased, Intermediate and Junior Championships were added in 1966 and, with the need to split the youngest age group still further, a Minor Girls Championship was started in 1970. The current distances for the Championships are:

Seniors: Not less than 4000 metres, nor more than 6000 metres
Intermediates: Not less than 3500 metres, nor more than 4000 metres
Juniors: Not less than 3000 metres, nor more than 3500 metres
Girls: Not less than 2500 metres, nor more than 3000 metres

As an indication of the growth in the younger areas of the sport, the 1980 National Championships had around 850 entries for *both* the Junior and Minor Girls events!

Selection for the England team to compete in the World Championships is traditionally the first four English girls to finish in the Senior race, plus two others (who are sometimes the fifth and sixth finishers, but the opportunity exists for the selectors to include up to two athletes who may have missed the race, or run badly, through illness).

The Scottish Women's CCU usually adopts a similar but unwritten rule of automatically selecting the first three or four home in their Senior Championships, held in mid-February, for their World Championships team.

In addition to the same four age groups in operation in England, the Scots also have a fifth age group, from nine to eleven years, known as the Minor Girls (with the eleven- to thirteen-year-olds called simply 'Girls'). Experimental events at this level were so successful that a Championship was inaugurated for them, and it is now the largest field, with nearly 300 runners taking part in the 1979 Championship, on a fixed distance of ¾ mile.

There is also a 4000 metres Championship for Intermediates and Seniors combined, held on a separate date, and confined to athletes with a Scottish qualification, whereas the main National Championships are 'open'.

Wales, the only one of the UK countries to have a joint men's and women's association controlling cross country, the Welsh Cross Country Association, only started holding Women's Championships in 1969, but now caters for the four standard age groups.

Their National Championships are normally held in mid-February in conjunction with the Men's Championships, although this is possible only because of the smaller fields (e.g. sixty finishers in 1979 in the most popular event, the Girls, compared to over 500 in the corresponding English National race).

The Seniors run approximately 3 miles (5 kilometres), the Intermediates 2¼ miles (3.6 kilometres), the Juniors 1½ miles (2.4 kilometres) and the Girls 1¼ miles (2 kilometres).

In Northern Ireland the Intermediate age group has almost disappeared in cross-country events, with all runners over fifteen often taking part in the same races. A special trial for the World Championships team selection is held, in addition to the normal National Championships, which take place in mid-February.

All four UK countries, as well as Eire, take part in an annual women's international match, known as the Five Nations meeting, in January. It was started in 1975 at Coatbridge, and the countries take it in turn to host the fixture. The winning team receives the Billy Morton Trophy, the award which was formerly presented to the winners of the International Championships proper, until the IAAF took control of the Championships in 1973.

World Championships

The women's race is now firmly a part of the World Cross Country Championships programme, but it was only in 1973, when the IAAF took over the Championships, that it became regularly so. The women's event had only started some six years earlier, in 1967, and was not even always staged with the Men's Championships. For example, in 1968 the men were at Tunis and the women at Blackburn; in 1970 the men were racing in Vichy, France, and the women at Frederick, Maryland. In other years, such as 1967 at Barry in Wales, and 1971 at San Sebastian in Spain, they were staged together. From 1973, at Waregem in Belgium, they were finally 'married' by the IAAF.

The distance of the Women's Championships is now standardized at 4–5 kilometres, and each country can enter eight athletes, with six to run and four to score. In practice, six are usually named, with two reserves.

The emphasis in both Men's and Women's Championships has always been on the team event, but these rules prevented the entry before 1978 of Grete Waitz of Norway, who that year, and in 1979, dominated the women's race. Before 1978 she could not raise a team from Norway, where there are very few female cross country runners. Ironically, in the year she did finally gather a team round her, the IAAF tried out experimental rules to permit individual entries from countries in the same position as Norway had been.

The age qualification for entry to the World Women's Championships is for the athlete to be at least fifteen years old on the day of the race. There is also an age group with no race! 'Junior Women', according to the IAAF Rules on the World Cross Country Championships, includes 'any female athlete under the age of 18 on December 31st in the year of the race, and not younger than 14 on the day of the race'. But, so far, although it has been discussed, a Junior Women's World Championship has not yet been staged.

As with the men, there is a big question mark over the future participation of the four home countries, as opposed to one team from the UK. Apart from the considerable cut in numbers of British athletes consequently able to take part, the three countries outside England fear that they might end up with few, if any, runners qualifying for a 'British' World Championships team, and that this could have a detrimental effect on the sport in their area. The opposite view, that it might lead to a raising of national standards, could also be argued, of course.

Cross country (Schools competition)

Many schools have an active cross country programme, particularly for boys, and some travel the length of the country to compete in invitation inter-schools races and relays during the winter months, such as the King Henry VIII School's Cross Country Relay at Coventry, or the Knole Run at Sevenoaks.

There are also a number of friendly inter-counties matches arranged between the more progressive of the schools county associations. But the main highlight for the ambitious competitor is the English Schools Cross Country Championships for boys and girls, which are usually, though not always, held separately, and the Home Countries Schools International match, which also caters for both boys and girls.

In England, the steps to that event start at each boy or girl's own school, which will at least have the chance to be a member of the local divisional schools athletics association. Not every school belongs, and not every school – particularly girls' schools – includes cross country in its PE programme, although the number is increasing.

Each local schools athletics association stages its own cross country championships for boys and girls to select eight runners in each of the three age groups to represent that local association in the County Schools Cross Country Championships. In some cases, particularly with Senior Girls, it may not even be necessary to stage an actual local race to select the runners because sometimes there may not *be* eight!

The successful runners then compete at the County Schools Championships which are often held in early February for the girls and late February for the boys. From these races the county selects its teams for the English Schools Championships.

The enthusiasm for and organization of cross country in schools varies widely according to the individual staff members. Some teachers (and not always PE teachers) spend many hours of out-of-school time coaching, encouraging and transporting their local runners to schools races; others go through the cross country season as though it isn't there. Often it is noticeable that a boy or girl who has shown up well in club races does not appear in a schools event in which they would have done well, and subsequent investigation shows that they simply did not know about the schools race, or that their school was not affiliated to the local schools athletics association, and so they could not compete.

Any schoolboy or schoolgirl runner at a secondary school should be eligible to compete in at least their local championship (after that it is up to them how well they do competitively), and if necessary a little prodding of the teacher by child or parent can help. Obviously PE teachers have to be interested in a wide range of sports which necessarily involve a lot of out-of-school time. But sometimes a little co-operation and forward planning can result in young athletes going as far as they are able in schools competition, instead of missing out altogether through no fault of their own.

English Schools Championships

The English Schools Athletic Association, which had staged a successful track and field championship since 1925, first promoted a National Schoolboys' Cross Country Championship in 1960, and a Schoolgirls' Championship in 1968.

The Boys' event is usually held on the fourth Saturday in March but moves to the third Saturday if it clashes with Easter. The Girls' Championship is held on the first Saturday in March, unless it is being staged jointly with the Boys' event, which sheer numbers often make difficult. All competitors must be in full-time attendance at school at the time of the Championships.

Basically, the events follow the rules of the ECCU for boys and the WCCA for girls, but one major difference is the age grouping. There are three age groups in schools competition, which are the same for both boys and girls, as shown below. County teams are able to enter sixteen athletes in each race, but only eight can run and six score. The maximum distances for the races are shown below.

		Boys	*Girls*
Juniors	Competitors twelve years and under fifteen at midnight on 31 August/1 September at the end of the current school year	5000 metres	3500 metres
Intermediates	Competitors fifteen years and under seventeen at midnight on 31 August/1 September at the end of the current school year	6500 metres	4000 metres
Seniors	Competitors seventeen years and under twenty at midnight on 31 August/1 September at the end of the current school year	8000 metres	4500 metres

Scottish Schools Championships

The Scottish Schools Athletic Association now stages a joint National Championships for boys and girls in March, with direct entry from any affiliated school allowed, to the limit of one team per age group. Eight runners per age group can be entered, with six to run and four to score, or up to three individuals per age group.

The Scottish team for the Schools International match is selected largely on these Championships, but the Scottish SAA reserves the right to select any athlete who did not compete in the Championships for reason of injury, ill-health, non-entry by school, and so forth.

Unlike the English Schools, four age groups are in operation, and the enthusiasm is such that the Girls eleven to thirteen race at Edinburgh in 1979 had 379 entries. The Girls over seventeen race, however, had just eight, reflecting one of the sport's universal problems, discussed earlier in the book.

The age groups are calculated differently for boys and girls, as indicated below.

		Distance
Girls (eleven to thirteen)	Ages at	1 mile approx.
Junior Girls (thirteen to fifteen)	1 September	2 miles approx.
Intermediate Girls (fifteen to seventeen)	preceding	3 miles approx.
Senior Girls (over seventeen)	race	3 miles approx.
Boys Group D (under thirteen)	Age at 1 April in year of race	2 miles approx.
Boys Group C (thirteen to fifteen)	Ages at	3 miles approx.
Boys Group B (fifteen to seventeen)	1 September	3 miles approx.
Boys Group A (seventeen to nineteen)	in year of race	4 miles approx.

Although direct access to the Scottish Schools Championship is possible for each school, there are also many inter-school competitions, and regions such as Ayrshire, Lanarkshire and Glasgow organize their own Championships, parallel to the National Championships.

Irish Schools Championships

The team representing Ireland in the Schools International match is chosen after the All-Ireland Schools Championships which are 'held on the Saturday immediately preceding March 17'. The venue for these rotates among the four provinces and, although the teams are officially 'selected', the leading finishers are normally those chosen for the International.

In the Girls' races, six athletes run with three to score, and in the Boys' events, eight run with four to score. Ages are calculated on 1 July in the year of competition, and the approximate distances of the races are as follows:

	Boys	*Girls*
Under fifteen	3000 metres	1500 metres
Under seventeen	4500–5000 metres	3000 metres
Under twenty	7000–7500 metres	2000 metres

Athletes in Ulster schools qualify for the All-Ireland Championships through the Ulster Secondary Schools AA Championships, held on the last Saturday in February. In the Boys' events, eight run with six to score, while in the Girls' races six run with three to score. The first three teams and six leading individuals outside those teams in each age group qualify, but there are some differences between the distances, and Ulster uses four age groups, again calculating the ages as at 1 July in the year of competition.

	Boys	*Girls*
Under thirteen	1500 metres	1500 metres
Under fifteen	3000 metres	1500 metres
Under seventeen	4500 metres	3000 metres
Under twenty	6000 metres	2000 metres

Qualification for the Ulster Championships in turn comes through the five District Championships:

1. County Down (including Belfast East of the Lagan)
2. South Antrim (Belfast West of the Lagan, Lisburn, Lisburn R.D., Newtownabbey, Carrickfergus, Whitehead)
3. The rest of County Antrim, County Londonderry, North Donegal
4. County Armagh, County Monaghan
5. County Cavan, County Fermanagh, County Tyrone, South Donegal

The District Championships are held on dates fixed locally, but not later than the third Saturday in February, one week before the Ulster Championships. Again, the best three teams and the leading six individuals outside those teams, qualify for the Ulster Championships.

Unofficial schoolboys' cross-country championships were held at both Ulster and All-Ireland levels in 1966, and the following year they were held officially, with the Ulster Secondary Schools AA being formed that year. From 1970, Ulster and All-Ireland Championships for schoolgirls were also staged.

Welsh Schools Championships

The Welsh Schools Athletic Association was formed in 1947, although Glamorgan and Monmouthshire Schools AAA were making steps towards such a formation in the immediate pre-war years. The first Welsh Schools Cross Country Championships were staged at Newtown in March 1961, with a first combined boys and girls championship held in 1967.

The Welsh Schools Cross Country Championships are usually held on the first Saturday in March, and are frequently staged at Newtown, Powys, although the summer track and field championships are held in turn in the eight constituent counties of the Welsh Schools AA (Clwyd, Dyfed, Gwent, Gwynedd, Powys, Mid Glamorgan, South Glamorgan and West Glamorgan).

Competitors qualify for the Championships through their school and then county events, although recently an extra national cross country competition for school teams has been tried out successfully.

The age groups for boys and girls are the same, and distance limitations are as follows:

		Boys	*Girls*
Junior	Competitors under fifteen years at midnight on 31 August/1 September at the end of the current school year	5000 metres	3500 metres
Middle	Competitors fifteen years and under seventeen years at midnight on 31 August/1 September at the end of the current school year	6500 metres	4000 metres
Senior	Competitors seventeen years and under twenty years at midnight on 31 August/1 September at the end of the current school year	8000 metres	4500 metres

Schools International Match

The Schools International Cross Country match, which is normally staged in late March or early April, has a fairly recent history, although a track and field International match has been held since 1962.

The real roots of the cross country match go back to 1969, when Ireland sent an under-nineteen and under-seventeen boys team to compete in the Scottish Schoolboys Cross Country Championships. No reciprocal match took place, but in 1972 the Scottish Schools invited the other countries to a cross country international for senior boys and girls at Clydebank. Ireland and Wales accepted the invitation, and in March 1973 the first match organized by the British Schools International Athletic Board (the association linking the four home organizations) took place at Newtown in Wales.

Again it was only for senior boys and girls, but the following year, when the match was held at Cashel in Eire, the age group was changed to '17 or under in year of competition'.

In the same year the track and field International match also switched from the senior to intermediate age group because it was felt that the Junior Commission of the British Amateur Athletic Board was by then providing sufficient competition for the leading athletes in that age group.

The age groups for the cross country match were amended again in 1975 to 'under 17 on August 31/September 1 in the current year', but the afternoon's programme of just two thirty-two athlete races (eight runners from each country, with six to score) seemed a little thin. Consequently, from 1977, junior boys and girls races were added to the programme, and the recommended maximum distances and age groups are now as follows:

		Boys	Girls
Junior	Competitors under fifteen years at midnight on 31 August/1 September at the end of the current school year	5000 metres	3500 metres
Intermediate	Competitors fifteen years and under seventeen at midnight on 31 August/ 1 September at the end of the current school year	6500 metres	4000 metres

Road running

Open races

Every weekend thousands of runners in the UK take part in a wide range of open road races of varying distances. These are advertised in the athletics press and elsewhere, and attract entries from all standards of competitors, from novice to Olympic. No other form of athletics event regularly gives you such a broad spectrum of competitor, and you never know with whom you will be running.

Most road races for Senior men are a minimum of 4–5 miles in length – a good distance for the novice to try, after some weeks of basic training – and they range up to the 53½ miles London to Brighton classic (and occasionally beyond). But the most popular races tend to be around 10 miles (there was an entry of 1100 for the 1979 Michelin 10 miles road race at Stoke-on-Trent), the distance which the Road Runners Club considers to be roughly the dividing line between races contested by those who run both road and cross country events and those whose interest is mainly on the road.

The following list, prepared with the co-operation of John Jewell, past president of the Road Runners Club, gives an indication of a cross section of open road races available, together with a brief course description, the year of inauguration where known, and the various RRC standards for the course.

The RRC Standards Scheme, which was started in 1954, gives a particular encouragement to the runners who do not normally expect to be among the prize-winners. Any RRC member who achieves a performance bettering the listed first- or second-class standards at three different distances of 10 miles and over within one year (calculated from 1 November to 31 October) is entitled to a certificate, which is sent without charge after the performances have been checked. The runner can also purchase a standards badge.

The standards are adjusted for various races to allow for any slight over-distance, a hilly course, and so forth, so that the standards are all of equal difficulty as far as can be judged. Races at 'odd' distances have standards calculated to the equivalent level.

There are separate standard schemes for Veterans over forty and over fifty, and also now for women although, in view of the more restricted number of races available at present, they are allowed to count two performances at the same distance towards their certificate. The full list of standards is published regularly in RRC Newsletter, which is sent free to members.

On the list published here, the venue is given if it is not immediately obvious from the name of the race, and exact distances if they are known to be slightly under or over. An asterisk indicates that the race includes a women's section although, even within the lifetime of this book, more previously all-male races may include women's sections, reflecting the rapid growth in this area of the sport.

			Men				Women	
			1stG	2ndC	Vet. 40	Vet. 50	1stC	2ndC
Tonbridge 10 miles*	Mar.	Two laps of 5 miles; mainly flat	53	1–01	1–03	1–10	1–04	1–13
Edinburgh University 10 miles*		Two circuits of 5 miles, including climb to the Braid Hills	54	1–02	1–04	1–11	1–05	1–14
Michelin 10 miles (Stoke)*	Jun.	Two 5 miles laps in partly built-up area, one hill each lap	54	1–01	1–03	1–10	1–04	1–13
Nuneaton 10 miles (1963)*	Sept.	Two 5 mile laps, mostly country roads, undulating	53	1–01	1–03	1–10	1–04	1–13
Rowntrees 10 miles (York)*	Oct.	One flat lap	53	1–01	1–03	1–10	1–04	1–13
Shaftesbury H 10 miles (Hendon 1954)*	Aug.	Two large laps, plus one small lap. Undulating, built-up area. Start and finish in Copthall Stadium	53	1–01	1–03	1–10	1–04	1–13
Walton 10 miles (1945)*	Oct.	Flat, three laps of perimeter of Burwood Park Estate	53	1–01	1–03	1–10	1–04	1–13
Witney 12 miles* (12 miles 400 yards/19.678 kilometres)	Sept.	Three gently undulating laps of traffic-free circuit in grounds of Blenheim Palace, Oxfordshire	1–06	1–17	1–19	1–27	1–20	1–30
Manchester YMCA 20 kilometres (12 miles 752 yards)	Jun.	One flat lap, built-up area, starting and finishing at YMCA Sports Field, Withington	1–08	1–18	1–20	1–29	1–21	1–32
Dartford Half-Marathon (1977)* (13 miles 1100 yards/21.927 kilometres)	Aug.	Two laps, undulating, around Wilmington	1–11	1–23	1–26	1–34	1–26	1–40

A cross section of open British road races.

			Men				Women	
			1stC	2ndC	Vet.40	Vet.50	1stC	2ndC
*Romford Half-Marathon**	Mar.	3½ mile lap, followed by 9½ mile lap. Hilly; country roads	1-11	1-23	1-26	1-34	1-26	1-40
Morpeth to Newcastle (1904) (13 miles 1100 yards/21.927 kilometres)	Jan.	Place to place, mainly flat, hill at 7 miles	1-14	1-26	1-29	1-37		
Sale 15 miles	Aug.	Four flat laps round outside of Wythenshawe Park	1-23	1-37	1-40	1-50		
Duncairn Nomads 15 miles (Belfast)	Apr.	Out and back course; hill at 12 miles	1-23	1-37	1-40	1-50		
Dudley 25 kilometres (14 miles 1306 yards/23.725 kilometres)	May	One lap, very undulating	1-24	1-39	1-42	1-53		
*Mitcham 25 kilometres (1952)** (15 miles 940 yards)	Jan.	Three laps of flat circuit in built-up area	1-26	1-41	1-44	1-55	1-44	2-00
Chichester to Portsmouth (1946) (16 miles 368 yards/26.086 kilometres)	May	Place to place on main roads through built-up area of Portsmouth to finish on Alexandra Park track	1-30	1-46	1-49	1-59		
Finchley 20 miles (Ruislip, 1933)	Apr.	Four laps of flat 5 miles on suburban roads	1-54	2-16	2-20	2-30		
Liverpool Pembroke 20 miles (1954)	May	Four flat 5 mile laps around housing estates and country roads; start and finish at King George V playing fields, Huyton	1-54	2-16	2-20	2-30		

			Men			Women	
		1st C	2nd C	Vet. 40	Vet. 50	1st C	2nd C
Spenborough 20 miles	Two undulating laps, with long climb at 1 and 11 miles, plus three laps of track		1-56	2-18	2-22	2-32		
Barnsley Marathon (1975)*	Dec.	Out and back course, mainly flat, from Barnsley Town Hall	2-35	3-05	3-10	3-25	3-05	3-42
Harlow Marathon*	Oct.	4 mile lap, followed by two 11 mile laps on road and cycle path within New Town; undulating	2-36	3-06	3-11	3-26	3-06	3-43
Isle of Wight Marathon*	May	One hilly lap through Newport, Godshill, Shanklin, Sandown and Brading. Start and finish on Ryde Esplanade	2-39	3-09	3-14	3-29	3-09	3-46
Milton Keynes Marathon*	Sept.	Unique specially constructed traffic-free circuit covered three times; undulating in parts	2-36	3-06	3-11	3-26	3-06	3-43
Polytechnic H Marathon (Windsor, 1909)*	Jun.	From castle grounds, one lap through Great Park and on country roads, undulating for the first 10 miles. Finish on track in Windsor	2-36	3-06	3-11	3-26	3-06	3-43
Rugby Marathon*	Sept.	Lap on country roads, covered three times, with steep hill at 3,11 and 20 miles	2-37	3-07	3-12	3-27	3-07	3-44

Event	Month	Description	Men				Women	
			1stC	2ndC	Vet.40	Vet.50	1stC	2ndC
Sandbach Marathon*	Jun.	Lap on country and main road, covered three times. Flat. Finish at Leisure Centre	2-35	3-05	3-10	3-25	3-05	3-42
Scottish Marathon	Jun.	Out and back course, flat, from Meadowbank Stadium, Edinburgh, through Musselburgh	2-35	3-05	3-10	3-25		
South London H 30 miles (1943)* (30 miles 616 yards/48.843 kilometres)	Sept.	Four laps of 7½ miles with gradual ascents, on suburban and country roads from Old Coulsdon, Surrey	3-09	3-44	3-50	4-10	3-47	4-29
Two Bridges (Dunfermline) (36 miles 616 yards/58.080 kilometres)	Aug.	From Dunfermline, following north bank of Firth of Forth to cross the Kincardine Bridge, returning along the south bank, through Grangemouth and Bo'ness to the Forth Road Bridge, through Inverkeithling to the Civil Service Sports Centre, Rosyth. Hills at 22 and 27 miles	3-58	4-39	4-46	5-15		
Isle of Man TT Course race (1955) (39½ miles/63.5 kilometres)	May	Starts and finishes on the Douglas Promenade to join the TT course. One lap, with total ascent exceeding 2000 feet. The 'mountain' Snaefell climb begins at 25 miles	4-32	5-16	5-25	5-50		

| | | Men | | | | Women | |
		1stC	2ndC	Vet. 40	Vet. 50	1stC	2ndC
London to Brighton (1951)* (53 miles 856 yards/86.078 kilometres)	Sept.	6–21	7–16	7–27	8–08	7–37	—

Longest annual running race in Britain. Starts at Big Ben, Westminster; follows the old Brighton road through Merstham, Horley, Crawley, Handcross, Bolney, Pyecombe and Patcham, to finish at Brighton Aquarium. Course ascends and descends a total of 1250 feet, with the highest point (504 feet) at the top of Handcross Hill (approx. 33 miles), and the last climb at Pyecombe (46 miles 406 yards)

(*with acknowledgement to John Jewell, Road Runners Club*)

AAA Marathon/Polytechnic Harriers Marathon

Although these two stalwarts of the fixture list, the AAA Marathon and the Polytechnic Harriers Marathon, are separate races, they have on occasions over the past half-century been held jointly. But the 'Poly' Marathon is the oldest in Britain, dating back to 1909, the year after the first London Olympic Games, where the marathon was a particular disappointment to Britain.

The Sporting Life subsequently presented a magnificent trophy to Polytechnic Harriers, the London club, and asked if they would promote an annual marathon for it. The event was first held in 1909, with an entry of sixty-eight runners. It was staged from Windsor Castle to Stamford Bridge, and won by H. Barrett of the promoting club.

The first AAA Championship Marathon was held in 1925, in conjunction with the Polytechnic race, and was won by Sam Ferris in 2 hours 35 minutes 58 seconds. Ferris, who was destined to be the 1932 Olympic marathon silver medallist, also won the joint races in 1926 and 1927. In fact, he actually won the Poly race each year from 1925 until 1933, except in 1930, when RAF duty forced him to miss it. The AAA Championship event was held separately in 1928, but from time to time the two events were amalgamated again. Often, though, the AAA Championship race, which continued throughout the Second World War on several temporary courses, has used a number of different routes within the same area, with the most famous being that from Windsor to Chiswick, on which Jim Peters produced some outstanding runs in the early fifties.

Now the race, known as the Goldenlay Polytechnic Marathon after its current sponsors, still starts in the private grounds of Windsor Castle but follows one long loop, finishing with a circuit of the all-weather track at Vansittart Road, Windsor. Despite an upsurge in the number of other marathons available in Britain, it still attracts a field of well over 300 runners each year, who all know that they are running in a race with a real history.

National Road Relays

The original, if unofficial, national road relay championship was always acknowledged to be the London to Brighton event, which was started in 1924. By 1950 it had become so popular (and the roads so busy) that qualifying races had to be held, and from 1951 the event became known as the 'National' Road Relay, although the qualifying race for southern clubs was held over the same course, and became known as the 'Southern' London to Brighton.

Until 1954, despite course alterations, it was a ten-stage race, and then from 1954 until 1957 it had eleven legs. A road diversion led to the inclusion of a twelfth stage from that date until its discontinuation after the 1965 National race, when the *News of the World* had to withdraw its financial sponsorship.

This left a yawning gap in the competition calendar of the clubs, and so an inaugural AAA National Road Relay Championship was held at Whetstone, near Leicester, on 1 April 1967, attracting thirty teams. Coventry Godiva Harriers won the race, with its alternate long and short stages on a figure-of-eight course, and went on to win again in the three succeeding years.

The event was first staged in 1970 at Sutton Coldfield, now its usual venue each April, and the current laps are alternate stages of 5 miles 900 yards and 3 miles 100 yards, for a total of twelve stages.

Approximately twenty-eight to thirty clubs take part, usually comprising eight from the Midlands, eight from the North, and ten from the South, plus the Scottish and Welsh Champions. The clubs qualify through their Area Championships, which are held about three weeks earlier.

In October 1969 the AAA six-stage road relay was inaugurated at Crystal Palace to a less than auspicious start, with just nine teams taking part and City of Stoke AC winning comfortably. But the numbers gradually increased over the years and, although it is still very much of a second-string event to the twelve-stage race six months later, it has now established itself more firmly on the calendar in October.

The inaugural Scottish National six-stage road relay was staged at Strathclyde Park, Motherwell, in 1978, attracting fifty-eight teams and being won by Edinburgh Southern Harriers. The 'blue riband' event in Scotland, however, has long been the eight-stage Edinburgh to Glasgow relay, held in November, and which used to act as the Scottish qualifying event for the National London to Brighton.

Birchgrove Harriers won the first Welsh Men's Road Relay Championship, held over six stages at Bridgend on 30 March 1968. The following year a Youths' road relay was added, followed in 1973 by a Boys' event and in 1974 by a Colts' relay too.

There is no official Northern Ireland road relay championship, but the NIAAA promotes the annual Guinness Road Relay in April. This is an eight-stage, 32 mile open event from Portadown to Belfast, with stage lengths varying from 2½ to 7½ miles.

Women's road races

One of the very earliest of women's road relays – if not the first – was that promoted by Ilford Athletic Club, and which began as an offshoot of a men's road relay, known as the Round Ilford Relay. The women's race of 5 × 1¾ miles was first staged in 1935 from the Bungalow Tea Rooms, Chigwell Row, and was won in the inaugural year by the host club in 1 hour 15 minutes 14 seconds, with London Olympiades second and Epsom Ladies third!

Now there are a considerable number of women's open road relays although, like the cross country events, the organizers sometimes turn the Senior age group events into straightforward races for individuals rather than a relay, if numbers are insufficient.

The first National Road Relay Championship in England was held at Huyton, near Liverpool, in November 1963, when Mitcham AC won the 4 × 1½ miles Senior race from nine other teams.

These days the National Championships are the highlight of the women's road relay season. They are held in November, following the county and area road relays in October. In 1979 nearly seventy teams took part in the National Junior Women's Road Relay Championship. The recommended distances are:

Seniors:	3 × 3000 metres
Intermediates:	3 × 2500 metres
Juniors:	3 × 2000 metres
Girls:	3 × 2000 metres

The applicable age groups are the same as for cross country, as the seasons coincide.

In Scotland, where the five age groups are in operation at national level, the National Road Relays have been switched in recent years from their former date in March to mid-October, to encourage more competitors to take part. The championship distances are:

Minor Girls (9–11):	4 × ¾ mile
Girls (11–13):	4 × ¾ mile
Juniors (13–15):	4 × 1 mile
Intermediates (15–17):	3 × 1½ miles
Seniors:	3 × 2 miles

The Welsh Women's Road Relay Championships were first introduced for Seniors and Juniors in 1971, and later a Girls group was added. The Championships are now normally held in late September or early October, with four runners per team.

Following the successful introduction of experimental rules by the Women's CC & RWA (as it then was) in 1975, to allow women to run long distance road races, the first official Women's AAA Marathon Championship was held in conjunction with the traditional Isle of Wight Marathon in May 1978, and won by Margaret Lockley of Luton in 2 hours 55 minutes 8 seconds. The future of the Championship was assured at Sandbach in June 1979 when Joyce Smith (2 hours 41 minutes 37 seconds) led three other women under the existing UK best.

The advance of women's marathon standards generally has reassured any doubters of the capability of women to run long distances with no ill effects. In September 1979 the Scottish runner Leslie Watson became the first woman to complete the London to Brighton road race (more than a double marathon), covering the 54 mile 460 yard course, extended because of road works, in 6 hours 55 minutes 11 seconds. From 1980 the race includes an official women's section, a further indication that this area of the sport – and indeed the whole world of running – is expanding at a fast, furious and very healthy rate.